THE
EFFICIENT
ORGANIZATION

THE
EFFICIENT
ORGANIZATION

Selwyn W. Becker / Duncan Neuhauser

ELSEVIER

New York / Oxford / Amsterdam

ELSEVIER SCIENTIFIC PUBLISHING COMPANY, INC.
52 Vanderbilt Avenue, New York, N.Y. 10017

ELSEVIER SCIENTIFIC PUBLISHING COMPANY
335 Jan Van Galenstraat, P.O. Box 211
Amsterdam, The Netherlands

Library of Congress Cataloging in Publication Data

Becker, Selwyn William, 1929-
    The efficient organization.

    Bibliography: p.
    Includes index.
    1. Organization.   2. Organization–Case studies.
3. Management. I. Neuhauser, Duncan, joint author.
II. Title.
HD31.B369943   301.18   75-8269
ISBN 0-444-99004-6

Manufactured in the United States of America

Contents

Preface   vii

Part I: **A THEORY OF ORGANIZATIONAL EFFICIENCY**

Introduction   3

1   Organizational Efficiency and Organizational Goals   39

2   Specification of Procedures   51

3   Complexity of the Task-Environment   69

4   Visibility of Consequences   77

5   Other Variables   85

6   A Model of Organizational Efficiency   91

Part II: **THE EMPIRICAL EVIDENCE**

Introduction   99

7   The Hospital Organization Study: The Administrative Component—Low-Complexity Task-Environment   105

8   The Hospital Organization Study: The Professional Component—High Complexity   125

9   The Hospital Organization Study: The Three Missing Observations—Case Studies   141

10   The Insurance Organization Study (with Juan A. Bustillo)   147

11   Discussion and Evaluation   159

Appendix A   The Hospital Study: Measuring Instruments   173

Appendix B   The Insurance Study: Measuring Instruments   177

Notes   195

Bibliography   215

Index   225

Preface

This book is intended for those interested in the nature of formal organizations, for those who are engaged in the study of organizations, as well as for those who teach others how organizations function. While it is not meant to be a "how to" text, the general nature of the theory being tested here might furnish a manager with insights into the relationship between his organization and our models and data, and thus perhaps prove of value in his efforts to improve or restructure his own organization.

The researcher and teacher will find that ours is a "contingency type" theory, in which the structure of the organization depends on environmental and task conditions. Within the framework of the theory several important issues are addressed and partially resolved: the role of participation in the decision-making process of organizations and the problem of organizational goals in the measurement of organizational efficiency. With these problems resolved, a general model of organizational efficiency is presented.

The model is evaluated by means of two comparative field studies. The first, a study of 30 hospital organizations, was completed in 1970, and the second, a study of 15 insurance companies, in 1973. The data from both studies offer strong support for the model of organizational efficiency.

This is one of the few books to present a comprehensive theory, as well as a test of that theory with relatively large numbers of organizations in which the "whole" organization is the unit of analysis and the organization's output the dependent variable.

The studies could not have been completed, nor the book written, without the cooperation of the 45 organizations involved in the research. Thanks are also due to the U.S.P.H.S., which supported the hospital study through a grant to the Center for Health Administration Studies of The University of Chicago and to the Ford Foundation, for which one of the authors acted as a project specialist during the research design and supervision of the fieldwork on the insurance study. Finally, thanks are due to the Instituto de Estudios Superiores de Administracion for its support, and to Professor Juan Antonio Bustillo, who conducted the insurance study.

Selwyn W. Becker
Duncan Neuhauser

PART I:

A THEORY OF ORGANIZATIONAL EFFICIENCY

Introduction

EFFICIENCY AND THE STUDY OF
FORMAL ORGANIZATIONS

The number of ways people claim to have studied formal organizations approaches the number of variables that affect the functioning of organizations. Some studies deal with the relationships between perceived authority structures and degree of centralization, others look at span of control as a function of hierarchic levels, while still others are interested in the relationship between the size of an organization and the degrees of succession in its top managerial ranks. One current lively controversy in the pertinent literature surrounds the relationship between size, complexity, and administrative ratio.[1] The question is whether size makes for complexity or whether growth rate does, and regardless of which causes which, how they relate to the administrative ratio.

Scientists, especially social scientists, are wont to tell their students that anything of interest to the scientist is worthy of exploration and study. But in the study of formal organizations such an approach can lead to misguided research activity. Organizations are formed to produce a good or service. The production of that good or service constitutes the output of the organization. How well, how efficiently, how effectively organizations produce a good or service constitutes the relevant output variable in the study of formal organizations. All other variables—size, succession rate, complexity, administrative ratio—are input variables. To be interested in how two input measures relate to one another solely for the sake of understanding that relationship is tantamount to dilletantism.

We do not wish to imply that everyone ought to be interested in organizational efficiency. Someone might conceivably be interested in the effect of different communication situations or different authority patterns on problem-solving. Well and good, but if he is, he should be aware that despite his use of an organization variable (a structural input variable like communication or authority pattern), he is not studying organizations but, rather, human problem-solving, which in the study of organizations is another input variable. One properly may confine one's interest to problem-solving, but if one wishes to understand the functioning of organizations, problem-solving behavior must be related to the purpose of the organization—the efficient output of a product or service—or else what he is doing is not a study of organizations.

The current interest in the relationship between size, complexity, and administrative ratio is significant not for its own sake, but because of the implied further relationship between these input variables and the output variable—efficient functioning of organizations. Our conclusion, then, is obvious. The study of organizational efficiency is important both from theoretical and practical points of view—to understand how the many input variables affect one another and in so doing how directly or indirectly they affect organizational efficiency.

If organizational efficiency is of paramount importance, why have other researchers failed to recognize this, or, if they have, why have they produced relatively few studies using efficiency as the dependent variable? In a recent textbook Hall states, "The interest in effectiveness has not led to a definitive set of studies or conceptual approaches to the issue. A good part of the difficulty in assessing effectiveness lies in the problems surrounding goals."[2] In effect, Hall has stated that effectiveness, or efficiency, has not been defined because the concept denotes efficiency at achieving some goal and that there are problems associated with identifying and measuring organization goals, and hence in measuring organizational efficiency.

In this book the problems associated with organizational goals and of defining efficiency are resolved within the framework of the Entrepreneurial Theory of Formal Organizations. The variables in that theory are then related to relevant literature, and a model of organizational efficiency is developed. The data from the two field studies, one of 30 hospital organizations and the other of 15 insurance companies, are presented to test the efficacy of the model. Since organizational goals and efficiency are discussed in the context of the Entrepreneurial Theory (E.T.), and since the model of efficiency utilizes variables from the E.T., it will be beneficial to review the theory in some detail.

THE ENTREPRENEURIAL THEORY OF FORMAL ORGANIZATIONS[3]

Almost everyone would agree that formal organizations are systems (i.e., they have a more or less enduring differentiation of structure and function), and that they are deliberately formed to achieve a goal. For instance, Blau states that formal organizations are social units ". . . established for the explicit purpose of achieving certain goals."[4] Barnard defines formal organization as a ". . . system of consciously coordinated activities or forces of two or more persons."[5] Based on these definitions it seems clear that organizations arise when someone expends resources and establishes some procedures for their use in order to achieve a goal. Little attention has been paid, however, to who provides the resources and what part of the system, or social unit, has property rights with regard to those resources. This is an important consideration, for only those who have rights to the resources have legitimate legal or societal sanctions at their disposal to enforce procedures for their use. In other words, only the holder of the property rights is socially sanctioned to impart direction to the system. The person(s) who by virtue of his rights to the organization's resources is allowed to shape and mold (as well as to dissolve, sell, or otherwise transfer) the organization to attain his goal is in essence the *owner(s)* of the organization. The owner may be a single individual, a small group like a committee or a board, or the citizenry of a nation.[6]

The assertion that formal organizations are owned means that they can be treated as property. The assumption that formal organizations are property is central to our theory, and since property has different meanings for different people, it is essential to explore carefully what we mean by the term "property" and "property rights."

According to Kingsley Davis, property "consists of the rights and duties of one person or group (the owner) as against all other persons or groups with respect to some scarce good."[7] This definition of property includes societal as well as legal sanctions. The characteristics of property rights are that they are transferable (either by exchange or transmission from one generation to the next) and that they do not imply actual use of the object by the owner. In discussing whether property rights refer only to concrete external objects, Davis states that "What property rights really refers to in all cases is the right to demand certain kinds of behavior from other individuals. . . ."[8] Davis also distinguishes between two types of property: public and private. "The term 'private property' should apply to rights by individuals or groups acting in their own interest, and 'public property' should apply to rights held by the community-at-large and administered by individuals or groups acting as agents of the community."[9]

In discussing the property rights in productive technology, Davis states that "there are *always* [italics ours] two mutually contradictory principles at work: (1) the tendency of men to retain their rights in productive property but to let others work it for them; (2) the tendency of those who work the property to acquire rights in it. The first is made possible by the separability of use and ownership; the second by a counteracting affinity between the two."[10] He further states that the persons actually connected with the productive instruments are in a position to use them for their own advantage, as opposed to the advantage of the titular owner, i.e., "The share of the product that goes to capital may not always be forthcoming if the persons who furnish the capital stand apart from the production itself."[11]

Our conception of formal organization, i.e., one that includes an owner, is based on the premise that a formal organization is property and that the property rights in it are transferable either by exchange or by transmission from one generation to the next. We recognize that the owner need not actually manage or operate the organization—he can allow it to be run by a manager or director. We further assume, following Davis, that property rights are not restricted to concrete objects but include the right to demand certain kinds of behavior from other individuals. Specifically, we are thinking of the owner's right to make certain demands on his labor force, his human resources.[12] At the same time, however, we recognize that the right may or may not be honored, because, following Davis, we assume that there is a tendency for those who work the property to acquire rights in it. The owner of a formal organization, then, has a dual problem: (1) to utilize his property so that his goals are attained; and (2) to prevent the erosion of his rights by those who operate the property.

In summary, ownership of a formal organization resides with the person or persons who have property rights to the total organization. The owner's resources are the elements that comprise the formal organization's differentiation of structure and function and arise, in part at least, as a result of the procedures established by him.

Definition: A *Formal Organization* is a purposely developed system, i.e., an ongoing interaction of procedures and resources, to which an owner has property rights.

We assume that the reason an owner seeks to attain his goal by creating (using, buying, renting, etc.) an organization is to obtain the economic or psychological advantages that result from coordination. We further assume that the rational owner aims to achieve his goal in as efficient a manner as possible and to prevent the operators of the organization from usurping his property rights. When the owner decides to attain his goals through organization, he acquires resources necessary for goal attainment and coordinates them in productive effort. He can do this in ways that give greater or lesser discretion to the human resources. When an owner informs the labor force of his goal, places capital at their disposal, and allows them to expend it for machinery and/or raw materials as they see fit, he is giving them maximal discretion. When an owner decides for what and how his capital will be expended, when he informs the labor force of his goal and also tells them exactly how to achieve it, he is giving them minimal discretion.

Maximal coordination by the owner is possible only when all discretion resides in him. By "coordinate" we mean imparting direction to the system, i.e., to specify procedures for the utilization of the resources of the system. The maximally coordinated organization is the end point of a continuum, and in the real world it usually is not reached. An owner may choose to coordinate the

resources by himself or delegate that responsibility to some decision-making components within his organization. The coordinating, decision-making components of the organization constitute
what we consider the managers of the organization. The coordinating, non-decision-making components constitute what we consider
the bureaucrats (clerks, bookkeepers, strawbosses, etc.). In other
words, the difference between a manager and a bureaucrat is the
degree of discretion each enjoys in determining his own organizational activities and those of others. Bureaucrats, though engaged
in the coordinating process, have little or no discretion in the
performance of their functions, nor do they determine the activities of others. Managers, on the other hand, have some discretionary powers over their own activities and also determine the activities of bureaucrats (and others) in the organization. Most coordinators fall between the extremes of having full discretion or none
at all. This variation in degrees of discretion allows us to classify
coordinators in terms of a ratio of discretionary to nondiscretion-
ary activities. Coordinators thus are operationally defined according to their activities within the organization.

Persons not primarily engaged in the coordinating process we
consider producers. Producers work toward the attainment of the
owner's goal directly through their own activities rather than by
facilitating or increasing the effectiveness of others. Consider, for
example, the different roles played by the craftsmen and the foreman in building a house. The foreman—i.e., the coordinator—does
not drive nails or saw wood. He performs no act directly, tangibly,
immediately related to the building of the house. His contribution
lies in increasing the efficiency of those who do. Although the
house could be built without a coordinator, it probably would be
more costly.

Producers, like coordinators, also have more or less discretion
over their organizational activities. Producers who determine their
own activities (i.e., have discretion) we designate as professionals.[13] Producers whose activities are determined by others we
term workers. These four organizational roles are determined by
their function and manner of performance, as shown in Table I-1.

To this point we have discussed some assumptions basic to
our view of formal organization. Next we will define and discuss
the variables that determine the bureaucratic structures of formal
organizations.

TABLE I-1

**Function and Manner of Performance
of Four Organizational Roles**

Function	Manner of Performance	
	Discretion	No Discretion
Coordinator	Manager	Bureaucrat
Producer	Professional	Worker

The Variables. It is our premise that the kind of organization which develops is determined by two variables: (1) the degree to which resources are stored in specific or general form, and (2) the degree to which procedures are organizationally specified.

We consider a resource any factor—labor or capital—that produces a good or service. Just as Davis considers "good will" an intangible associated with property rights, so do we consider as a resource any organizational property, intangible or not, which is exchangeable for capital or transferable in any way. Both good will and credit are examples of exchangeable or transferable intangible resources. Property rights, whether associated with tangible or intangible resources, may be owned outright or they may be leased. Rights to owned resources may be held indefinitely, while rights to leased resources are obtained only for a limited period of time. While most resources can be either leased or owned, labor, except under unusual circumstances, must always be leased.

Storage of resources refers to possession of them during the period of time between their acquisition and their consumption. We define organizational resources as those resources stored within an organization. The "specific-general" dimension is analogous to the notion of committed and uncommitted resources. When a resource is in specific form it is earmarked for a particular use; when it is in general form its use is undetermined.[14] The analogy is not a perfect one, however, because the factor of storage as well as commitment enters into our concept.

Definition: Any resource stored by an organization in the form necessary to implement a program with the owner's intent that it be used, modified or consumed within the organization in the process of obtaining his goal is a *Specific Resource.* Any resource stored by an organization with the expectation that it will be converted to a specific resource is a *General Resource.*

Operationally, the ratio of specific to general resources is the present investment in specific resources over the present value of general resources, with present investment equaling the initial cost of the specific resources times the unused proportion of those resources and present value equaling the market price of the general resources. (The present investment in leased resources is the total payment [rental fee, contract, or salary] times the remaining unexpired percentage of the lease period.)

Uncommitted money, or the ability to borrow, is the most usual general resource. However, organizations that utilize and consume money internally to implement a program at the behest of an owner also can store it as a specific resource. Money might be a specific resource to a lending institution or foundation since their programs require its consumption by or within the organization rather than its conversion to another resource. Even these institutions, however, may maintain money as a general resource if they store it prior to determining its use.

Labor usually is a specific resource; however, it too can be a general resource. For example, when a baseball team buys a player merely for trading purposes, that player is stored as a general resource until a trade involving him is made. If no trade is completed, the player can be converted to a specific resource by the decision to use him on the team—by fiat allocating him for consumption by or within the organization.

The lending institution example illustrates how a usually general resource can be employed as a specific one; the baseball team illustrates how a normally specific resource can be used as a general one. In both cases the resources can be converted from one form to another by the owner's fiat. These are exceptional cases, however, for usually money is a general resource and labor a specific one. Conversion of resources from one form to another by fiat also is rare because conversion frequently involves recourse to the goods and services of an individual outside the organization or to another, autonomous organization.

The second variable is the degree to which procedures are

self- or organizationally-specified. A procedure is self-determined when the person is given discretion in achieving the organization's goal. He is given general instructions to achieve an organizational objective but no specific instructions about how to achieve it. We refer to self-determined procedures as general procedures. Procedures are conceived of as distributed on a continuum from absolutely specified to totally generalized.

Definition: Procedures are *completely specified* when an owner or his agent requires a volitional resource to perform a series of planned activities so that the entire working period is consumed in the performance of these acts. Procedures are *completely generalized* when the volitional resource is required by the owner to specify his own procedures in attaining the organization's goal.

Operationally, the ratio of specified to generalized procedures is the proportion of time spent by volitional resources in carrying out procedures planned by others above them in the administrative hierarchy over the total time spent on organizational activities.[15]

We hypothesize that the structure of the formal organization and its concomitant authority pattern is dependent on the ratio of specified to generalized procedures and on the ratio of stored specific to stored general resources.

The variables proportion of specified procedures and proportion of resources stored in specific form are continuously distributed. Nevertheless, for expository purposes we will consider only the end points of these two continua. Where P+ stands for a high proportion of specified procedures and P- for a low proportion, and R+ for a high proportion of stored specific resources and R- for a low proportion, four possible combinations of procedures and resources exist: (1) P+R+; (2) P+R-; (3) P-R+; (4) P-R-.

In the first situation, P+R+, a high proportion of the procedures are specified and a high proportion of the resources are stored in their specific forms. The P+R+ organization is exemplified by an automated factory in which all the machinery and people necessary to achieve the goals of the organization are stored, and where all their activities are planned or programmed.

In the second situation, P+R-, the owner specifies a high proportion of the procedures, but he stores a low proportion of the organization's resources in specific form. In the construction industry, for instance, the owner does not know whether he will use glass, brick, or cement on his future construction projects. To store all resources for any construction exigency would obviously be costly and in most enterprises, impossible. This is true of any industry, whether fashion or show business, with a relatively unpredictable demand.

The third case, P-R+, is one in which the owner stores the specific resources necessary to goal achievement but does not or cannot specify the procedures for their coordination. Hospitals, research organizations, and universities are more or less characteristic of this type of organization, in which resources are stored in specific form (surgical instruments, doctors, computers, professors, etc.) but the owner does not specify their use.

The last situation, P-R-, in which there are few specified procedures and few specific resources is one with a low probability of the emergence of a viable organization. With little planning and few resources to coordinate, there is little reason to maintain even the semblance of a formal organization. Other than this last case, each of the (projected) combinations of procedures and resources results in a distinctive pattern of formal organization.

Bureaucratic Structures

The Complete Bureaucracy. The most widely discussed type of formal organization is the monocratic bureaucracy. Weber states that one characteristic of monocratic bureaucracies is that they are "organized in a clearly defined hierarchy of offices."[16] He also states that this form of organization is ". . . capable of attaining the highest degree of efficiency and is . . . the most rational known means of carrying out imperative control over human beings."[17] This can be taken to mean that, among other things, bureaucracy is a control mechanism to insure coordination.[18] In Weber's formulation, coordination and control are achieved within the framework of an executive authority pattern. Marcson describes this authority pattern as "a system of controls in which a superior in a hierarchical organization exercises ultimate control over his subordinates. It is . . . based on incumbency in a position and occurs within the framework of pre-existing rules of the organization."[19]

The Weberian ideal bureaucracy exists only when the owner (or his surrogate) exercises executive control over and coordinates the activities of the people and tools necessary to achieve the goals of the organization. Effective executive control and coordination is dependent upon extensive planning. Planning and coordination only can be carried out when people and other resources necessary to their planning and execution are available within the organization. Thus, conditions necessary for the emergence of an organizational form approximating the Weberian Model are, in our terminology, a high proportion of specified procedures (P+) and a high proportion of stored specific resources (R+). The Weberian ideal bureaucracy can only occur when virtually all procedures are specified and all resources required for goal achievement stored in specific form. We term this kind of organization a Complete Bureaucracy.

Definition: A *Complete Bureaucracy* is a formal organization which in the process of goal attainment stores all the managerial hierarchies necessary to maximize coordination and control.

As previously implied, the automated factory is one of the closest approximations to the complete bureaucracy. Here the activities of all the resources, including the human ones who tend the machines—pushing buttons, watching for warning lights, etc.— are completely programmed. Almost all the resources are stored in specific form and almost all the procedures are specified. They are specified by the owner, and (generally) via a chief executive passed down the hierarchical levels to the worker. This kind of authority pattern, called an executive-authority pattern, is associated with the complete bureaucracy. Although a complete bureaucracy maximizes coordination, it is often undesirable or even impossible for the owner to specify a high proportion of the procedures or to store specific resources. Failure to do one or the other modifies the complete bureaucracy.

The Truncated Bureaucracy. First, let us examine the effect on the organization of failure to store a high proportion of specific resources. As we stated earlier, this situation is characteristic of industries such as fashion and construction with relatively unpredictable demand. It is our contention that when demand is unpredictable, human resources are among the first specific resources not to be stored. This is so because people are among the more expensive storable resources. The high storage costs are primarily due to the fact that human resources cannot, except in unusual circumstances, be owned outright. Human resources almost always must be leased. A major difference between owned and leased resources is the rate at which they lose value when in use and when not in use. Owned resources tend to depreciate more slowly when not used. On the other hand, because the rent for leased property remains constant, the rate of depreciation of leased property is unaffected by use. Therefore, per dollar invested, it frequently costs more to store leased than owned resources.[20] Consequently, when demand is unpredictable, i.e., when the probability of nonuse of stored specific resources is high, human resources are among the first not stored by the organization.

Generally the more unique the skill of the resource, the less available and the more costly its replacement. As a result, an owner prefers to store unique or difficult-to-obtain resources rather than more prevalent or easily obtained ones. Among the unique skills a human resource can possess is an understanding of how and why a particular formal organization operates. This applies more generally to the manager than to the worker—especially the higher each of them is in the organizational hierarchy. Not only the uniqueness of skills increases as one moves from the lower to the higher administrative levels, but the responsibility for coordination and planning also does. Consequently, the potential benefits to be derived from the coordination and planning associated with each bureaucratic level increases as one moves up the administrative ladder. Thus, owners prefer to store higher-level rather than lower-level managers. When all necessary levels are stored, the higher ones are leased for longer periods of time. That is, high-level managers are contracted for on an annual basis, while lower-level managers are hired by the month or week. The tendency of organizations with unpredictable demand not to store lower administrative levels (or, if stored, to lease them for shorter periods of time) is reinforced by the fact that storage costs vary inversely with level. That is, the combined salaries of a given level generally exceed the combined salaries of the level above it.[21] The failure or inability to store the lower levels results in what we call a truncated bureaucracy.[22]

Definition: A *Truncated Bureaucracy* is a formal organization in which one or more of the lowest managerial levels necessary to maximize coordination and control in the production of a good or service are not permanently stored within the organization.

Where the lower administrative levels needed for coordination and control are not stored within the organization and cannot be obtained on demand, their functions must be performed by persons outside the organization.[23] In the construction industry, the craft union in large measure has fulfilled these functions. It is difficult for organizations other than craft unions to judge the ability of workers who move from job to job in the practice of their occupations. The definition of acceptable performance and the rating of employees based on that definition is an administrative service performed by the craft union for the owner of the formal organization. The craft unions, then, perform a dual function. On the one hand, they represent their members in bargaining with the formal organization, and on the other, they function as an administrative adjunct to the organization. Since these functions are performed outside the truncated bureaucracy, we characterize the attendant authority pattern as an executive-external one. Obviously the importance of the external authority, and the consequent loss of authority by the owner, is directly related to the degree of truncation.

Thus, when procedures are highly specified and resources stored in general rather than specific form (P+R-), the departure from a complete bureaucracy occurs through the truncation of the lower administrative levels. The pattern of authority associated with this form of bureaucracy is the executive-external authority pattern. This departure from the complete bureaucracy differs radically from the one observed when procedures are not highly specified and when resources are stored in specific form (P-R+).

The Enucleated Bureaucracy. In a P-R+ organization the owner does not tell the volitional resources how to achieve the organization's goals, he merely tells them what they are. In this situation the owner relies on the specific resource to define its own procedures, to decide how and when to achieve the organization's goals. An example of such an organization might be a small school whose owner gathers together ten professors, a building, a library, pencils, and paper. In his effort to fulfill the stated objective of the organization—teaching the young the wisdom of the ages, how to think—the individual professor will, of course, use his own methods. No one tells him how to transmit his knowledge: he specifies his own procedures. Conforming to our definitions of organizational roles, the producers in our hypothetical school are, therefore, professionals rather than workers.

Where producers specify their own procedures, the necessity for a coordinator is, of course, sharply reduced. Self-regulation, however, generally is not so extensive that some coordination of resources may not prove beneficial. Where feasible, the professionals tend to act as the coordinators, since only they can anticipate which procedures they will employ and which resources they will need. Thus the faculty in our example, acting as a collegial group, determines the allocation of resources and regulates the use of common resources such as classrooms.

In the P-R+ organization we have described, the need for coordination is reduced and, where necessary, self-coordination occurs. Therefore, the number of managerial levels between the owner(s) and the producers is sharply reduced. In fact, if each volitional resource specified *all* his own procedures, all levels between the owner and the producers would or should be eliminated. Such an organization we call a totally enucleated bureaucracy. Though the extreme enucleation which we have described occurs rarely, if ever, approximations are readily found in such professional organizations as law firms, medical groups, universities, research institutes, etc.

Definition: A *Totally Enucleated Bureaucracy* is a formal organization in which all the hierarchic levels between the owner and the producers necessary to maximize coordination and control are eliminated.

To the extent that the producers coordinate their own activities, they perform the function of the enucleated bureaucratic levels. This coordination is achieved by what we term a consensual specification of procedures and allocation of resources. Divisions of labor are agreed upon and uses of physical facilities planned through the professionals' consensus rather than by executive directive. When administrative functions are performed by a group each member of which has a voice in decision-making, and when those decisions are based on a consensus, coordination is achieved through collegial decision-making.[24] In the totally enucleated bureaucracy, the professionals constitute such a decision-making body. It seems clear then that a collegial authority pattern is associated with the totally enucleated bureaucracy.

In the last remaining combination of procedures and resources, P-R-, no formal organization occurs. If the procedures are not specified, the hierarchy between the owner and the lowest management levels is enucleated; if resources are not stored in specific form, the lowest levels of management are truncated; if all the levels of the hierarchy below the owner are excised there can be no formal organization. The patterns are summarized in Table I-2.

Optimal Bureaucratic Structures. Both the truncated and enucleated bureaucracies are modified forms of the complete bureaucracy. The proposition that these modifications occur under certain conditions suggests that the complete bureaucracy is not always the optimal organizational form for attaining the owner's goal. Indeed, as we will show, the complete bureaucracy rarely, if ever, is an optimal form of organization.

An optimal bureaucracy is one which stores *only* that number of levels which maximizes the *benefits* of coordination, while the complete bureaucracy stores all the hierarchical levels neces-

TABLE I-2

**The Determinants of Bureaucratic Types and
Associated Authority Patterns**

Determinants*	Bureaucratic Type	Authority Pattern
P+R+	Complete bureaucracy	Executive
P+R-	Truncated bureaucracy	Executive-External
P-R+	Enucleated bureaucracy	Collegial
P-R-	No organization possible	None

* P+ symbolizes a high proportion of specified procedure, P- a low proportion; R+ a high proportion of stored specific resources, R- a low proportion.

sary to maximize coordination itself. A maximally coordinated organization has available, as needed (1) all the volitional and nonvolitional resources necessary to perform all the interdependent tasks, and (2) plans all the interdependent tasks to the extent that the performance of any one of them will not hinder, and, when possible, enhance the performance of any other task. A complete bureaucracy not only stores the hierarchies necessary to plan all the interactions of the human and nonhuman factors of production, but also stores the hierarchies necessary to insure that planning is being carried out, thus attaining both coordination and control. Just as benefits can be gained from coordination, so are there costs associated with the processes of coordination and control. The optimal bureaucracy occurs at the point when the gains that would accrue to the owner from increased coordination and control are outweighed by the costs of obtaining that increase—namely, that of adding an additional hierarchical level.

One example of movement from a complete toward a more nearly optimal bureaucracy was described in *Time* magazine. In that example, the reductions in coordination and controls made by the owner of a retail chain resulted in a net gain for his organization. Inventory replacement cards, sales receipts, time clocks, etc. were eliminated. Undoubtedly, there was some loss due to the lessening of coordination and controls, but the owner ". . . wiped out so much record keeping that he has junked 120 tons of paper forms, saved $14 million. He was able to cut prices 5% and was rewarded with an 18% sales increase. . . . Some 8,000 jobs out of 28,000 have been eliminated. . ."[25] Each of the changes made eliminated a specified procedure and so decreased the ratio of specified to generalized procedures. In effect, the granting of increased discretion to the lower administrative levels tended to change the organization from a more complete to a more enucleated one.

Whether change toward the optimal condition takes the form of greater enucleation, as in the example, or of greater truncation, generally is determined by the nature of the organization's interaction with its external environment.[26] The speed with which an owner can specify procedures is directly related to the complexity of the organization's interaction with the environment. Complexity increases as: (1) there is an increase in the number of environmental factors to be considered before an appropriate response can be selected; and/or (2) there is an increase in the intricacy and difficulty of the response. Stocking a nation-wide chain of supermarkets is an example of a complex interaction on a response, or procedural, level. When the interaction is complex and rapid specification of procedures is required of the organization, the owner is forced to allow the lower hierarchic levels to specify their own procedures, and this tends to enucleate the bureaucracy.

Given the tendency to enucleate, coordination by means of a collegial system is desirable if the producers in the organization share common resources. Because the producers, in this case professionals, specify their own procedures, only they can determine what resources they will need. Further, they are best able to allocate these resources across the entire organization (i.e., among themselves), and so take advantage of economies of scale.

However, coordination by a collegial system depends on the emergence of consensus and thus tends to be time-consuming. Consequently, this system is efficient to the extent that resource requirements remain relatively stable.

An enucleated bureaucracy employing a collegial system facilitates rapid specification of procedures but limits the speed with which resources can be converted. When both rapid change of resources and rapid specification of procedures are required, alternate, more complex organizational structures must be employed. However, as we shall see, these structures further reduce the benefits of coordination. Enucleation of the bureaucracy, then, is optimal (a) when environmental interaction is complex, making owner specification of procedures difficult, and (b) when there is need for rapid response, making owner specification nearly impossible. Coordinating an enucleated bureaucracy by a collegial system is optimal (a) when the professionals share common resources, and (b) when the resource requirements are stable.

In addition to complexity, the interaction between an organization and its external environment also can be characterized by its diversity. By diversity we mean an environmental state where, to achieve the goal, a number of different functions must be performed, each of which requires a more or less different set of procedures and resources. That is, given one environmental condition, the owner achieves his goal by utilizing one subset of procedures and resources, and given a different environmental condition, he employs a separate subset of procedures and resources. The more diverse the interaction, the more diverse will be the resources required for goal attainment by the organization. The more sporadic the demand for each of the diverse functions, the greater the costs and risks associated with storing all the necessary resources. When the storage costs outweigh the benefits of coordination, the owner should obtain the necessary volitional and non-volitional resources only *after* the demand for them has been made. This tends to truncate the bureaucracy. Thus, when interaction is diverse and, in addition, the environment is unstable, the optimal organizational form tends toward a truncated bureaucracy.

This tendency is mitigated, however, if the organization is forced to respond rapidly to environmental demands. It takes time to acquire resources, so in order to respond rapidly, the organization must have on hand the resources necessary to make any of its diverse responses. Storage of large quantities of alternative specific resources which perform no immediate function, and indeed may never perform a function, is costly. Highly diverse interaction, coupled with sporadic demand and the necessity for rapid response, normally increases the cost of storage of all the necessary resources to the point where organization does not occur. There are, however, some instances where the possible costs of not storing all alternative resources are so great that they outweigh the costs of storage. This holds true particularly of the military establishment, which must be prepared to respond rapidly to a highly diverse environment, and where demand for military action is sporadic. Ordinarily the costs of such storage would lead to a truncation of the organization. When extraordinary conditions, like national defense, require storage of a wide range of reserve weapons systems and of alternative hierarchic levels necessary for the rapid use of those systems, the resulting organization is an overcomplete bureaucracy.

Definition: A formal organization is an *Overcomplete Bureaucracy* when it stores (for long periods of time) more hierarchic levels than are necessary to maximize coordination and control.

In summary, a complete bureaucracy is optimal when the environment is stable. Once the environmental factors in a stable environment are understood, there is no need to reexamine them. A stable environment thereby decreases the effect of complexity of interaction. Further, a stable environment by definition eliminates sporadic demand. Thus, in a stable environment where the owner can specify the organization's responses, the optimal organizational form approaches the complete bureaucracy. Since these conditions rarely, if ever, occur, a complete bureaucracy rarely, if ever, is optimal.

Movement away from a complete bureaucracy depends on the interrelationship of three variables: (1) complexity of environmental interaction; (2) diversity of environmental interaction; and (3) the need for rapid response. An increase in the complexity of interaction tends toward enucleation. The tendency is enhanced as a function of the need for rapid specification of procedures. An increase in the diversity of interaction together with sporadic demand tends toward truncation.

Complex Organizational Structures. To this point we have only considered "simple" organizational types and the authority patterns associated with each of them. An organization is a complex one when its authority relationships cannot be described by a single authority pattern. An example of such a complex organization is a hospital, where the administrative and medical groups each operate under a different authority pattern: the administrators under an executive-authority pattern, and the doctors under a (more or less) collegial system. Obviously, attainment of the hospital's goals is directly dependent on the activities of the members of the collegial group. The function of the administrative component is to facilitate the work of the colleagues. The nature of the activities performed by the administration are, therefore, dependent on the needs of the collegial group. When the activities of one group are directly determined by the needs of another within the same organization, the first group is coupled and in service to the second group.

Definition: An *Internally Coupled Bureaucracy* is a formal organization containing two or more authority patterns, one in service to the other.

The when and why of internally coupled organizations can be understood by looking at the organization from the owner's point of view. He must maintain procedures at the specified end of the continuum and store resources in their most specific form if he is to maximize coordination. Should achievement of his goal require the use of volitional resources for which he cannot specify procedures, then a collegial coordinating mechanism may be optimal for maximizing the benefits of coordination. Should the colleagues require some services or functions to be performed for which procedures can be specified (and if these are of sufficient number and size to make it economically or psychologically feasible), the rational owner will couple a small, more complete bureaucracy to the collegial group to perform those functions. Under these conditions, the complete bureaucracy is in the service of the colleagues, and their activities are determined by the needs of the colleagues.

On the other hand, when the owner of a complete bureaucracy, for better attainment of his goals, requires the performance of some functions without being able to specify procedures, then he will couple a collegial authority pattern to his executive-authority pattern, and the activities of the colleagues will be determined by the needs of the complete bureaucracy. A research-and-development division whose research objectives are established by the sales organization is a case in point.

Another sort of coupling occurs when the services of two kinds of bureaucracies are needed to produce a good or a service but the owner of one of the bureaucracies does not store all the specific resources necessary to staff two bureaucracies. An example of this type of coupling might be a manufacturer who needs the services of a market-research organization. Because he does not need them frequently enough to couple internally, he temporarily converts some general resources to specific ones by hiring independent researchers. We call such a situation external coupling.

Definition: Externally Coupled Bureaucracies are formal organizations wherein one bureaucracy specifies or approves the procedures (or determines the goals) of the other.

External coupling by specifying or approving procedures occurs when an organization like Sears Roebuck hires a "job shop" to make a part for one of its appliances. The job shop's procedures are specified or approved through Sears' setting up minimum requirements. The earlier example of a manufacturer hiring a market-research organization illustrates external coupling through goal determination. These examples highlight two differences between internal and external coupling: (1) in external coupling no volitional resources are common to both organizations, and (2) internal coupling always involves two different authority patterns. A distinction also should be made between externally coupled organizations and two independent commercially interacting organizations. In both situations there is an exchange of goods and services. In an externally coupled relationship, however, the bureaucracy in service to the other cannot exist without the dominant organization. In other words, an oligopsonistic relationship must exist between the two organizations before they can be considered externally coupled.

A third type of complex organization is the decentralized organization. As we use the term, decentralization is related to the degree of autonomy across organizational units. Autonomy is equated with the extent to which the activities of one component of an organization are independent of the activities of other components of the organization. In other words, the degree to which an organizational unit is autonomous varies inversely with the degree to which its activities are coordinated with other organizational units. The autonomy of an organizational unit theoretically can vary from total interdependence to almost total independence. Total independence of organizational components would be indicative of separate organizations rather than one decentralized organization. If all organizational units, however autonomous, are less than totally independent, then there must be interdependent areas that require coordination. A central bureaucracy can coordinate the activities of the autonomous units wherever feasible and also take advantage of possible economies of scale.[27] Based on these assumptions, we arrive at the following definition:

Definition: A *Decentralized Bureaucracy* is a formal organization when it consists of two or more semiautonomous units neither of which is in service to the other.

Autonomy arises when a unit manager is given discretion not only over his unit's procedures but also over the conversion of general resources to specific ones. When a manager is given a goal and specific resources to achieve that goal, his range of activities is much more curtailed than when given general resources to use at his own discretion in achieving the owner's goal. The former condition we consider as delegation, the latter as autonomy. Delegation results in a single enucleated bureaucratic structure,[28] while autonomy leads to two or more semi-independent organizational units. Granting a manager authority to convert resources independently is tantamount to the establishment of a semiindependent organizational unit.

The degree of organizational decentralization can be measured by the degree of autonomy given to organizational units, that is, the amount of general resources over which the unit's manager has control. Stated more formally, the degree of organizational decentralization is determined by the general resources managers are permitted to allocate without approval from the owner or his chief operating executive, divided by the total resources of the organization.[29] The extent to which a subunit is decentralized can be determined as follows: the general resources of the subunit which can be allocated by the manager of the unit without the permission of either the owner or of any other managers, divided by the total resources of the unit.

When an owner decentralizes he gives up control over some of his resources. As a consequence, the possibility of usurpation is increased and some potential benefits from coordination foregone. Thus decentralization involves costs which, for the rational owner, must be offset by gains resulting from decentralization. We contend that the potential benefits from decentralization increase as the necessity for rapid response increases. In fact, we will demonstrate that the necessity for decentralization arises as a result of time pressures.

We hypothesize that decentralization arises as a function of the complexity of the organization's interaction with its external environment and the rapidity with which the organization must respond to that environment. As we have stated, complex interaction results either from procedural or environmental complexity. We further hypothesize that the optimal form of decentralization differs as a function of the various kinds of complexity. When procedures are so complex that a great deal of time is required in order to specify the appropriate responses, one way of saving time is to specify some of these procedures simultaneously rather than sequentially. This can be accomplished by allowing components of the organization to specialize in a set of procedures leading to the achievement of subgoals. In this way, each component simultaneously specifies the procedures for achieving its subgoals. Presumably, near simultaneous achievement of the set of subgoals results in achievement of the organization's overall goal.

Organization of autonomous units around sets of different subgoals is, in effect, functional decentralization, an example of which might be the Scott Paper Company, which has timber, paper-processing, and paper-towel divisions. All the divisions specify their own sets of complex procedures, and they do so simultaneously. However, since the supply and demand of the units affect one another, their activities must be interrelated if the final goods are to be efficiently produced. That coordination is provided by a central bureaucracy.

When complex interaction arises from environmental complexity and response must be rapid, the time needed to make a decision can be reduced by setting up parallel bureaucracies to deal with different segments of the environment. (The environment can be segmented on the basis of population or geographical differences or any other relevant characteristic.) This has the effect of reducing the number of hierarchies through which information from the environment must pass. Let us take a simplified view of a supermarket chain. If a complete bureaucracy were to deal with all segments of the population, the number of administrative levels would be greater than if parallel bureaucracies were set up to handle individual population segments. The latter results in a larger number of managers at each level (one of the costs of decentralization) but fewer levels. Though each orders from a central warehouse, the bureaucracies are parallel because each one semi-independently buys, sells, and displays its own merchandise. Every merchandising decision is duplicated, and each decision is simultaneously and independently arrived at by the parallel bureaucracies. Since the actions of one parallel bureaucracy have relatively little effect on another, little coordination is required of the central bureaucracy. The role of the central bureaucracy lies primarily in the prevention of usurpation and the maximization of economies of scale. In the case of our supermarket chain, such an economy might be effected if the central bureaucracy buys staple items for national distribution while local units determine the weekly specials.

The advantages of parallel bureaucracies in dealing with an unstable environment become apparent if one makes two assumptions: first, that knowledge of changes in the environment enters the organization through the bottom layers and travels through the intermediate to the top layers; second, that the time necessary for a given quantity of information to pass through a layer of bureaucracy is a constant. Under these assumptions, as one adds or subtracts a bureaucratic layer, there is a corresponding arithmetic increase or decrease in the time required to perceive, initiate, and evaluate new procedures to cope with an environmental change. This can be illustrated by comparing a two- with a three-layer bureaucracy. In the two-layer bureaucracy the lower level reports an environmental change to the upper level, the upper level specifies a new procedure to deal with the changed environment, and the lower level reports on the adequacy of the new procedure. Three communication time-units have been consumed. In a three-layer bureaucracy each of the three steps requires two communication time-units, or a total of six time-units, to complete the cycle. This is illustrated in Table I-3. In the same time that a two-level bureaucracy can make and evaluate three independent changes, a four-level bureaucracy can institute and evaluate only one procedural change.

The major benefits of parallel decentralization result from processing information through fewer hierarchic levels. However, because the parallel bureaucracies also are simultaneously specifying procedures, there is a time-saving in response rates. Function decentralization, on the other hand, derives its major benefits from the savings in response rates due to simultaneous specification of procedures. This situation also has secondary benefits. If a single bureaucratic unit were to specify all the complex procedures, a larger number of hierarchies would be necessary, so functional decentralization realizes some benefits from more rapid information-processing.

Since both forms of decentralization (differentially) eliminate some hierarchic levels between the owner and the producers, the distinction between these organizational forms and enucleation may not be entirely clear. It rests on the different coordinating mechanisms used by these organizations. Coordination in an enucleated bureaucracy is accomplished by the colleagues who

TABLE I-3

Communication Time and Bureaucratic Levels

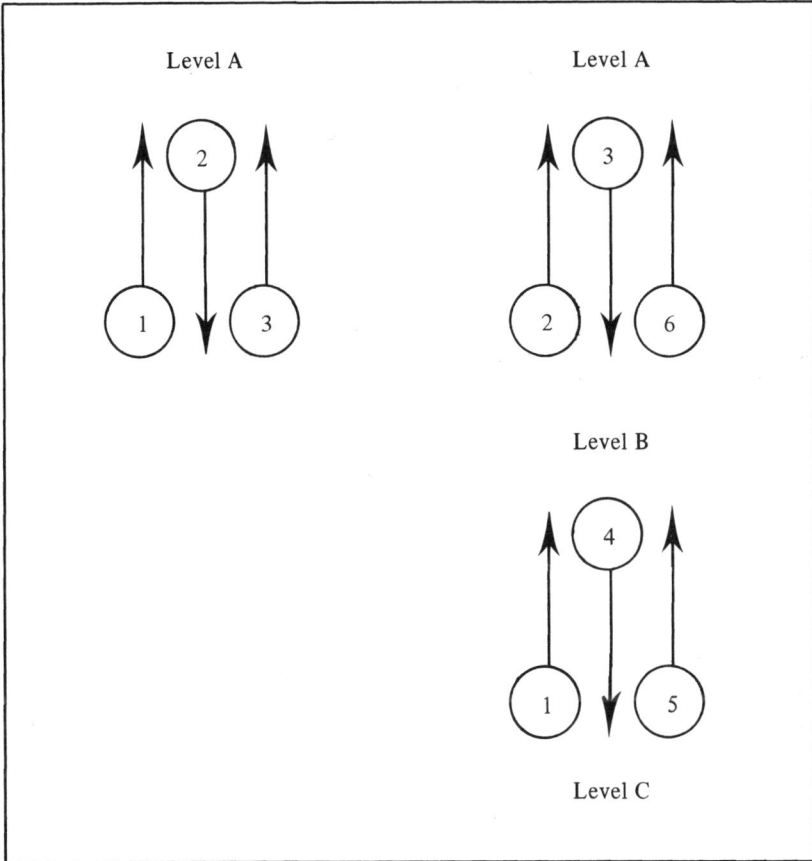

Level A   Level A

(2)

(1) (3)

(3)

(2) (6)

Level B

(4)

(1) (5)

Level C

form themselves into a single bureaucratic unit for that purpose, while coordination in a decentralized organization is achieved within and between multiple semiautonomous units.

A collegial system dependent upon the emergence of consensus requires considerably more time for decision-making than does a small number of single executives, each making decisions independently. A single coordination mechanism, however, is better able to allocate resources across the entire organization. On the other hand, a decentralized mechanism enables more rapid response although limiting the extent of coordination. Whether enucleation or decentralization is optimal depends on the necessity for rapid decisions about resources.

In summary, the decision to decentralize and extent of decentralization is a function of (a) the necessity for rapid specification of procedures and rapid resource decisions, and (b) the degree of complexity of the interaction between the organization and its environment. Given the necessity for rapid decision, slow response is costly. When the costs of slow response exceed the benefits gained from coordination, the result is a decentralized organization. When the slow response is due to procedural complexity, we hypothesize that functional decentralization will occur whereby each unit simultaneously specifies a set of procedures to attain a part of the organization's goal. In order for the overall goal to be efficiently attained, the central bureaucracy must coordinate to some extent the efforts of the functionally decentralized units. Parallel decentralization results from environmental complexity, where each of the duplicated bureaucracies achieves a small portion of the overall goal of the organization. The major function of the central bureaucracy is to take advantage of economies of scale in purchasing and allocating resources commonly used by the parallel units.

In developing this typology for purposes of exposition, we have dealt more or less with pure organizational forms. Before concluding this section on complex organizational patterns, we will try to point out just how intricate these patterns can become. In an organization with autonomous units, the central bureaucracy may have one type of structure, while the decentralized units have other structures. For instance, a university may have an enucleated dominant bureaucracy (colleagues) and a series of parallel bureaucracies (research projects), each of which may approximate a complete, enucleated, or truncated bureaucracy. Each of these parallel bureaucracies, in turn, may have decentralized units. Another example might be General Motors, where some parts of the organization are decentralized on the basis of function, others on the basis of environmental differences, and still others remain under the direct control of the central bureaucracy. Obviously, a very large number of possible combinations of organizational units are possible.

In an unpublished paper, Gordon and Becker define the third variable, "visibility of consequences" (hereafter C_V), as the degree to which the owner of an organization can and does evaluate the costs of obtaining a given level of goal attainment from a procedure-resource interaction.[30]

Consequences are conceived of as ranging from high visibility, wherein the owner of the organization can and does evaluate both the cost of a program (i.e., the cost of a resource-procedure interaction) and its relative contribution to goal attainment to low visibility, wherein the owner is unable or unwilling accurately to assess the value of a program in terms of his goal. Visibility rather than knowability or measurability was selected as the relevant dimension along which consequences are distributed because of situations where the consequences, in terms of the organization's goal, are relatively knowable or measurable in some abstract sense, yet for some reason are not accessible to the owner.

The consequences associated with the programs in state and municipal hospitals might serve as examples of such a situation. The owners of these organizations constitute the appropriate electorates. Holding constant such factors as interest in the organization, sheer physical distance makes a difference to these owners not only in terms of the time required to evaluate consequences, but also in the accessibility of information about them. Distance from the organization tends to reduce the visibility; yet the inherent knowability or measurability of the consequences does not differ substantially for the two organizations.

Visibility of consequences can be associated with a single procedure-resource interaction, with a set of procedure-resource interactions, or with the overall program of procedure-resource interactions for goal attainment. Visibility of consequences can be operationalized at either a macro- or a micro-level. For example, the board of directors of an organization can decide whether the activities of a division are optimal in terms of overall goal attainment, while the division manager attends to procedure-resource interactions and the subgoals to which they are related.

In an organization characterized by high C_V, an owner is able to evaluate the costs of, and the degree to which, a current resource-procedure interaction contributes to goal attainment. He is able to test the efficacy of new procedures or resources and, if they should prove superior to his current practices, adopt them. With low C_V, the owner not only is unaware of how much a current program contributes to goal attainment, he also is unable to judge whether an alternate program would be superior. Just as it is difficult to associate degrees of goal attainment with various programs under low C_V conditions, so it is difficult to determine if the owner's property rights are being usurped.

We have assumed that there is a tendency for those who work a property to acquire rights in it.[31] The acquisition of those rights either by seizure—i.e., theft—or by misuse of resources constitutes usurpation. Misuse of resources can take two forms: (1) exploitation of organizational resources by the operators of the organization for their personal benefit; or (2) ritualization of procedures for personal benefit. Theft of resources involves their actual removal from the organization. Other possible forms of usurpation, exploitation, and ritualization allow the organization to retain (nominal) ownership of the resources.

Exploitation of organizational resources for personal gain can range from total monopolization of the resource to part-time use to sporadic use. Exploitation encompasses actions such as use of a company car or the services of a secretary for personal or nonorganizational matters, after-hours use of office equipment, appropriation of more office space than actually needed, refusal to hire competent assistants lest they not "fit in" with the group in control.

Ritualization as a form of usurpation occurs when an operator insists on certain procedures not necessarily in the best interests of the organization simply because they benefit him personally. The following practices fall under this category: use by a foreman of manual wiring instead of printed circuits because the manual operation provides him with more subordinates; the retention of judgmental sampling when a statistical sampling approach to quality-control would obviously be superior; preventing the elimination of an obsolete course from a curriculum simply because it is the only course the operator can teach. In each of these examples ritualization is beneficial to the operator because a procedure is retained in which he is expert, thus enhancing his position. Further, having prevented change, he is not faced with the problem of having to cope with new procedures, and so in addition to status he also gains security.

The organizational structure determines whether usurpation takes the form of exploitation, ritualization, or theft. The dynamics of usurpation, when it is likely to be attempted or likely to succeed, are determined by the owner-operator goal relationship and by the perceived and actual visibility of consequences.

Organizational Structure, Relative Ease, and Form of Usurpation. All usurpation involves an abuse of resources either through manipulation of procedures (exploitation and ritualization) or violation of procedures (stealing). All things being equal, usurpation is easiest where a person specifies his own procedures. One simply specifies a procedure that makes possible the exploitation of a resource and its use for personal benefit. This is characteristic of the enucleated bureaucracy, the organizational form that most favors usurpation. The ease with which usurpation can be carried out in this form of organization is perhaps best illustrated in Hall's study of the informal organization of the medical profession.[32] Hall detailed how new procedures for the selection of interns were specified in a hospital so that a group of doctors could monopolize the resources for their own benefit. Competitive examinations for prospective interns were eliminated because Jews frequently received the top scores and the ruling group of doctors wished to keep Jews out of their hospital. In this case the operators obviously exploited the resources of the organization for their personal benefit.

As the proportion of organizationally specified procedures increases, it becomes correspondingly difficult to usurp by specifying one's own procedures. Rather, usurpation takes the form of defending the use of an already specified, preferred procedure in the face of one possibly more efficient from the owner's point of view.

The hypothesis that exploitation as a means of usurpation is more likely in an enucleated than in a complete bureaucracy, and that ritualization as a means is more likely in a complete than in an enucleated bureaucracy, does not rule out the possibility that stealing can occur in both. We assume that monopolization of a resource provides as much gain for the usurper as does stealing, but that stealing is considerably more risky. Therefore, a "rational usurper" will monopolize resources rather than steal them. If, however, the resources cannot be exploited or procedures ritualized, theft will be the characteristic form of usurpation.[33] Since human resources in the truncated bureaucracy are only temporarily stored in specific form, the opportunities to benefit personally from exploitation or ritualization are severely curtailed, so if usurpation is to occur, it usually involves the removal of resources from the organization. Pilferage of building materials, notorious on almost all construction projects, is one example of usurpation in the truncated bureaucracy. Others include: the theft and resale of fashion designs, or work slowdowns to maximize the pay for work performed.

So far, we have hypothesized that usurpation is easiest and will occur as exploitation in an enucleated bureaucracy because of its low proportion of specified procedures. In the complete bureaucracy with its high proportion of specified procedures usurpation is more difficult. Further, because the specified procedures make exploitation difficult, usurpation occurs as ritualization. In the truncated bureaucracy with a low proportion of stored specific resources, ritualization is legitimized by contract, and exploitation of resources is only temporarily beneficial, so usurpation takes the form of theft.

In associating each bureaucratic type with a particular form of usurpation we do not mean to imply that only one form of usurpation can occur in any given organization. In fact, it is likely that all forms of usurpation occur in all organizations. By linking bureaucratic forms with kinds of usurpation, we merely identify the dominant form of usurpation in that organization. Though we expect, for instance, ritualization to be the dominant form of usurpation in a complete bureaucracy to the extent that procedures are not specified in some areas of the organization, to that extent will exploitation be the more likely form. Generally, procedures are less specified the higher the hierarchic level in the complete bureaucracy; therefore, usurpation will occur as exploitation at the top of the organization and as ritualization nearer the bottom.

Ease of usurpation is dependent on bureaucratic structure only to the extent that C_V is held constant. Regardless of structure, ease of usurpation is inversely related to visibility of consequences; high C_V makes usurpation more difficult, because the owner can associate misuse or abuse of a procedure with lower levels of goal attainment.

By looking at both bureaucratic form and C_V, we can determine the ease with which a particular form of usurpation can be accomplished, but it is an inadequate basis on which to predict attempted usurpation. The operators' perception of C_V is more important than the actual C_V, for they will act in accord with their perceptions. However, perceptions of C_V alone do not forecast usurpation; the attempt to usurp is made only when there is a motive to do so.

Motive for Usurpation. Usurpation is not inevitable, for the operators of an organization may or may not desire to usurp the owner's property rights, depending partly on whether their goals and those of the owner coincide or conflict. Goal congruence or goal conflict is, in Etzioni's terms, a function of the kind of compliance relationship that develops between the owners and the operators.

Where a normative compliance relationship exists, high goal congruence may be expected.[34] A normative compliance relationship develops when the owner applies normative power to gain compliance and the operators have moral involvement with the goals of the organization. Moral commitment can be based on an internalization of the organization's goals, or on sensitivity to pressures from primary-group members. Voluntary membership in organizations like church groups, political parties, etc., exemplifies moral commitment through the internalization of goals; groups of professionals in organizations like law firms, hospitals, or universities represent operators who develop moral commitments (partly) through primary–group pressures.

Lower goal congruence can be expected from a utilitarian compliance relationship.[35] This relationship develops when an owner's use of remunerative power interacts with the operators' calculative involvement. Most profit-making organizations develop primarily utilitarian compliance relationships.

Obviously, in the absence of a motive, usurpation will not take place. It would make no difference whether usurpation was perceived to be easy or difficult, when the owners and operators are in a normative compliance relationship, the subversion of the owners' goal would be tantamount to the subversion of one's own goal. Our hypothesis about attempts to usurp and the outcomes of those attempts all presume low goal congruence.

With low goal congruence between the owners and operators, we hypothesize that maximal usurpation will occur in an organization in which visibility of consequences is low and is perceived to be low by the operators.

Based on this hypothesis it can be implied that (a) minimal usurpation will occur in an organization in which visibility of consequences is high and is perceived to be high by the operators; (b) usurpation will be attempted unsuccessfully where visibility of consequences is high but erroneously perceived as low by the operators; (c) fewest attempts at usurpation will be made, and, if made, be least successful, where visibility of consequences is high and is perceived as high by the operators. The predictions about usurpation attempts and outcomes are summarized in Table I-4.

Usurpation and Complex Organizations. The hypotheses about usurpation are deemed relevant either in simple or in complex coupled organizations since they refer to individual functioning in any type of organization. However, in complex organizations, either decentralized, coupled, or a mixture of both, usurpation can occur at a departmental as well as at a personal level. Departmental usurpation is exactly like individual usurpation in that the organization's resources are exploited for the benefit of the department to the detriment of the total organization, and hence to the detriment of the owners. For example, take a small psychology department in a college or university which also has a mathematics and statistics department. The psychology department has no statistician of its own, so psychology majors take the required statistics courses under the auspices of the statistics department.

TABLE I-4

Relationship Between C_V, Usurpation Attempts, and Outcomes
under Conditions of Low Goal Congruence

	High C_V Perceived	Low C_V Perceived
High C_V Actual	Few Attempts—Unsuccessful	Many Attempts—Unsuccessful
Low C_V Actual	Few Attempts—Successful	Maximal Attempts—Successful

The psychology department requests a budget increase to hire a statistician, for, so they argue, their students will learn more if the teaching material deals with psychological variables. Moreover, the faculty, it is claimed, will be aided in their research (even though the researchers almost never consult a statistician *before* collecting their data), etc. Because in the posited situation C_V is quite low— the learning argument does not lend itself readily either to proof or refutation, and nobody is likely to check the department's research activities after the hiring of the statistician—the department is granted the requested budget increase. Now the psychology department has a larger budget—which, should the statistician quit, may be used to hire another clinician who will argue for a budget increase to hire yet another statistician—a larger faculty, and a greater voice in the faculty senate, while the college or university ends up with an overstaffed statistics department and with statisticians in the psychology department, the business school, etc.

Another example of usurpation might be in the simultaneous development of missile and antimissile systems by the army, navy, and air force. Again, in this situation, C_V is quite low; the arguments for and against a centralized missile system are technical enough so that the owner—i.e., the public—is unable or unwilling to absorb the data.

The example of the psychology department and the missile system illustrates usurpation involving one or more relatively equal semiautonomous units. With such units, usurpation is accomplished by direct acquisition of resources. The semiautonomous units each control their own procedures (except for those specified by the hierarchically superior coordinating unit) and so cannot affect one another's. When usurpation involves coupled organizational units, e.g., units with different authority patterns one servicing the other, usurpation can be achieved through the manipulation of procedures. When one unit services another, its procedures can affect the functioning of the other. This is true either when a collegial group services an executive group, an R and D unit in a production organization, or when the executive pattern serves the colleagues, universities, hospitals, etc. For example, physicians may obtain the right to schedule voluntary operations on Saturdays because it benefits the collegial group, thereby needlessly increasing overtime pay and inefficiencies in the administrative sector. Quality of care may not be improved, but the organization's costs are.

Usurpation in a coupled organization was observed but not otherwise documented by one of the authors at a U.S. Naval Mine Defense Laboratory. Due to the nature of the work—developing defenses for not yet developed offensive weapons—C_V was very low. Consequently, to prevent usurpation, many procedures to control resources were specified. At one point, the comptroller department realized that as the number of controls increased, so did the resources assigned to the department. More and more controls were recommended by the department. Each set of adopted controls was followed by a rewriting of job descriptions in the comptroller department. The rewritten description included the coordination of the new controls, which sometimes justified a higher civil service classification (and, hence higher pay) or the hiring of assistants, which ultimately meant revised job descriptions. Eventually, the colleagues—physicists, mathematicians, oceanographers, and engineers—were so busy filling out time cards (and punching time clocks), allocating time for various tasks, filing weekly, monthly, and quarterly progress reports, filling out requisitions for everything from a single brass screw to a large minesweeper, that almost no time was left for scientific work. Morale in the collegial group was scandalously low, and the comptrollers were happily designing new and broader control systems.

As with individual usurpation, successful departmental usurpation presupposes low goal congruence as well as low visibility of consequences. If an organization ends up with duplicate statisticians, duplicate missile systems, or an all-powerful comptroller department, and these departments did not intend to benefit at the expense of the owners, then their decisions reflect stupidity or low C_V rather than usurpation.

Visibility of Consequences and Other Organizational Variables. Usurpation is frequently camouflaged to make detection difficult, yet its occurrence is strongly affected by visibility of consequences. It is quite easy to see how other areas of organizational functioning not subject to deliberate camouflage also could be affected by this variable. Conflict in organizations, for example, is one such area.

Conflict, according to the E.T., is the advocacy or implementation of competing programs (interactions of procedures and resources) designed to attain organizational goals. Conflict is overt behavior that consumes organizational resources.

For example, arguing about alternative procedures or resources is organizational conflict only when the arguments consume organizational time or other resources. We consider arguments that consume an organization's time but are not related to its goals usurpation, not organizational conflict. Conflict in an organization can arise over use of existing procedures, over choice between existing and new alternative procedures, or over the allocation or use of resources.

An organization's tolerance for conflict is a function of bureaucratic structure, with a complete bureaucracy having less tolerance for conflict than either a truncated or enucleated bureaucracy. While tolerance for conflict partly determines the speed with which conflicts are resolved and the actual levels of conflict in an organization, visibility of consequences is the stronger determinant.

When there is a basis for conflict resolution (high visibility of consequences) and when tolerance for conflict is low (complete bureaucracy) resolution will be rapid, and, other things being equal, levels of conflict low. When there is no basis for resolution (low visibility of consequences) and great tolerance for conflict (truncated or enucleated bureaucracies), resolution will be slow and levels of conflict greatest. We believe that there will be more conflict in a complete bureaucracy with low visibility of consequences than in a truncated or enucleated organization with high visibility of consequences, because the organization that cannot tolerate conflict yet has no machinery for resolving it will probably develop some rational or seemingly rational though time-consuming conflict-resolving mechanism, like a grievance procedure.

Organizational conflict is not unlike organizational change and adaptation in the sense that change and adaptation refer to changing procedures and resources, or to the specification of either fewer or more procedures. To the extent that conflict and

change are similar, the effects of high or low visibility of consequences are similar. There are some differences, however. Conflict
arises within the organization and involves antagonistic positions,
while the impetus for change may come from the organization's
environment and need not involve an antagonist. Although outside
information can enter the organization at any hierarchic level, if
it does not enter at the appropriate decision-making level it must
pass through one or more levels before a response can be considered. Every one of the levels acts as a filter, reducing the amount
of information passed on, and consuming time in deciding whether
or not to pass on the information. Each of the filters must decide
if the information and suggested response are relevant to organizational goal attainment. If the filter is aware of the outcome of
procedure-resource interactions (high visibility of consequences),
he can make such decisions more reliably and more rapidly. Therefore, the higher the visibility of consequences, the more rapidly
will the necessity for change and/or suggested responses to environmental changes reach the appropriate decision apparatus.

Once the information reaches the appropriate bureaucratic
level, the decision process is analogous to that of conflict resolution. When environmental conditions can be responded to more
appropriately by changing organizational structures or resources,
such changes will occur more rapidly and more frequently in organizations having high visibility of consequences.

By now it is fairly obvious that visibility of consequences is
an important variable in the E.T. It is related to organizational
control systems, control of usurpation, and conflict, to coordination, change, and adaptation to environmental and task conditions. All of these problems in turn affect organizational efficiency, so that visibility of consequences as well as ratio of specified to generalized procedures and degree of task-environment
complexity are variables in our model of efficiency.

In Chapters III, IV, and V, these variables will be discussed in
relation to the relevant literature. However, before we can discuss
those variables and the related literature in the context of organization efficiency, we must resolve the problem of defining efficiency in relation to organizational goals. We shall attempt to deal
with this in the next chapter.

CHAPTER 1

Organizational Efficiency and Organizational Goals

Both conceptually and operationally, the lack of agreement on what constitutes "efficiency" presents a major obstacle to the synthesis of research on organizational efficiency, and consequently to the construction of models of the efficient organization. On a conceptual level it seems evident that efficiency can only be thought of in relation to a goal. Almost everyone, though by no means all, agrees with that assumption, but with very little beyond that. First, assuming some goal, there are disagreements on what efficiency is and how it is measured; second, there are disagreements on defining the relevant goal; and finally, there are disagreements on whether the relevant goal is intra- or interorganizational. In this chapter we will discuss and attempt to resolve some of these disagreements.

OPERATIONALIZATIONS OF EFFICIENCY

The different ways of measuring efficiency arise from an unclear understanding of the concept, or, if it is understood, from an inability to operationalize it. First, let us understand the concept, which has been called by many different names. In its simplest form, organizational efficiency refers to the way in which the resources of an organization are arranged. In the maximally efficient organization the resources (whether land, labor, capital, goodwill, or any combination thereof) are so arranged that no other method would produce as profitable a return. (Return can refer to profitability, quality of health care, election of a political candidate, or whatever the goal of a given organization.)

In order to operationalize this concept it is necessary to define organizational goals, measure the degree of goal attainment as well as the value of organizational resources, and know all possible alternative arrangements for these resources. Short of such perfection, researchers have measured "efficiency" and labeled their findings variously as: efficiency, quality, performance, effectiveness, goal achievement, or success.

Efficiency. Efficiency is generally measured by the ratio of outputs (returns, benefits) to inputs (costs, effort). Ideally, all inputs and outputs are included. (Feldstein, Berry, and Hage are among those who have measured efficiency in this fashion.[1]) The researcher who applies this measure of efficiency assumes the organization has inputs, a production process, and outputs. The unit of measurement in empirical research in which these yardsticks have been used is that part of the organization which includes the production process, frequently the entire organization.

Quality. When efficiency is measured as a ratio of inputs to outputs, it frequently is assumed that the units of output are a constant. In organizations or organizational units where quality differences are great and cost differences negligible, the opposite assumption is more appropriate. In the case of fine restaurants, artists' studios, hospitals, universities, research institutes, for example, it might be more appropriate to measure differences in quality of output for a constant level of inputs.[2]

Productivity. Productivity, like efficiency, is expressed as a ratio of outputs to inputs. Unlike efficiency, it is concerned with only a subset of all inputs. For example, labor productivity describes the number of units of output or the dollar volume of outputs produced per man hour worked or per dollar of wages (economic definition).[3] Frequently, sociologists and psychologists measure productivity by the number of units of output produced by a single worker or small group of workers (controlling for the number of workers). (See, for example, Dubin *et al.* and Sutermeister.[4]) When productivity is measured in this fashion, subunits of organizations rather than organizations as a whole constitute the typical unit of analysis.

Performance. This word is the most nebulous of those being compared here. Sometimes it is related to goal-directed activities and sometimes it is not. It seems to be a catch-all term for a variety of approximate measures of efficiency, including morale, share of the market, innovation, etc.[5] Sometimes it simply seems to mean what is happening in the organization, which might include a baseball team's league standing or an army's combat record, factors which may or may not be related to the goals of the organization.

Goal Achievement (Goal Attainment, Degree of Goal Attainment). Most organizational goals are never reached, only approximated (e.g., zero costs, infinite profits, no accidents). Therefore, the *degree* of goal achievement is what is usually implied and would therefore be a more appropriate designation. This may or may not be measured as an output-input ratio.

Success. The attainment of a goal (or subgoal).[6]

Effectiveness. In the literature on organization this is perhaps the most widely used term of this group.[7] Some writers, among them Etzioni,[8] equate effectiveness with degree of goal achievement. For others, effectiveness is not only goal-oriented but also broader in scope than efficiency. Under effectiveness they subsume low costs, high profits, good morale, plant and equipment maintenance, maintaining a favorable public image, etc. Katz and Kahn emphasize this difference between effectiveness and efficiency; their position will be discussed below.[9]

Except for the rather nebulous concept performance, and the variety of organizational behaviors subsumed in that category, a good deal of agreement exists on how to measure organizational efficiency, although some differences are evident. The differences arise from assumptions about what constitutes an appropriate unit of measurement and from confusions about what constitutes an appropriate output variable. Sometimes the entire organization is selected as the unit of measurement, while other studies are devoted to organizational subunits or even individual workers. Sometimes innovation or high morale is selected as an output variable even though a given organization may not value innovation or morale per se, but only as avenues leading to behavior more directly linked to goal achievement.

These differences aside, almost all attempts either measure goal-oriented behavior or performance of a central function which, it is assumed, is related to achievement of the organization's goals. Frequently these measures are deflated as a function of the amount of resources necessary to achieve a particular level of whatever output is being measured. The selection of any output for measurement is predicated on an understanding of organizational goals. Most of the time, unfortunately, these goals are defined by the researcher rather than by the organization.

GOALS

Although efficiency generally is thought of in terms of striving to achieve a goal, the concept itself, the goal, raises several major problems.[10] It is often said that the publicly stated goals of an organization may differ from those actually being pursued. A number of paired words have been used to describe goal-related activity, and they reflect this distinction: manifest-latent; formal-informal; official-unofficial; open-hidden; public-private; de jure-de facto. Meanings may overlap and distinctions may be unclear, but the general idea is that there are differences between what one *says* one does and what one *actually* does.

Second, some people are able to formulate their goals more precisely than others. For example, in otherwise similar companies one owner may say that his goal is to maximize profits, another that his goal is to maximize return on investment, a third that he is trying to sell as many widgets as possible, and still another that he is out to make the world a better place.

On the other hand, if one wishes to find out what the "real" goals are, one may start by observing the behavior of the owner. Do his actions support or belie his words? If they contradict or are not congruent with his assertions, then goals may be inferred from the observed behavior. However, measuring efficiency in terms of an inferred goal can lead to error.

A relatively inefficient organization might be presumed efficient because its inferred goal might be the achievement of a particular objective in a particular fashion, i.e., its goal might be inefficiency. This is an extreme position, since intent can also be inferred from behavior; however, inferring organizational goals from behavior could lead to the assumption that all organizations achieve their goals all the time. The concept of efficiency would then become meaningless.[11]

Assuming goal structures to be measurable, whose goal is the relevant one? The owner's, the worker's, the manager's, the consumer's, or society's? These may be very different; for example, a company's stockholders may wish to create a monopoly, while society might benefit more from competition.

The problem, then, is twofold: first, the question of whose goal is the relevant one, and second, the stated goal, because of motivational or other factors, may differ from the actual goal.

Universal Goals. A number of writers have attempted to circumvent these dual problems by establishing universal goals that would apply to all organizations, for example, "organizational survival," "increasing the share of the market," or "achieving a record of accomplishment." Survival is obviously analogous to Social Darwinism and ecological studies. However, the biologist is concerned with the survival of a species rather than of an individual. For example, individual mosquitoes do not have a very long life span, but as a species they are quite successful. Similarly, the average restaurant stays in business for only a year or two, but the restaurant industry as a whole is long-lived. On the other hand, most larger organizations survive for many years, thus making research using survival as a criterion very difficult indeed.[12] Occasionally one comes across firms which do not have survival as a goal. For example, when the American Tobacco Company Trust was buying up its competitors at the turn of the century, one entrepreneur sold his firm to them for a profit, moved to a new city, started another firm, again sold it to the trust at a profit, and then moved again. Quick profit, not survival, was the goal. Survival as a goal also does not hold true for organizations with finite time horizons. Expositions, regional olympics committees, foundations set up to find cures for specific diseases, etc., all have finite time horizons, and so survival is an inappropriate measure.

Share of the market has been used to measure efficiency, the assumption being that the inefficient firm eventually will be driven out of business while the more efficient enterprise will survive (Stigler, 1958). This is a more short-run measure than survival and therefore possibly a more useful one. One must, however, be careful in using this as a measure of efficiency, because of cases where share of market and efficiency are unrelated. For example, share of the market may depend on luck, environmental influences, and governmental policy rather than on a firm's efficiency.

Another attempt to find universal goals has been made by Talcott Parsons. His AGIL schema provides these four categories of necessary activities for all organizations:[13]

A. Adaptation to the environment
G. Goal attainment
I. Integration (social stability)
L. Latency (pattern maintenance, or maintenance of cultural symbols and motivation)

Theodore Caplow proposes a similar schema.[14] Caplow says that organizational effectiveness can be measured by the following variables: stability over time, integration of organizational components, volunteerism (maintaining member participation), and achievement of organizational goals. These generalized schema must be operationalized for specific organizations before they can be useful for research purposes.

Katz and Kahn make a distinction between efficiency, which for them is akin to the goal attainment of Caplow and Parsons, and effectiveness, which is the "maximization of return to the organization by all means."[15] By efficiency Katz and Kahn appear to mean the cost of producing a unit of output where cost includes only the salaries of production personnel and supplies. They rightly argue that in addition the organization must be concerned with morale, public image, legal constraints, wear and tear on the plant, etc., in other words, organizational maintenance. For them, effectiveness includes both the narrowly defined accounting measures of efficiency and appropriate organizational-maintenance activities. This is schematically portrayed in Table II-1.

To some degree this distinction between efficiency and maintenance parallels the distinction between line (efficiency) and staff (maintenance), and between direct costs (efficiency) and indirect costs (maintenance).

TABLE II-1

Relations Between Efficiency and Effectiveness for Some
Organization Theorists Who Use the Systems Approach

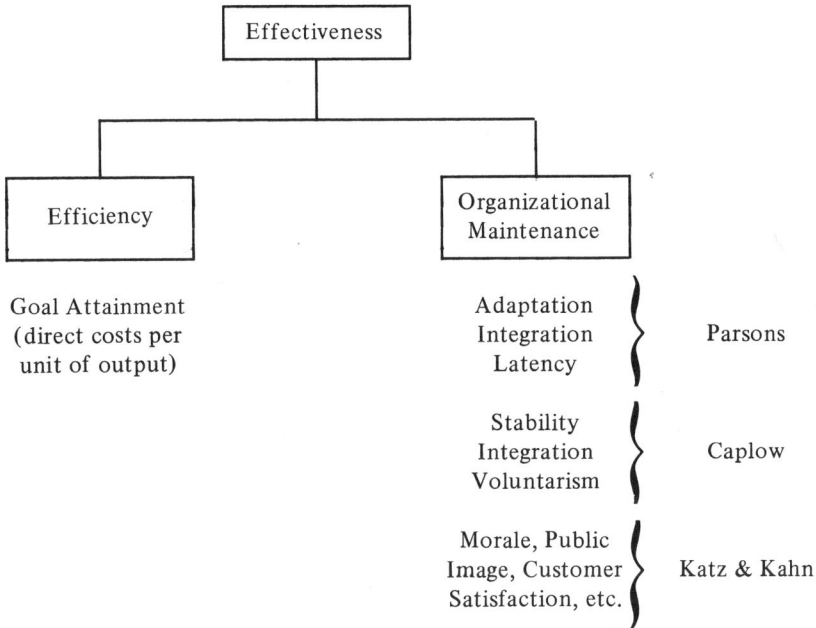

```
                    ┌─────────────────┐
                    │  Effectiveness  │
                    └─────────────────┘
              ┌────────────┴────────────┐
     ┌────────────────┐        ┌──────────────────┐
     │   Efficiency   │        │  Organizational  │
     │                │        │   Maintenance    │
     └────────────────┘        └──────────────────┘
```

Goal Attainment	Adaptation	
(direct costs per	Integration	} Parsons
unit of output)	Latency	

	Stability	
	Integration	} Caplow
	Voluntarism	

	Morale, Public	
	Image, Customer	} Katz & Kahn
	Satisfaction, etc.	

SYSTEMS APPROACH VERSUS GOAL APPROACH

The "systems resource approach" developed as a reaction to
the use of narrow operational measures of efficiency that include
only direct production costs and exclude indirect costs and the
intangibles accountants call "goodwill."[16] Researchers using the
systems approach, e.g., Seashore and Yuchtman, have measured
effectiveness using many different variables, such as growth, per-
unit costs, business volume, maintenance costs, etc. Owners or
managers are concerned with all these variables, but the pitfall of
this approach is that some of them represent means to an end
rather than an end in itself. Spending money and effort on maintenance or lifting worker morale is not usually the owner's goal
but rather a means of keeping the organization together so that his
long-range goals, whatever they may be, can be achieved. In other

words, those utilizing the systems resource approach incorrectly include measures of input variables in their operationalization of the output variable.

RESOLVING SOME ISSUES

Our task now is to devise a measure of efficiency which retains the informative quality intended by users of the systems approach and which also conforms to our definition of the concept. Theoretically, organizational efficiency refers to the degree of return on investment, where "return" is defined by organizational goals. It is impossible to make this concept operational, since estimating the maximal return requires familiarity with every possible arrangement of resources. However, we can conceive of and measure relative organizational efficiency either across independent organizations or for the same organization over a period of time. This measure of organizational efficiency requires identification of goals and measures of degree of goal attainment relative to some base, either another organization or set of organizations, or relative to previous goal attainment of the same organization.

In either case, be it attainment relative to other organizations or relative to past functioning, problems of size may arise. Larger organizations usually have more resources invested, and this could result in higher output; however, this does not necessarily denote greater efficiency. To adjust for size, relative efficiency should be measured as a ratio of outputs to inputs.

Which organizational behavior constitutes outputs and which inputs depends on the goal structure of the organization, and this brings us back to the two problems mentioned earlier: (1) whose goal structure is the relevant one; and (2) how can differences between stated and "actual" goals be resolved? We resolve the first problem by fiat and the second by expediency.

Whose goal structure is the relevant one is quite clear in the E.T. In that theory, an organization is defined as "a purposely developed system . . . to which an owner has property rights." It is assumed that ". . . a rational owner aims to achieve his goal in as efficient a manner as possible. . . ."[17] To be consistent with this theory, the relevant goal is that of the owner. In a broadly owned organization like a community hospital or a publicly held business corporation, where questioning the owners about goal structures may not be feasible (although survey sampling techniques have made it possible), and assuming no usurpation of the owners' rights, the goal structure of the owners' surrogates can be measured. Boards of trustees or directors and chief operating executives are typical examples of surrogates.

Having identified the relevant goals, we still have the problem of the various methods of verbalizing them. This confronts us with a dilemma, and our solution is based on expediency. First, we confine analytic studies to organizations with similar central functions; by that we mean comparing a certain type of hospital, for example, with others of the same type, or comparing insurance companies providing certain kinds of services with others offering similar services. In this way we compare organizations doing the same thing, functioning in the same market (environment) at the same time and under the same legal restraints or advantages. Given all these similarities we feel justified in assuming that the goals of these organizations are similar enough to justify a comparison of their relative efficiency. This assumption can be partially verified by talking with the owners or their surrogates. If, ignoring minor differences in wording, the stated goal structures are in accord with the central function of the organization, then measures of how efficiently the central function is achieved constitute a good gauge of relative organizational efficiency.

This expedient solution is not without cost. It implies that analyzing organizations with major multiple goals poses major problems. Consider a set of, say, ten organizations, each with at least two major goals. Suppose further that each has precisely the same number of major goals and also the same combination of goals. In order for us to be able to compare these ten organizations, it is further necessary that the ten owners not only list their goal preferences in identical order—i.e., goal 1 above goal 2—but also that they assign similar relative priorities to the two goals—i.e., goal 1 is one and a quarter times as important as goal 2.

It would appear almost inconceivable that an identical set of organizations can be found, yet many organizations do in fact have multiple goals. Are we to ignore them entirely? Certainly not. But again, the solution is only an expedient one rather than a theoretical *tour de force*. Simply reconsider the utility of the contemplated unit of analysis. If the organizations within the set cannot be compared because of differences in goal structures, then we must redefine the relevant systems to be studied. Take, for instance, ten universities, each with graduate and undergraduate programs as well as professional schools. Because each of the ten organizations values its professional schools differently vis-à-vis its graduate and undergraduate schools, these ten institutions cannot be compared for relative efficiency, and the individual university cannot be the unit of analysis. If, however, there is interest in specific divisions of the universities, then the unit of analysis can be redefined so as to encompass only those divisions. For instance, the teaching hospitals of the ten universities could be studied. If the goal structures of these ten hospitals are fairly similar (as detailed above), then comparisons of their relative efficiency can be made.

If we accept the assumptions and assertions that allowed us to resolve the issues and problems surrounding goal structures, then the formal definition of relative organizational efficiency is a straightforward one.

DEFINITION OF EFFICIENCY

Discounted Present Value. Underlying our definition of relative organizational efficiency is the assumption that the organization owner's interest in goal attainment is a continuing factor, as valid tomorrow as it is today. We also assume that trade-offs between the two are possible. An owner may spend money today on plant maintenance, advertising, and research to obtain profits in the future even though this may reduce current profits. We also assume that $100 today is worth more than the certainty of obtaining $100 a year from now, which is worth more than getting $100 two years from now, and so forth.

The present value of $100 next year is P, where $P = \dfrac{A}{(1 + r)}n$, with r being the rate of interest; n, the number of years; and A, the face value at the end of one year. If r = .10, n = 1, and A = $100, P equals $90.91. In other words, given a discount rate of 10 percent, it makes little difference whether one has $90.91 today or $100 a year from now. (If the $90.91 were invested at an annual rate of 10 percent for one year, one would have $100 at the end of the year).[18]

The Assumption of Scarcity. We assume that resources are scarce (and therefore have a price) and that the organization's owner does not have an infinite amount of time, energy, and capital to invest in the pursuit of his goals. His time, energy, and capital are assumed to be scarce. If this is true, then the owner will want to achieve his goals with a minimal expenditure of scarce resources. That being the case, his goals can be stated in terms of a ratio of benefits or outputs to inputs.

If the assumption about scarcity is not tenable, then the concept of efficiency is irrelevant. Without scarce resources, efficiency can be maximized by maximizing output even though costs or inputs go to infinity!

With the assumption of scarcity, however, we can represent goal attainment in terms of an output-input ratio. Adding the concept of discounted present value of benefits to costs, changes in the discounted present value of benefits to costs represent changes in organizational efficiency. For a number of reasons efficiency can be defined in terms of discounted present value of benefits to costs.

1. Trade-offs between present and future goal attainment are taken into account.

2. Important organizational variables utilized in the systems or effectiveness approach are taken into account in achieving an over-all goal. From Table II-2 it can be seen that this approach is not inconsistent with concern for morale, human relations, customer satisfaction, growth, innovation, maintenance, personnel skill levels, coordination, etc., which are not included in the financial report of the organization. These may all be important means to the owner's long-range goal attainment. We modify Table II-2 in the following way.

3. The final reason for selecting this measure is that it can be applied both in for-profit and not-for-profit organizations. Of course, implementation and measurement become more difficult, though not impossible, when happiness or "utility" or some other generalized concept like quality of medical care is the output variable.

TABLE II-2

The Goal Attainment Approach to Organizational Efficiency

The Degree of Goal Attainment:

$$
\text{The discounted present value of the ratio of benefits to costs (in comparison to other alternatives)} = \frac{\text{Output and Discounted Future Output}}{\text{Input, Including Production Costs \& Maintenance Costs}}
$$

CHAPTER 2

Specification of Procedures

In the first chapter we stated that for every environmental state there is an optimal organizational structure and that this optimal form is most efficient when dynamic conditions (to be discussed) are fulfilled. In the E.T., one determinant of an organization's structure is the degree to which the owner (or his agent) specifies the procedures to be followed by the human resources in the attainment of the owner's goal. The specification-of-procedures variable is a complex one. Not only does it affect organizational structure, as we contend, but organizational control and authority patterns as well. It is a highly important variable, and it plays a major role in the E.T. as well as in many others as can be seen in Hickson's review of the concept.

In his review of theories of organization, D. J. Hickson[1] found that the variable specificity of the roles of organizational members, although disguised under many different names, turns up repeatedly in theoretical and empirical research on organizations. Hickson called this concept specificity of role prescription. His summary of this literature is reproduced in Table III-1. As with so many other overlapping concepts in this literature, each writer's designation has different nuances, and Hickson had to judge whether a particular concept was intended to convey specificity of role prescription or not. He omitted centralization (more specified)-decentralization (less specified), perhaps because he focused on superior-subordinate relationships, while centralization-decentralization is a more macroscopic concept, referring to relationships between departments and divisions. By and large, however, we agree with Hickson's ideas on the importance of the variable and of what it means, although we shall continue to call it specification of procedures.

TABLE III - 1

**Hickson's Typology of the Terminologies Used by Various Students of
Organizational Structures for Specifity of Role Prescription[2]**

Students of Organizational Structures	Terminologies for Specificity (or precision) or Role Prescription	
	Higher Specificity	Lower Specificity
Structure Analysts (Sociologists and Administration Theorists):		
Weber	Traditional, bureaucratic	Charismatic
Burns, Stalker	Mechanistic	Organic (or organismic)
Barnes	Closed System	Open System
Whyte	Formalized	Flexible
Hage	High formalization (standardization)	Low formalization
Crozier	Routinized	Uncertain
Gordon, Becker	Specified procedures	Unspecified
Thompson	Overspecification	Structural looseness
Litwak	Weberian	Human relations
Janowitz	Domination: manipulation	Fraternal
Frank	Well-defined (and overdefined)	Underdefined
Simon	Programmed	Nonprogrammed
Presthus	Structured perceptual field	
Bennis	Habit	Problem-solving
Structure designers (Management Writers):		
Taylor	Scientific task determination	Personal rule of thumb
Fayol, Urwick, Brech	Clear statement of responsibilities	Personalities predominant (rather than intended design)
Brown	Explicit authority and accountability	Undefined roles and relationships
Structure critics (Social Psychologists):		
Likert	Authoritative	Participative
McGregor	Theory X	Theory X
Argyris	Rational organization	Self-actualization

A procedure is a unit of work performed by an organizational member. Some words and phrases are similar in meaning to procedure, among them behavior, tasks, role, activities, and "what a worker does." In the Entrepreneurial Theory,[3] a procedure is specified "when an owner or his agent requires an organizational member to perform a (series of) planned activitie(s) in a given manner in the attainment of the owner's goal. . . . "[4] Conversely, a procedure is generalized (unspecified) "when an organizational member is required by the owner to specify the member's own procedure in attaining the organization's goal."[5] The theory defines the degree to which procedures are specified in an organization as the proportion of time spent by organization members performing procedures specified by others above them in the administrative hierarchy to the total time spent in the organization. The variable also may be defined as the proportion of specified procedures to the total number of procedures.

Hickson states there is no consensus on the relationship between specification of procedures (and similar concepts) and efficiency.[6] Before examining the different positions on this issue, let us look at how specification of procedures has been measured. By first examining the various implementations we shall gain greater understanding of the variable whose relationship to efficiency we are attempting to explicate.

SPECIFICATION OF PROCEDURES

Techniques for Measurements. Control, centralization, participation, and other concepts akin to specification of procedures have been measured empirically in a variety of ways. Attitudinal, observational, and structural means have been used, but none of the methods is completely satisfactory.

By far the most frequently used approach is attitudinal, that is, asking people in the organization "Who makes the decisions around here?" Endless variations of that question have been used to elicit the desired information. Some involve one or two simple questions, while others use measures like Likert Scales or the more elaborate Initiating Structure (I.S.) questionnaire[7] and Control Graph.[8]

Observational measures require that an observer determine the percentage of employees participating in decision-making and the actual span of control. The smaller the percentage of managers, the lower the specificity of role prescription. Because of the effort and time involved, this method is practical only for in-depth case studies of one or two organizations.

Another, more structural group of measures utilizes the existence of, and compliance with, formal rules. Rosner[9] in his study of hospital medical staffs used: (1) the percentage of incomplete medical records; (2) restrictions on the use of drugs; (3) consultation requirements; and (4) a perceived measure of control to develop his hospital control index. Jerald Hage[10] proposed as measures of "formalization": (1) the proportion of jobs that are codified, and (2) the range of variation allowed within organizational jobs.

Hill and French[11] in their study of the power exercised by heads of academic departments developed a checklist of tasks which either the department head or others (such as the professors themselves) might perform. The greater the number of these tasks performed by the department head and the smaller the number performed by the individual professors, the more specified the procedures.

Brech[12] proposes to measure specificity by whether the job is changed to fit the man (low specificity) or whether the man is made to fit the job (high specificity). Another structural measure is Jacques' concept,[13] "time span of discretion," which refers to the period of time that marginally substandard discretion can be exercised by a worker before his boss hears about it. The longer the time span, the less specified the role. This can be measured by (1) the frequency with which the superior reviews the subordinate's performance, and (2) the amount of damage, or rejected work, the subordinate can produce before the superior hears about it.

Related measures include such yardsticks as the percentage of employees in the organization who participate in decision-making,[14] the span of control,[15] and the size of the managerial component.[16] Whisler[17] based a different measure of centralization of control on the distribution of compensation among the managerial group. In his opinion a company is more centralized if a relatively high proportion of all salaries, wages, and fringe benefits go to top management than if a relatively high proportion goes to lower management.

Whisler *et al.*[18] provide one of the few attempts to validate different control (specification) measures. They obtained three measures of centralization of control: (1) the distribution of individual compensation, (2) the span of control, and (3) perceived control (Tannenbaum's control graph). They found that these measures were highly related in the departments of an insurance company with repetitive tasks, but not in those with complex tasks.

Tannenbaum in his own work[19] argues that it is not the perceived distribution of control up and down the hierarchy that leads to efficiency, but rather the absolute volume of perceived control. The higher the total amount of perceived control, the more efficient the organization.

Tannenbaum's conclusion notwithstanding, it is not surprising that Hickson finds no consensus on the relationship between specification of procedures and efficiency. The variable has been measured in a bewildering variety of ways, with almost no attempt to compare or validate the various implementations. Thoroughly confounded in this melange of measures is perceived control, actual control, and degree of formalization (potential actual control). Furthermore, it is possible to conceive of different kinds of perceived control and actual control. Even when different kinds of measures are related,[20] the relationship changes from task to task and from condition to condition.

Under these conditions it is impossible to expect anyone to find systematic relationships between specificity of role prescription and efficiency. If, however, it is realized that the variable specificity of role prescription is in fact a composite of at least three variables, then it is not illogical for the researcher to hypothesize relationships between perceived control and efficiency, actual control and efficiency, or perhaps even between formalization and efficiency. At the very least, however, it is incumbent on the researcher to define more sharply the variable in question. The variable of interest to us—the proportion of procedures specified for a given organizational role—is a measure of actual control and is differentially related to efficiency as a function of different organization-environment interactions.

The Argument for a High Proportion of Specified Procedures. A number of writers have emphasized "that clear lines of authority and responsibility are desirable, as is clear role definition."[21] These authors tend to emphasize monocratic control of the organization through the use of rules and regulations specified by hierarchical superiors for subordinates and sanctioned by the authority of office. This approach was described by Max Weber[22] as a bureaucratic authority pattern, which he considered the most efficient authority pattern. Henri Fayol also took a similar position when he suggested that "the soundness and good working order of the body corporate depend on a certain number of principles, laws, and rules."[23] Frederick W. Taylor chose the same philosophy in his scientific management. "If you allow each man to go his own way, just exactly as he pleases, without any regard for science, science melts right away. You must have standards."[24]

Other writers who emphasized the importance of managerial controls in organizational efficiency are L. Urwick, Webster Robinson, and more recently E. F. L. Brech,[25] who held that good formal organization and good direction would draw support from the informal organization and that the organization should ordinarily be "formulated according to deductive principles" rather than take individual personality differences into account. The basic Weberian position was adopted by Hage as recently as 1965, when he stated in his axiomatic theory:

> The combination of centralization [of decision making] and formalization [specification of procedures] is nothing more than coordination. There are individuals who supervise and who have rules or standards by which to evaluate the performance of their subordinates which not only result in more uniformity of behavior but in a higher volume of production as well.[26]

John Pfiffner's study of forest rangers provides empirical evidence to support this approach. He found that the use of written rules and regulations led to stability and predictability of performance and consistency of treatment of subordinates. This in turn had a positive effect on "the individual's sense of security and confidence about his role."[27]

A number of studies employing the Ohio State concept of "initiating structure" (IS) support the view that close supervision by a well-informed supervisor can prove effective. IS is conceptually similar to hierarchical supervision . . .[28]

Initiating Structure (IS) defines the extent to which the supervisor delineates the situation for his subordinates to facilitate coordination aimed at goal attainment. It would include clarification and definition of what the supervisor expects of his men, establishing routines and procedures of work, and prescribing ways for getting the job done.[29]

With respect to American general hospitals, Georgopoulos and Mann conclude:

Formal organizations typically depend on attaining predictability regarding performance through a structure of explicitly defined and regulated statuses and roles and an elaborate system of programmed coordination. The greater the pressure for exact and prompt coordination, moreover the greater the tendency toward explicit regulation of behavior, hierarchical relationships, impersonality and ultimately well-defined patterns of deference and social distance. To a large measure, the community general hospital exhibits this structure.[30]

Although Georgopoulos and Mann say that many decisions in hospitals are made by employees, they note that:

The emphasis on formal organizational mechanisms and procedures and on directive rather than "democratic" controls along with a number of other factors, gives the hospital its much talked about "authoritarian" character which manifests itself in relatively sharp patterns of superordination-subordination, in expectations of strict discipline and obedience, and in distinct status differences among organizational members. . . .[31]

They suggested that a hospital's low tolerance for error and concern for maximum efficiency and predictability of performance tend to make the authoritarian control pattern more functional:

> Increased professionalization and specialization have also
> had the effect of sharpening some of the status differences
> among the people working in the hospital—and sharp status
> distinctions bespeak of some authoritarianism.[32]

Their empirical evidence supports their contention that the clarity
of organizational rules and regulations and specific supervisory
practices lead to increased organizational coordination, both formal and informal. Coordination in turn is related to good patient
care. It is important to note that these findings refer primarily to
nurses, technicians, and other hospital employees, not physicians.[33]

Their findings may not apply to physicians. In general, hospital administrators tend to believe that more control over physicians would increase hospital efficiency by lowering hospital costs
and improving the quality of care.[34] Because physicians are often
adamantly opposed to any attempt by others to specify their procedures, administrators rarely find it politic publicly to express
these opinions. Noltingk's observation concerning research scientists fits the attitude of many physicians.

> One feature of administrative bureaucracy which can be
> particularly galling to the scientist is the feeling that deci-
> sions, vitally affecting himself and his work, are being taken
> by people with little first-hand knowledge of his prob-
> lems . . . and so the scientist is very chary of submitting his
> case to the layman and very loath to have to accept the
> latter's judgment.[35]

Specification of Procedures Questioned. A number of points that
have been raised about the efficacy of managerial controls or specified procedures are of importance to the theoretical framework
we plan to develop. They are:

First, that hierarchically imposed rules have "unintended
consequences" which do not always aid the owner in achieving his
goals. According to Robert Merton

> Unchallenged insistence upon punctilious adherence to for-
> malized procedures . . . may be exaggerated to the point
> where primary concern with conformity to the rules inter-
> feres with the achievement of the purposes of the organiza-

tion, in which case we have the familiar phenomenon of the technicism or red tape of the official.[36]

Second, rules may or may not be adhered to. Gouldner, in his study of a mining firm, found that many rules were ignored. He called this phenomenon "mock bureaucracy."[37]

And third, rules may be imposed in a manner which workers find intolerable. Rules may be imposed in a cruel, arbitrary, or contradictory manner. This form of authoritarian leadership was the independent variable in a famous laboratory study of leader behavior by White and Lippitt.[38] Because this study involved small children and artificially induced styles of leadership, it may not be relevant to organizations. However, Baumgartel[39] investigated similar variables in a study of a research organization. He found that participatory leadership was more efficient than either directive or laissez-faire leadership styles.

Leadership style and hierarchical control are distinct concepts (a distinction ignored by some writers, e.g., W. G. Scott, Georgopoulos, and Mann).

P. Blau and W. R. Scott do make this distinction: "An authoritatian approach, which is not to be confused with the exercise of effective authority, involves a somewhat rigid and domineering pattern of close supervision."[40]

Fourth, rules may or may not be appropriate to the intent of the owner. To quote Harold Leavitt, ". . . like other tools, authority can be used expertly or blunderingly."[41]

And fifth, hierarchically imposed rules are sometimes considered to be contrary to the idea of professionalism, particularly by the professionals themselves.

The Case against Specification of Procedures. The "human-relations school" differs in some important ways from the monocratic approach discussed above. Generally, for efficient decision-making, adherents of the human-relations school advocate a participatory, democratic process, by which a group of peers arrives at a consensus through education rather than through the authority of office. The human-relations school has been concerned with a cluster of other different variables, but only one—participatory decision-making (generalized procedures)—concerns us here.

Stephen Sales summarizes the central focus of the human-relations school as follows:

> It is commonly assumed that with other conditions held constant, employees will produce more under democratic supervision. (Such an assumption, of course, lies behind the entire human relations movement.)[42]

According to him, autocratic (hierarchical) supervision is

> ... characterized by the relatively high degree of power wielded by the supervisor over the work group. As contrasted with democratic supervision, both power and all decision-making functions are absolutely concentrated in the person of the authoritarian.
>
> Democratic supervision, on the other hand, is characterized by a sharing of power and by participative decision-making. Under democratic supervision, the work group becomes in some ways co-equal with the supervisor; responsibility is spread rather than concentrated.[43]

The case for low specification of procedures is made by Katz and Kahn:

> By and large, those organizations in which influential acts are widely shared are most effective. The reasons for this are in part motivational, having to do with implementation of decisions, and in part non-motivational, having to do with the excellence of decisions.[44]

Douglas McGregor also advocates this approach in his Theory Y, as does Rensis Likert in his theory of participative management: "The low producing managers, in keeping with traditional practices, feel that the way to motivate and direct behavior is to exercise control through authority."[45]

Chris Argyris, in emphasizing the value of self-actualization, says "As management controls are increased, the degree of frustration, failure, short-time perspective and conflict will increase . . ." and "Increasing the degree of directive leadership, increasing the degree of management controls increases the antagonisms of workers toward the organization."[46] The human-relations school has tended to support the idea that "no normal person is happy in a situation which he cannot control to some extent."[47] This is reflected in the effect of participatory management on morale. However, it is not established that high morale or job satisfaction is always related to higher organizational efficiency.[48]

PARTICIPATION AND MOTIVATION

Underlying the human-relations approach are assumptions about human motivation consonant with Maslow's theory of personality. Maslow says that once a worker's basic needs for food, clothing, and shelter are satisfied, he becomes increasingly concerned with ego-esteem and self-actualization. These needs include a desire to control one's environment, to take pride in one's skill. The best way to satisfy these and many other higher-level needs is through participation in decision-making, assuming " ... that democratic supervision allows productivity to be a path to the satisfaction of self-actualization and ego-esteem needs, whereas autocratic supervision does not serve such a purpose."[49]

It seems unlikely that workers performing highly routine tasks can derive satisfaction from high performance, regardless of the supervisory style. Some tasks, like washing pots and pans in a restaurant, are too dull and too lowly to promote self-esteem under the best of circumstances.

In contrast, highly skilled jobs like scientific research, medicine, engineering, or management provide a far greater potential for self-actualization. If Maslow and Likert are correct, with work of this sort one would expect the greatest gains in productivity from participation in decision-making.

A number of empirical studies provide support for the participatory decision-making (generalized-procedures) approach. William F. Whyte's description of the toy-factory assembly line paints a vivid picture of the increased productivity that can result from letting workers set the speed of the assembly line—in this case, at some loss in coordination. A number of studies by the Survey Research Center of the University of Michigan have shown that close supervision is related to lower productivity for clerical workers,[50] in a tractor factory,[51] in two industrial plants,[52] and in a refinery,[53] to name only a few.

In another group of studies on scientific researchers it is shown that the professionals prefer participatory decision-making to hierarchically imposed controls. The work by Pelz and Andrews is the most extensive study in this area.[54]

The Human-Relations Literature Questioned. In their recent reviews of this literature, Katz and Kahn and Lowin report that in some cases participatory management has helped to increase efficiency and failed in others. Lowin concludes his review of the literature by saying that the major studies are "at best suggestive" in support of participation, while the minor ones are "inconclusive." Lowin says, "among all the minor reports we have cited, only that by Coch and French can be said to clearly document the value of participatory management."[55] Blau and Scott disagree: "The Coch and French study makes no claim that their experiment involved democratic decision-making, only 'participation in planning the change.' "[56]

Indeed, Coch and French do not say in what areas the workers at the Harwood factory specified their own procedures. Could they have rejected the production changes proposed by management? Could they have changed the piece-work rate? Were they allowed to change starting times, coffee breaks, or working conditions? Unfortunately, the report does not make this clear.

French *et al.* report that participation in the Harwood factory consisted largely of interactive discussion. In their own words:

> Admittedly, interactive discussion is a minimal form of participation. Naturally, it is better to have the workers actually share in designing the change, if it is possible. When, as in this case, the nature of the problem calls for skilled engineering, employee participation must necessarily take a more limited form.[57]

This seems to be more consistent with F. W. Taylor's viewpoint than with Likert's.[58]

Morse and Reimer[59] found, in a study of clerical workers, that the group using hierarchical controls was more efficient than the group using participatory decision-making, but this increased efficiency in the hierarchically controlled group was achieved at the cost of poor work attitudes, lower loyalty, and poor motivation among the workers. Likert uses this study to support his views of the positive effects of participation by concluding that the short-range gains from hierarchical control would be lost in the long run as a result of low morale and high turnover.[60] Unfortunately, no empirical evidence is presented to support this contention. Without such evidence, Morse and Reimer's study can hardly be said to support the contention that participatory management is more efficient.

The most extensive experiment in participatory management is, to our knowledge, never referred to in the human-relations literature. Long before the birth of the human-relations school in the U.S., Lenin was advocating direct management of Russian factories by workers. After the Russian Revolution of 1917, worker participation in management was undertaken, but in practice was soon abandoned in order to preserve "labor discipline and productivity."[61]

Attempted Resolutions of Conflicting Findings. Among the attempts to resolve the contradictory findings are what we call the personality explanations. Some of these explanations rest on the assumption that some people prefer to impose or be subservient to hierarchical controls, while others prefer participatory decision-making. According to Koontz and O'Donnell:

> The implications of autocratic methods for various types of personality cannot be overlooked. Not only may the uneducated and timid react best to autocratic methods, but often hostile and overly aggressive individuals require the firm hand of a strong manager.[62]

Lowin builds his model on this assumption. He hypothesizes that the effect is cumulative in that supervisors will pick the leadership style they prefer. This in turn will attract workers who prefer this style, and, therefore, the organization will operate most efficiently by using this leadership style. Lowin says the result is a stable condition.

Tannenbaum and Schmidt[63] also suggest that the appropriate leadership style depends on the manager's value system, confidence in subordinates, leadership inclinations, and feelings of security in the face of uncertainty. They say it depends on the subordinates' need for independence, readiness to assume responsibility, tolerance for ambiguity, interest in the problems involved, identification with the organization's goals, and knowledge and expectations. It also depends on the values and traditions predominant in the organization. Pelz and Andrews[64] found that a scientist in a loosely coordinated situation (generalized procedures) had to be strongly motivated or stimulated in order to be productive. Schein, after summarizing the conflicting findings, does not share the belief that certain personality types prefer to be either controlled or not controlled, and hence seek appropriate positions. He states that the opposite ought to be the case, that whatever the personality type of the subordinate, he manages accordingly. Schein states:

> ... the successful manager must be a good diagnostician and must value a spirit of inquiry. If the abilities and motives of the people under him are so variable he must have the sensitivity and diagnostic ability to be able to sense and appreciate the differences. ... If the needs and motives of his subordinates are different they must be treated differently. ... He may be highly directive at one time with one employee but very nondirective at another time with another employee.[65]

With the assumptions, ideas, and data generated by the emphasis on personality, one could conclude that personality is a more important determinant of organizational control systems than are size, complexity, task, environment, etc.

Another explanation emphasizes professionals in organizations and conflicts between hierarchical or managerial controls and the professional's desire for autonomy.[66] Apparently, professional workers prefer a participatory approach to decision-making, peer-group consensus. Empirical evidence to support this is provided by Meltzer, Gerard, Pelz, and Pelz and Andrews.[67] Pelz concluded:

> We are becoming more and more convinced that this active interest in the ongoing work, combined with a hands-off policy concerning its direction, is one of the most fruitful things that a research chief can do—particularly with his younger personnel.[68]

Here, the appropriate conclusion is that democratic control should be increased in organizations as the degree of professionalism of the organization increases.

It is our belief that the conflicting data arose because of two kinds of errors: first, the confusion of managerial style, i.e., democratic vs. autocratic, with participatory decision-making. It is possible for procedures to be highly specified and for supervisors to be employee-centered democratic managers.

If it were possible to look at output and its relation to how decisions about the work are made, holding managerial style constant, we would still expect to find that high productivity sometimes is associated with participatory decision-making and sometimes with rigid specification of procedures. We would also expect that the nature of the task was the variable underlying the expected diverse finding. Indeed such a position could have been taken by Vroom and Mann as early as 1960, when they found that workers in one kind of job preferred one type of supervision, while workers in another preferred a different type.[69] Indeed, one might reinterpret the data on professionals in organizations and conclude that preferences for participation in decision-making are not due to the professionals' personality or need for self-actualization so much as to the nature of the task they perform.

The Task-Environment Explanation. The Entrepreneurial Theory of Formal Organizations predicts that as the interaction between the organization and its environment increases in complexity, there will be a tendency for the organization's owner to specify fewer and fewer procedures.[70]

Blau and Scott, in reference to a study by Janowitz, also hypothesize a relationship between control and complexity:

> Rigid discipline stifles professional judgments. Conversely, hierarchical authority is weakened by increasing technological complexity in an organization with its resulting emphasis on technical expertness for all personnel including those on the lowest operating levels.[71]

Katz and Kahn also suggest that "complexity and skill requirements of the job" are relevant. "Emphasis on legal compliance can bring about acceptable levels of individual performance both in quantity and quality. The more routine the activity, the more likely this is to be true." When the job itself is complex and the worker derives a sense of satisfaction from doing his job well (craftsmanship), then self-expression and self-determination are "most conducive to the achievement of high quality and quality of role performance."[72]

In the Entrepreneurial Theory it is argued that the need for rapid response to the demands of the task-environment will force the owner to allow lower-level personnel to specify their own procedures (increased enucleation). In contrast, Katz and Kahn, Tannenbaum and Schmidt, and Lowin[73] predict that the need to make decisions rapidly will make hierarchical control more efficient.

Unlike the other theories discussed above, the Entrepreneurial Theory holds that optimal organizations are structured by matching authority patterns to the appropriate task-environment. This is called coupling. Lowin seems to make the opposite hypothesis when he says that participative decision-making tends to be most effective when the entire organization is included.

These contradictory hypotheses can perhaps be evaluated by reference to some empirical data. A number of recent studies have taken the complexity of the task-environment into account. Lawrence and Lorsch[74] categorize this literature as the contingency (relativity) theory of management.

Empirical Studies and Contingency Theories of Management. In these theories, the management style which leads to efficiency will vary according to circumstances. This is something of a departure from many writers who implicitly espouse a "best way" of managing all organizations under all circumstances.

Several studies fall into this category. Joan Woodward[75] in her study of 100 English industrial firms found that management characteristics varied according to the technology involved. Her primary technology categories were unit production (job shop), mass production (an assembly line), and process production (e.g., refineries). She found that the ratio of managers to hourly workers increased with the predictability of the production techniques, implying more hierarchical control for simple technologies.

Burns and Stalker[76] in a study of 20 British firms found two different management styles, which they called "mechanistic" and "organic." The mechanistic style was more formal and hierarchical and appeared to be appropriate to stable conditions. The organic style, less formal and involving much lateral interaction rather than vertical command, appears to be appropriate for unstable conditions.

Lawrence and Lorsch, in their study of 10 American corporations, also found that the appropriate management style varied according to "technical and economic conditions outside the organization."[77] They found that hierarchical-centralized organizations were appropriate for stable environments, while more loosely organized, decentralized organizations were best for uncertain unpredictable environments.

The high-performance organizations were more likely to match their organizational structure to the environment in an appropriate manner. Parts of organizations sometimes faced different environments: the production department may have faced a stable environment and been hierarchically organized, while the research-and-development department may have faced an uncertain one and been more decentralized. These different organizational structures co-varied with managerial attitudes toward interpersonal and time orientations. Organizations facing different environments required differentiation in order to be efficient, and integration in order to coordinate these divergent subcomponents.

Separate and special integrative activities (e.g., cross-departmental committees) appeared to be unnecessary when the organization was undifferentiated and facing a stable environment, for then the hierarchy could carry out the integrative activities;[78] for organizations facing multiple environments ("coupled," in terms of the Entrepreneurial Theory), their findings produced the following paradox:

> The two organizations with the most successful performance records had, in fact, achieved the highest degree of integration of the six and were also among the most highly differentiated.

They summarize by saying

> If organizations have groups of highly differentiated mana-
> gers who are able to work together effectively, these mana-
> gers must have strong capacities to deal with interdepart-
> mental conflicts. A high degree of differentiation implies
> that managers will view problems differently and that con-
> flicts will inevitably arise about how best to proceed. Effec-
> tive integration, however, means that these conflicts must
> be resolved to the approximate satisfaction of all parties
> and to the general good of the enterprise.[79]

The contingency theory of management marks a sharp departure from some of the previous literature in organization theory,
which was divided into hostile camps of writers, some preferring a
hierarchical bureaucratic structure and others participatory decision-making. As does Schein and some others in the human-relations movement, the contingency theory says that both are right,
depending on the circumstances. This reconciliation can be viewed
as a major advance in organization theory.[80]

The Entrepreneurial Theory, although using variables other
than differentiation and integration, is a contingency theory of
formal organization. In that theory not only are different structural forms associated with different environmental conditions,
but it postulates that if an organization faces a complex environment, it is efficient for that organization to contain as many different structures as is necessary to cope with the environment.
Furthermore, implicit in the differing structural forms are differences in managerial style. The fewer the number of procedures
specified by the organization, the more decentralized or enucleated (removal of managerial levels between the owner and the
worker) will be the organization or the organizational component,
and the more enucleated or decentralized the unit, the greater the
amount of collegial decision-making and the greater the participation of organization members in decisions.

It is this contingency theory of formal organization, a theory
in which organizational structure and managerial style are simultaneously changed as a function of environmental complexity,
which will be tested by the empirical work reported here.

CHAPTER 3

Complexity of the Task-Environment

In the previous chapter we argued that the optimal organizational structure (and hence the optimal ratio of specified to non-specified organizational procedures) is contingent on circumstances. However, we did not elaborate on the nature of the circumstances. In the E.T., the optimal organizational structure is a function of the complexity of the task-environment and of the desirability of rapid specification of procedures or conversion of general resources to specific ones. In this chapter we will define and elaborate on the concept of task-environment and relate our use of the variable to other investigations of organizational complexity.

The terms task, technology, task-environment, and environment have all been used (1) to define the organizational boundary, and (2) to distinguish between what machines do and what people do. A task is defined by Bell as the smallest indivisible unit of work an employee performs.[1] This is similar to the definition of procedure in the Entrepreneurial Theory. Technology generally refers to the types of equipment employed in the organization, but it can also include techniques not primarily equipment-related, like the types of surgery performed in a hospital. Joan Woodward uses "technology" to subsume the categories of unit production, mass production, and process (flow) production.[2]

Where Woodward uses technology, Lawrence and Lorsch use environment, which they define as follows:

> While what we call "environment" is fairly self-evident as applied to research and marketing, the use of this term in relation to production requires some explanation. Contrary

69

to conventional usage, we have chosen to conceive of the physical machinery, the non-human aspect of production as part of its environment. Production executives must draw information from this equipments' performance and analyze it in terms of costs yields, and quality, just as they must also draw information from outside the physical boundaries of the firm about newly available equipment and alternative processes. It is this information and knowledge from all these sources that we are interested in characterizing as certain or uncertain. Readers who find this awkward may prefer to think in terms of "the production task" rather than of the "techno-economic environment."[3]

Task-Environment. In the Entrepreneurial Theory the concept task-environment is seen as an interaction between the organization and its environment. It includes the type of work being performed and the demands placed upon the organization by the environment. To some extent the owner creates his task-environment by his choice of product or service to be rendered, plant location, technology used, raw materials, and labor and sales markets. Even after these basic decisions have been made, the organization may or may not be able further to modify the demands of the environment. For example, a state may compel its hospitals to treat all patients who come to its emergency clinics. Such hospitals would be unable to modify that aspect of their environment, while hospitals in another state may be free to accept some patients and turn away others. The latter would have more control over the demands made by their environment than would the former. The concept of task-environment takes this difference into account and implies that the tasks performed by the organization are partly imposed by the environment and partly controlled by the organization.

Operationally, "task-environment" might be equated with "industry." An industry is a set of individual organizations producing similar goods or services for sale in a similar market, i.e., the steel industry in the United States. To the extent that the organizations in an industry use the same technology (equipment and tasks) and sell a similar product in the same market, "industry" can be equated with "task-environment."[4]

Complexity of the Task-Environment. According to the Entrepreneurial Theory, complexity of environmental-organizational inter-action has two components: procedural complexity and response-selecting complexity. The complexity of an organization's interaction with its environment increases "as there is an increase in the number of environmental factors to be considered before an appropriate response can be selected; and/or as there is an increase in intricacy and difficulty of response."[5] Given an increase in complexity, it is argued in the Entrepreneurial Theory that it is optimal for the owner or his agent to reduce the proportion of specified procedures *should it also* be necessary to specify those procedures rapidly.

The complexity of an organization's interaction with the environment then is a function of (1) the number of different tasks performed; (2) the degree of interdependence of the various tasks; (3) the problem of choosing the appropriate task or of performing it; and (4) degree of control over the environment. Optimal organizational structures and their relationship to demands on the organizational and environmental factors are shown in Figure 1, Chapter I.

Although complexity of the task-environment has not been empirically investigated to any great extent, based on studies of task complexity it can be assumed that organizations with complex environmental interactions develop complex structures. This assumption is tenable because the measures of organizational task complexity are strongly related to the definition of complex environmental interaction.

Anderson and Warkov characterized Veterans Administration hospitals treating one type of patient as having low complexity and those treating a mix of different patients as having high complexity. Heydebrand used the same measure, as well as a complexity index based on the number of different types of technical personnel employed in the hospital. Georgopoulos and Mann used the scope of services offered by the hospitals and the range of cases cared for. Jerald Hage defines organizational complexity by the mean level of training required for organizational employees and the number of different occupational specialties. Victor Thompson proposes the extent of specialization and the extent of departmentalization as measures of complexity. Bass and Udy propose measures of interdependence of tasks called "interaction complexity" by the former and "combined effort" by the latter as measures of complexity.[6]

In none of these studies, however, is complexity related to efficiency, nor does the Entrepreneurial Theory state a direct relationship. However, it implies a relationship in the discussion of optimal organizational structures as a function of environmental demands. In all cases, if organizations have a complex interaction with the environment, and speed of response by the organization is necessary, some degree of decentralization or enuclearization is optimal. All the optimal structures under these conditions require reduced specification of procedures by the owner or his agent, and greater self-specification of procedures by those at lower levels in the organizational hierarchy. Presumably, optimal organizational structures are synonymous with structures designed to attain the organization's goal most efficiently.

The relationship between complexity and efficiency, as derived from the Entrepreneurial Theory, is that the greater the complexity of the efficient organization's environmental interaction, the lower the proportion of production procedures specified by the owner. In effect, it is predicted that the efficient organization facing a complex interaction with its environment will deal with that environment by adopting some form of decentralized structure or enucleated structure and by coordinating structures in a more collegial fashion.

This is a somewhat different prediction from that made and empirically supported by Lawrence and Lorsch. They predict that as the environment becomes more complex (uncertain), the efficient organization becomes more differentiated and also develops integrating mechanisms to insure coordination between the differentiated units. Their prediction was sustained in studies of the plastics, food, and containers industries.[7] The E.T. prediction of decentralization or enucleation is similar to Lawrence and Lorsch's differentiation, but no specific integrating mechanisms are posited in the E.T.

Another treatment of environmental complexity is Galbraith's, who equates it with task uncertainty. Uncertainty is the difference between the amount of information necessary to complete a task and the amount the organization already possesses. When this difference is large, many deviations from the organization's rules and programs occur, and the organization must adjust by reducing the need or by increasing its capacity for information-processing. According to Galbraith,[8] when too much uncertainty makes coordination by means of rules, hierarchy, and goal-setting impossible, the organization must adjust one or more of four possible ways:

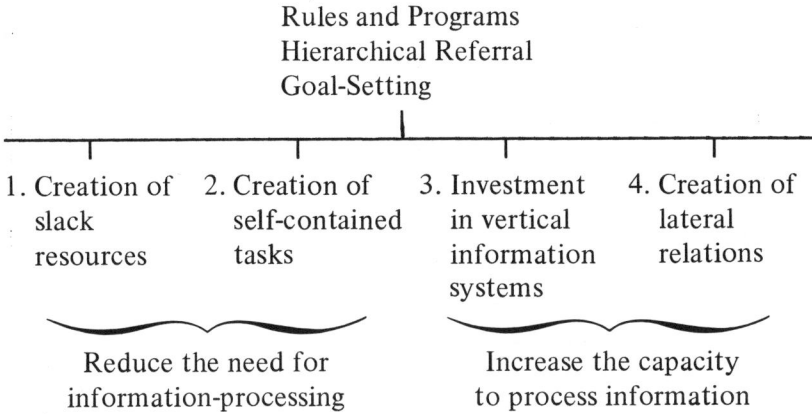

Rules and Programs
Hierarchical Referral
Goal-Setting

1. Creation of slack resources	2. Creation of self-contained tasks	3. Investment in vertical information systems	4. Creation of lateral relations

Reduce the need for information-processing   Increase the capacity to process information

The creation of self-contained tasks resembles functional or parallel decentralization in the Entrepreneurial Theory. In the E.T., with an increase in the number of environmental factors to be considered before an appropriate response can be selected, some forms of decentralization are appropriate. Galbraith's treatment of the need to process information and the creation of self-contained tasks as a means of reducing that need is quite similar to that of the E.T.

Creation of lateral relations is much like Lawrence and Lorsch's integration mechanisms and, as previously stated, not specifically dealt with in the E.T. The other two design strategies, creating slack resources and investment in vertical information systems, are not treated as structural changes by the E.T., but rather as changes in goals or procedures (reducing required level of performance to create slack) or as changing some specific resources to other specific resources (changing from manual calculators to computers or increasing the number of assistants processing information).[9] To the extent that increasing the organization's capacity to process information also increases knowledge about the transformation process, Galbraith's vertical information systems and lateral relations function like visibility of consequences.

While the E.T. makes specific predictions about how and when to decentralize and what form to choose for different environmental conditions, Galbraith merely states that the choice of strategy depends on which is least costly to the organization.

Two other major treatments of technology are those of Thompson and Perrow.[10] Thompson describes three types of technology: long-linked, mediating, and intensive. Long-linked technology occurs when organization acts are serially interdependent, as on a mass-production assembly line. Mediating technology occurs when an organization links customers or clients who wish to be interdependent, as in the case of a commercial bank that links depositors and borrowers. Intensive technology occurs when a variety of techniques are utilized in changing some object, as in the construction industry, where a variety of crafts and skills must be applied in an appropriate order to get the desired product.

According to Thompson, the design of the organization is affected by the type of technology it utilizes. Organizations employing long-linked technologies expand their domain through vertical integration; those employing mediation technologies increase the populations served; those employing intensive technologies incorporate the object worked on. These changes in design are expected to buffer the organization against crucial environmental contingencies.

Thompson's and the E.T.'s predictions about how organizations respond to differences in the task-environment are not mutually exclusive; in fact, both may be correct at different times in the life of an organization. Perhaps organizations first seek to reduce uncertainty by buffering and then respond to continued task-environment complexity by restructuring the decision-making elements which cope with the complexities. Whether both theories are correct is an empirical question, but both agree that different technologies or task-environments require different organizational structures for efficient functioning.

Perrow attempts to relate technology, goals, and structure. He classifies technology on the basis of the number of exceptions encountered in the work to be performed, and on whether or not the resultant search for a solution lends itself to analysis. Where he has a technology with few exceptions and analyzable search processes, Perrow posits that the task structure will be such that supervisory and technical personnel will have low discretion over their activities (high specification of procedures in the E.T.); in a technology with few exceptions and unanalyzable problems, supervisory personnel will have high discretion and technical personnel low; in one with many exceptions and analyzable problems, supervisory personnel will have low, and technical personnel high, discretion; and in one with many exceptions and unanalyzable problems, both types of personnel will have high discretion (low specification of procedures in the E.T.).

This description of Perrow's work, while condensed, does allow us to see that there is great similarity in the predictions made by the E.T. and by Perrow when similar topics are discussed. Perrow also discusses social interactions and differences in goal structures as functions of technology. These issues are not dealt with in the portions of the E.T. presented and tested in this work.

We can conclude this discussion the same way Thompson began his.

> Clearly, technology is an important variable in understanding the actions of complex organizations. A complete but simple typology of technologies . . . would be quite helpful. Typologies are available for industrial production and for mental therapy but are not general enough to deal with the range of technologies found in complex organizations.[11]

If, however, one assumes that jobs which require more technical personnel or more formalized training or greater specialization or are more interdependent pose greater difficulties, and hence results of performance are less predictable or controllable, then one can discuss similarities spanning all the studies. Despite differences in terminology and despite the fact that earlier researchers ignored the environment, it seems likely that two variables underlie all the studies of technology and complexity: the first is degree of control over the processes of production, and the second, degree of control of the environment affecting either inputs to the process of production or outputs of the process. The contingency theorists, E.T., Lawrence and Lorsch, Thompson, Per-

row, and Galbraith, all agree that efficient organizational structures will vary as certainty of the production process and certainty
or stability of the environment vary.

CHAPTER 4

Visibility of Consequences

In Chapter I we referred to Becker and Gordon's definition of visibility of consequences: "The degree to which the owner of an organization can and does evaluate the costs of obtaining a given level of goal attainment from a procedure-resource interaction." They explicitly relate visibility of consequences to goal attainment, and since we have related efficiency to resources expended (inputs) and degree of goal achievement (outputs), obviously visibility of consequences affects organizational efficiency. Becker and Gordon maintain that:

> In any form of bureaucracy, given high visibility of consequences an owner is able to evaluate the costs of and the degree to which a current resource-procedure interaction contributes to goal attainment. He is able to test the efficacy of new procedures or resources and install them if they are more beneficial than current practices.[1]

While the other variables related to efficiency, like specification of procedures and task-environment, were frequently defined and utilized differently by different researchers, no such confusion exists with visibility of consequences. Because this variable is a new one, having been constructed by uniting existing, simpler variables into a single concept, it is relatively unused and unconfused. The "can evaluate" or "knowable" part of the concept includes ideas like feedback, communications, and awareness, which are not specifically goal-related, as well as March and Simon's idea of operationality of goals, which is.[2] The "can evaluate" part of the concept simply refers to whether the owners of an organization make the association between goal-achievement and procedure-resource interactions, and thus also implicitly includes all the complex intellectual, attitudinal, and motivational variables which underlie any act of human behavior.

Thus far, the variable has been used only a few times. Pelz and Andrews used it to explain some of their findings about teams of scientists working in organizations. The more innovative teams were those whose supervisors could and did make critical evaluations of the team's output. Gordon and Marquis also found innovative scientists related to visibility of consequences. Rosner found that higher visibility of consequences was associated with innovation in hospitals. More rapid testing and more tests of new drugs took place in hospitals having higher visibility of consequences.[3]

Innovative activity need not necessarily be positively related to efficiency, so the demonstrated relationship between visibility of consequences and innovation does not establish a relationship between efficiency and visibility of consequences. We can, however, project that such a relationship does exist, first, on the basis of the Becker and Gordon theory, and second, by inference based on research using related variables.

Besides stating that high visibility of consequences allows the organization to test and select procedure-resource interactions beneficial to goal achievement, Becker and Gordon also relate visibility of consequences to other organization variables. Organizational efficiency goes beyond the mere selection of the best procedure; it also requires control over resources and prevention of usurpation of property rights, the ability to handle and resolve conflict between organization members, the development of goal congruence between the formal and informal organizations, and the ability to change or adapt as demanded by environmental conditions.

Visibility of consequences affects all these areas of organizational functioning, according to Becker and Gordon, and therefore we presume it is directly related to organizational efficiency. They hypothesize that successful usurpation of property rights by the operators of the organization is negatively related to visibility of consequences, while the type of usurpation and the motive for usurpation are determined by other variables. They reason that if an owner is aware of how procedure-resource interactions affect goal achievement, i.e., high visibility of consequences, then abuse of any of the procedures or resources for purposes of usurpation will be detectable and correctable.

Organizational tolerance for conflict, the existence of conflict, and the content of conflict are related to other variables, but resolution of conflict is (partially) related to visibility of consequences. Other factors being constant, high visibility of consequences is associated with more rapid and more rational resolution of conflicts. Given high visibility of consequences, the contested procedures or resources can be evaluated in terms of goal achievement and settled on a rational basis. Presumably, the rational basis for conflict resolution will lead to more frequent and more rapid settlement of disputes. Hence, high visibility of consequences should be associated with lower levels of conflict.

Although the functioning of the informal organization—its strength, potential importance, and goal structures—is largely determined by factors other than visibility of consequences, still C_V is an element to be reckoned with. Other factors being constant, an informal organization's potential influence on the formal organization is greater where there is low visibility of consequences. With low visibility of consequences the informal organization can more easily specify its own procedures either for purposes of organizational goal-attainment or for usurpation of the organization's property rights, and thereby strengthen its influence on the formal organization.

If the organizational tasks performed by the informal organization can be achieved only through interdependent activity, a condition where visibility of consequences is lower than in the case of each individual's output being determined solely by his own activity, then the members develop shared goals. Hence, if low visibility of consequences arises from interdependent activity, it will be associated with stronger informal organizations because of the members' shared goals. Consequently, the informal organization's potential influence on the formal and its influence on its membership increase as the organization's visibility of consequences decreases. Whether a strong informal organization enhances or impedes efficiency is a function of the degree of congruence between its goals and formal organizational goals, and visibility of consequences. These relationships are shown in Table V-1.

In summary, with high visibility of consequences the informal organization has less potential influence on the formal, has less coercive power over its members, will enhance efficiency with

TABLE V-1

**Relationship Between Organization Efficiency,
Visibility of Consequences,
and Goal Congruence**

		Visibility of Consequences	
		High	Low
Goal Congruence	High	Maximum Efficiency	Intermediate Efficiency
	Low	High Efficiency	Lowest Efficiency

high goal congruence, and will find it difficult to impede efficiency with low goal congruence.

Finally, high visibility of consequences, along with many other variables, enables an organization to detect the need for change and to select the most appropriate new alternative. This is the case because changes in environmental demands which reduce organizational efficiency will be detected if there is high visibility of consequences, and such an organization also could determine which of the available alternatives would lead to maximum efficiency.

Accepting the arguments that high visibility of consequences enables the organization to deal constructively with the problems of usurpation, conflict, informal organizational functioning, and change, and knowing that these problems must be solved in order to function efficiently, we simply generalize and predict that visibility of consequences is positively related to organizational efficiency. If this is indeed the case, then it also seems reasonable to assume that procedures designed to enhance visibility of consequences are related to efficiency. Becker and Gordon did not distinguish between kinds of procedures. They related optimal levels of procedure specification to environmental conditions, but they failed to distinguish between procedures designed purely to control resources and those designed to coordinate. We wish to distinguish between procedures designed to increase visibility of consequences and all others. Procedures to increase visibility of consequences are designed specifically to permit an owner to assess the outcomes of procedure-resource interactions, the degree to which procedure-resource interactions contribute to goal attainment. Thus, for example, a requirement that financial or statistical information be compiled and distributed in a particular way, at some particular time, might be considered a visibility procedure, akin to performance reports, feedback, information systems, etc. It includes both formal and informal reporting mechanisms designed to increase visibility of consequences. The greater the specification of C_V procedures, regardless of differences in environmental demands, the greater will be the organization's potential visibility of consequences and potential efficiency.

The wisdom of this hypothesis has been questioned by some of our colleagues, perhaps because of a less than complete understanding of the concept visibility of consequences. Perhaps the reader's grasp of the concept will be enhanced if we discuss our colleagues' reservations as well as our response. The question has been asked whether an increase in visibility procedures invariably results in greater visibility of consequences. If the transformation process remains basically mysterious and intuitive, then C_V procedures may be "noisemakers," not information, and if the transformation process is clear and obvious, redundant feedback may be generated. Our questioners presume that in either case visibility of consequences is not improved and (by implication) the additional cost of the redundant or noise-producing procedures represents a reduction in efficiency.

Our response is: Yes, noise, and redundancy may result from additional C_V procedures, but only temporarily. The reason we say "only temporarily" is due to the relationships among C_V procedures, visibility of consequences, and the transformation process. If the transformation process is relatively mysterious, then procedures that lead to higher visibility of consequences must of necessity somewhat reduce the mystery of the transformation process. Increasing visibility of consequences is increasing knowledge of *how* the transformation process works. If C_V procedures do not increase visibility of consequences, the rational manager will delete the procedures, hence the "yes, but only temporarily." Further, we agree that given the unlikely event that the transformation process is known, additional visibility procedures would be redundant. However, in most organizations the transformation process is not perfectly clear, or if parts of it are, others are murky. Therefore, we do make the prediction that increasing C_v procedures increases visibility of consequences, which in turn is related to increased efficiency. This prediction is based on our assumption that maximum efficiency can be achieved only with complete knowledge of the transformation process.[4]

Based on available research reports, we cannot directly relate visibility of consequences and efficiency, but if we assume that variables like those we characterize as visibility procedures are more often than not related to both visibility of consequences and efficiency, we can draw some inferences.

For example, in the floundering pajama factory successfully reorganized by the Harwood Company, an increase in feedback of information to managers and workers (increased visibility of consequences) was among many changes introduced. The increased productivity reported by Coch and French may be due more to increased information flow (visibility of consequences) than to the negligible increase in workers' decision-making. Pelz and Andrews, in their study of the performance of scientists and engineers, found that effective scientists both sought and had more contact with their colleagues, and apparently these contacts increased visibility of consequences. Doris Cook asked 134 managers to evaluate the usefulness of the reports they received. They rated daily reports as most useful and annual reports as least useful, implying that rapidly available information is an important component of efficient managerial functioning.[5]

Georgopoulos and Mann, in their study of community general hospitals, found that communication increases understanding and acceptance of rules, helps to clarify problems, promotes common understanding, and transmits ideas and suggestions. "Effective day-to-day communication between superiors and subordinates about the work process and work problems provides an additional key mechanism for coordination." They found that such coordination was positively related to good patient care, the goal of a hospital organization.[6]

A most interesting study related to visibility of consequences is that of Woodruff and Alexander. Comparing 10 successful small metal-fabricating companies with 10 similar companies that went bankrupt, they found no single cause for the business failures. Rather, each unsuccessful firm had more than one problem. However,

> Inadequate or misleading financial records probably caused more trouble than any other error of management. The records of one (unsuccessful) company consisted of masses of unsorted papers stuffed in boxes and then stuffed into an old-fashioned safe. This conglomeration plus the checkbook and journal of bank deposits comprised the record keeping system.
>
> Serious losses could later be traced to a series of little leaks, each one a seemingly insignificant dribble, but collectively equivalent to a substantial breach in the financial dike. Management was unaware of these leaks at the time because records were missing, were too cumbersome for quick analysis or were too long delayed in reaching the proper desk.
>
> Disaster awaits uninformed management which acts without adequate records. Information to meet the needs of those who use it must be simple, clear and promptly available. Observers were amazed that several companies (that closed) well machined and equipped, had no records of cost or performance control. Without records, they were conducting ineffectual operations and making blind decisions.
>
> None of the unsuccessful firms had really good financial records and nine of them had extremely poor records, so that management lacked navigational aids through the business shoals and mudbanks. All of the ten successful companies, in contrast, had well informed management, kept complete records, and made full use of the records that were kept.[7]

Unlike the relationship between specified roles and efficiency, the positive relationship between efficiency and variables we take as proxies for visibility of consequences is quite well established.

Measurement of Visibility of Consequences. The formulation of the variable includes the owner and the degree to which he can and does evaluate outcomes of procedure-resource interactions. This concept was operationalized precisely as stated in the study of hospital organizations by interviewing presidents of boards of trustees. We also measured the variable with respect to the chief administrative officer and (probably erroneously) tested him for the same knowledge as the board chairman.

Two issues are involved, one of them the difficulty with the concept of owner. Who is the owner of a not-for-profit organization, for instance a state-owned hospital? It is fine to say that the citizens of the state own it, but it is quite another thing to operationalize the concept at that level. Here the idea of usurpation becomes relevant. If it can be demonstrated (or assumed) that the chief operating executive (or members of the governing board) are not engaged in usurpation, then they clearly function as proxies for the owner, and it becomes proper to operationalize visibility of consequences at the level of board member or chief executive.

The second problem is whether the variable applies only to the top level or to lower organizational levels as well. To the extent that the chief executive does not specify all organizational procedures, an impossibility in all but the smallest organizations, then it is logical to measure visibility of consequences at all levels in the organization where responsibility has been delegated.

If this position is a correct one, then the second problem is whether the same operational mode is appropriate at all levels or whether each level requires different modes. Consider a chief executive of a decentralized organization. He might attend to the rate of return of each of the subunits, the costs of central coordination, policy decisions and their outcomes, etc., while the duties of the division head might involve changing one machine design for another, the outcomes of the test marketing of a new product, etc. It is rational for the manager at each level to attend to different tasks, and so it is rational that visibility of consequences be measured differently at each level. The determination should be appropriate to the content of the manager's particular task, technology, and environment.

While these considerations about operationalization were not fully developed for the study of hospital organizations, they were more closely adhered to in the study of the insurance companies.

CHAPTER 5

Other Variables

We have argued that specification of procedures, organizational interaction with the environment, and visibility of consequences are related to efficiency, and indeed we will use those variables as the basis for our relatively simple model of organizational efficiency. By using so few variables in our model, we do not wish to imply that no others are related to efficiency; quite the contrary. However, we do believe the variables in the Entrepreneurial Theory have greater generality and explanatory power than others which might have been selected, an argument we will attempt to support by placing a relatively exhaustive list of such other variables within the context of the Entrepreneurial Theory. Such a listing also will serve the additional purposes of (1) providing material for later revision or expansion of the theory; (2) providing knowledge of which other variables must be statistically or conceptually controlled by researchers testing hypotheses using subsets of these variables; and (3) acquainting managers with the complexity of their tasks and the potential costs of ignoring any of the variables.

To place these variables within the context of the Entrepreneurial Theory we need simply state that in the E.T. an organization consists of a combination of resources (people and things) and procedures (ways of doing things by, to, and with resources). The owner sets the goal and attempts to achieve it by storing in specific form a higher or lower proportion of the organization's resource (R±), and by specifying a higher or lower proportion of the organization's procedures (P±). The owner's ability efficiently to combine the appropriate resources and procedures, to cope with the limitation imposed upon him by the environment, depends on his ability to specify procedures to increase potential

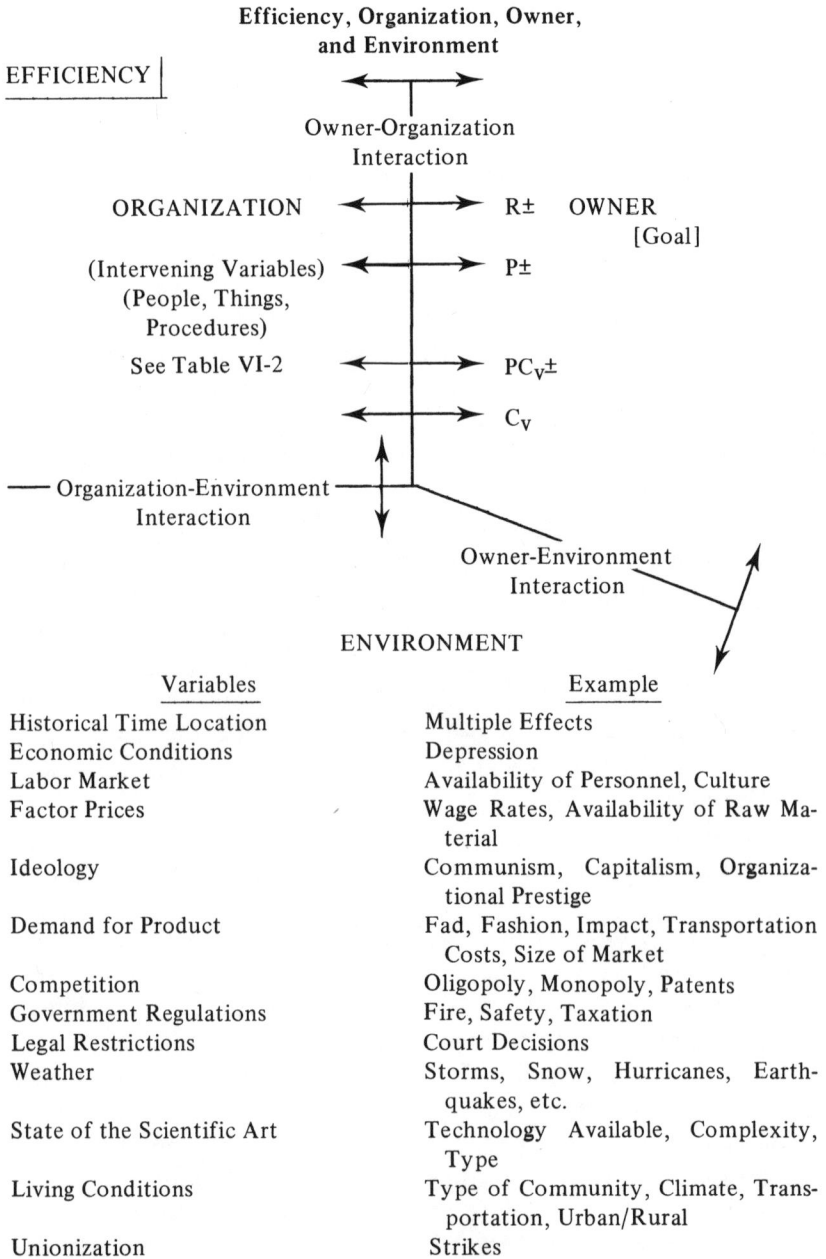

TABLE VI-1

Efficiency, Organization, Owner,
and Environment

EFFICIENCY

Owner-Organization
Interaction

ORGANIZATION ← | → R± OWNER
[Goal]

(Intervening Variables) ← | → P±
(People, Things,
Procedures)

See Table VI-2 ← | → $PC_v\pm$

← | → C_v

— Organization-Environment
Interaction

Owner-Environment
Interaction

ENVIRONMENT

Variables	Example
Historical Time Location	Multiple Effects
Economic Conditions	Depression
Labor Market	Availability of Personnel, Culture
Factor Prices	Wage Rates, Availability of Raw Material
Ideology	Communism, Capitalism, Organizational Prestige
Demand for Product	Fad, Fashion, Impact, Transportation Costs, Size of Market
Competition	Oligopoly, Monopoly, Patents
Government Regulations	Fire, Safety, Taxation
Legal Restrictions	Court Decisions
Weather	Storms, Snow, Hurricanes, Earthquakes, etc.
State of the Scientific Art	Technology Available, Complexity, Type
Living Conditions	Type of Community, Climate, Transportation, Urban/Rural
Unionization	Strikes

—and so on—

visibility of consequences (PC_V) so as to increase his actual visibility of consequences (C_V), his awareness of what is going on. The three axes in Table VI-1 reflect the relationships in the theory.

The environmental variables in Table VI-1 interact with the owner and with the organization. In the Entrepreneurial Theory, environment-organization interaction is characterized as either stable or unstable. Instability arises from difficulty in selecting proper procedures or responses, or because demands on the organization are either diverse or sporadic. Each of the listed environmental variables can be considered in terms of the theory as contributing either to the stability or instability of an organization's interaction with its environment. Treating the environment at that level of abstraction, e.g., as either stable or unstable rather than considering the actual events which produce stability or instability, allows prediction only about optimal organization structures—i.e., type of simple bureaucratic structure, coupling, degree and form of decentralization—while considering the content (rather than the effect) of any of the listed variables might lead to predictions about content of procedures or resources.

Obviously, concern with the content of variables is important first in deciding to organize, and second, in changing or controlling organizational conditions. With regard to change or control, the owner has relatively more control over his environment in the long run. He can vary plant location, size, industry, or technology. He can decide to bake bread in St. Louis or raise cattle in Texas. In the short run, once he has decided to bake bread in St. Louis, most of the environmental constraints are beyond his ability to control. (There is no satisfactory definition of when the short run ends and the long run begins. It will vary with the circumstances.) This distinction between controllable and uncontrollable variables which affect organizational efficiency is important for theoretical as well as practical reasons. Practically, the manager wants to know about those variables affecting efficiency that he can control. Theoretically, if we wish to observe the effect of specification of procedures on efficiency, we must control for differences in the environment. Fortunately, by comparing organizations with the same goal using the same basic technology, in the same industry, in the same area, under the same legal and governmental jurisdiction, in the same time period, one can come quite close to con-

TABLE VI-2

Organization: Expanded Intervening Variables and Efficiency

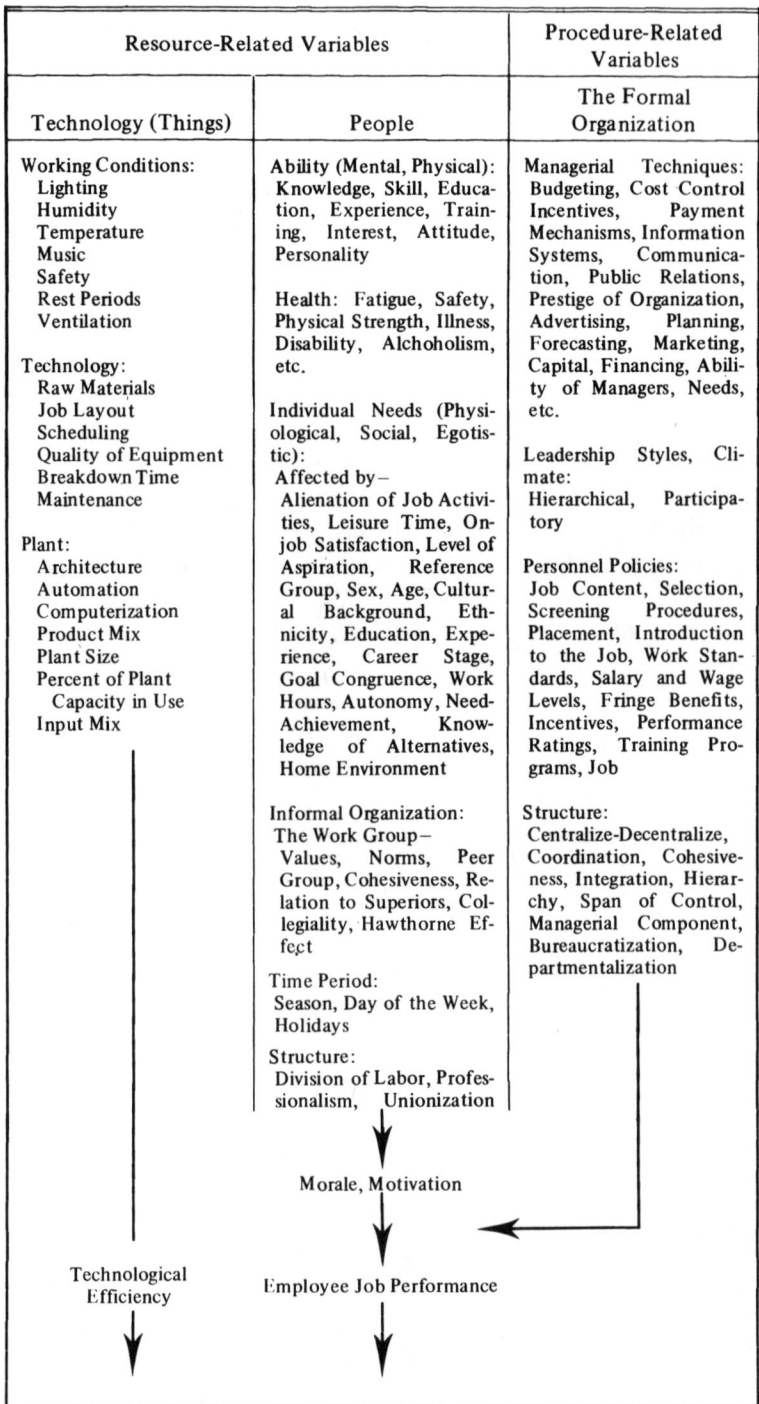

Resource-Related Variables		Procedure-Related Variables
Technology (Things)	People	The Formal Organization
Working Conditions: Lighting Humidity Temperature Music Safety Rest Periods Ventilation Technology: Raw Materials Job Layout Scheduling Quality of Equipment Breakdown Time Maintenance Plant: Architecture Automation Computerization Product Mix Plant Size Percent of Plant Capacity in Use Input Mix	Ability (Mental, Physical): Knowledge, Skill, Education, Experience, Training, Interest, Attitude, Personality Health: Fatigue, Safety, Physical Strength, Illness, Disability, Alchoholism, etc. Individual Needs (Physiological, Social, Egotistic): Affected by— Alienation of Job Activities, Leisure Time, On-job Satisfaction, Level of Aspiration, Reference Group, Sex, Age, Cultural Background, Ethnicity, Education, Experience, Career Stage, Goal Congruence, Work Hours, Autonomy, Need-Achievement, Knowledge of Alternatives, Home Environment Informal Organization: The Work Group— Values, Norms, Peer Group, Cohesiveness, Relation to Superiors, Collegiality, Hawthorne Effect Time Period: Season, Day of the Week, Holidays Structure: Division of Labor, Professionalism, Unionization	Managerial Techniques: Budgeting, Cost Control Incentives, Payment Mechanisms, Information Systems, Communication, Public Relations, Prestige of Organization, Advertising, Planning, Forecasting, Marketing, Capital, Financing, Ability of Managers, Needs, etc. Leadership Styles, Climate: Hierarchical, Participatory Personnel Policies: Job Content, Selection, Screening Procedures, Placement, Introduction to the Job, Work Standards, Salary and Wage Levels, Fringe Benefits, Incentives, Performance Ratings, Training Programs, Job Structure: Centralize-Decentralize, Coordination, Cohesiveness, Integration, Hierarchy, Span of Control, Managerial Component, Bureaucratization, Departmentalization

Morale, Motivation

Technological Efficiency   Employee Job Performance

ORGANIZATIONAL EFFICIENCY

trolling for most of the important differences due to the environment.

Although we have added other variables to the table, Table VI-2 is largely taken from the Sutermeister wheel,[1] one of the few systematic efforts to catalogue all the major variables affecting productivity. Productivity, according to the Entrepreneurial Theory, is greatly affected by the owner, who defines the technology, selects the people who work in the organization, and determines the organizational structure (degree of specified procedures, ratio of resources stored in specific form) for the purpose of reaching his goal with maximum efficiency.

One assumption in the theory is that the owner is rational, and that with rationality and high visibility of consequences all the variables listed in Table VI-2 will be handled most expeditiously. Just as the environment is dealt with at a higher level of abstraction in the theory, the procedure and resource variables also are more general than are the variables listed in Table VI-2. In the theory there is no concern with the content of a procedure or resource, but rather with the specified state of procedures and resources. Since all organizations have procedures more or less specified and resources stored in more or less specific form, our model of organizational efficiency is applicable to all organizations despite differences in the content of their procedures and resources.

CHAPTER 6

A Model of
Organizational Efficiency

In the preceding chapters we have defined efficiency and discussed the variables specification of procedures, task-environment, visibility of consequences, and specification of procedures to increase visibility of consequences. We have also related these variables to others that affect efficiency, and compared their levels of abstraction and generality. We concluded that because our variables were more abstract than others use, we could not predict the content of procedures, but we could draw conclusions relevant to all organizations about the states of procedures. Presumably, then, if our model is composed of variables common to all organizations, the model of organizational efficiency should be generalizable to all organizations.

The model will be developed following the logic of the Entrepreneurial Theory. We can summarize the theory as follows: By definition, each formal organization has a legal owner who creates the organization to achieve his goal.[1] The owner has the right to specify procedures for his employees, as well as the right to hire a manager, specify procedures for him, and allow him to specify procedures for others in the organization.[2] Presumably, the owner or his agent prefers to specify procedures and thereby maximize the benefits of coordination. That way he can retain control over his resources and also achieve his goal. The owner will relinquish control only if he can increase goal achievement.

The more complex the task-environment, the greater the number or the intricacy of the procedures involved in performance. As the number or intricacy of organizational procedures increases, the owner or his agent cannot specify the same proportion of procedures as in the case of fewer or less intricate ones. Moreover, as complexity as well as the necessity for rapid specification of procedures increases, the owner should hire employees able to specify their own procedures.

An organization may be faced with multiple task-environments, some more complex than others. An authority pattern appropriate for one of the task-environments might not serve the others. Therefore, given multiple task-environments, it would be more efficient to divide the organization into subcomponents with authority patterns matched to the appropriate task-environment. In this way loss of control is minimized. Instead of handing over all control to others, because part of his organization's task-environment is complex, the owner can retain control in the noncomplex areas. The Entrepreneurial Theory defines an organization containing different authority patterns as "coupled." This is similar to Lawrence and Lorsch's concept of differentiation in organizations.

As stated in Chapter IV, a procedure specified by the owner or his agent may be inappropriate, unenforced, or have unintended consequences. Therefore, linking specification of procedures with the appropriate task-environment is essential but not sufficient for achieving efficiency. If the owner's objectives are to be realized and unintended consequences minimized, the owner must be aware of the effects of his actions. The extent to which the owner can be and is aware of the effects of his actions and the functioning of his organization is defined as "visibility of consequences."

Let us assume a rational owner, that is, one who will attempt to achieve his goals in an efficient manner. Given high visibility of consequences, the owner will be able to specify those procedures which will maximize efficiency and eliminate inappropriate procedures or, without specifying procedures, bring the appropriate personnel for goal attainment into the organization. In short, high visibility of consequences is more likely to produce optimal organizational structures and functioning.

Although no distinctions have been made in the Entrepreneurial Theory between kinds of procedures, perhaps the theory can be made more precise by dividing procedures into two categories: those concerned with production activities and those concerned with visibility of consequences. Production procedures are those which are directly related to the production process, which directly facilitate the manufacture of goods and services by the organization. Visibility procedures are those which are designed primarily to make the owner aware of the degree to which his organization is meeting its objectives. A production procedure, for example, is one that specifies the grade of a raw material, the operating speed of the production machinery, or the number of work hours per week. A visibility procedure, for example, is one that calls for a monthly compilation of cost reports and for sending them to the corporate board.

Integrating the idea of production and visibility procedures into the theory leads to some modifications. Given high complexity of the task-environment, the owner will find it efficient not to specify production procedures, but instead, employ workers who can specify their own procedures. Whatever the degree of complexity, however, specifying visibility procedures will increase potential efficiency. Thus, the theory previously required a lower proportion of specified procedures for optimal functioning in a complex environmental interaction situation; now we hypothesize that to be true only of production procedures rather than all procedures.

Based on the logic of the Entrepreneurial Theory it is a simple matter to outline our model of Organizational Efficiency (see Table VII-1) and to restate the model as hypotheses, so that substantiation of the hypotheses will lend credence to the claim that the model is an accurate description of reality.

Hypotheses:

1. Specification of production procedures is positively related to efficiency in organizational components with low task-environment complexity, and negatively related to efficiency in components with high task-environment complexity.

2. Specification of procedures designed to increase visibility of consequences is positively related to efficiency.

3. Visibility of consequences is positively related to efficiency.

4. In combination, specification of procedures and visibility of consequences are more strongly related to efficiency than is either variable by itself.

TABLE VII-1

A Model of Organizational Efficiency

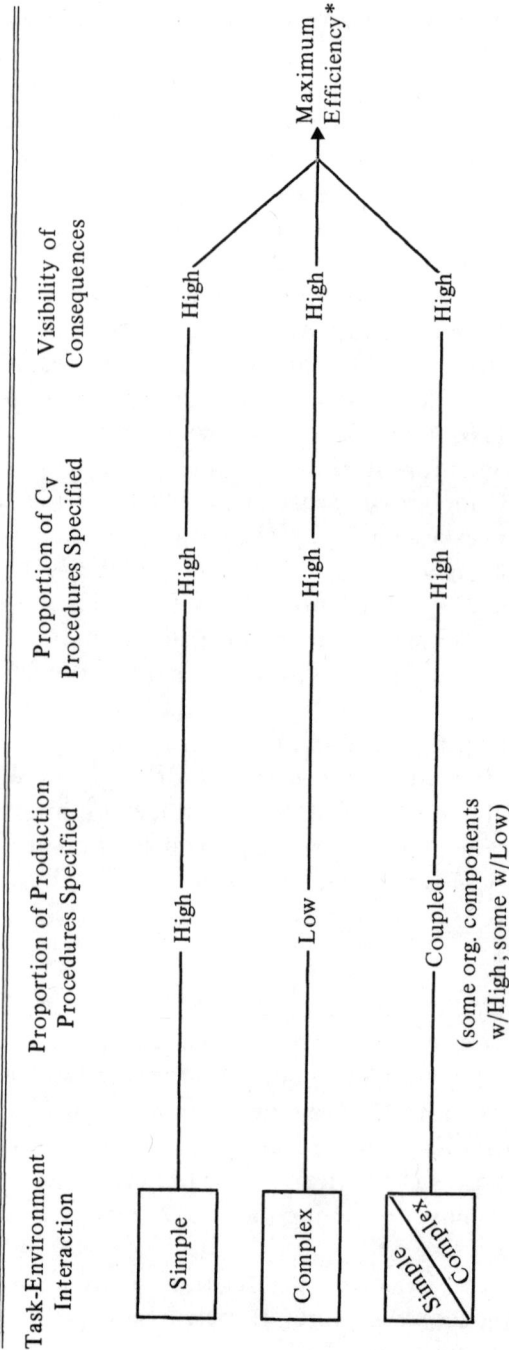

Task-Environment Interaction	Proportion of Production Procedures Specified	Proportion of C_v Procedures Specified	Visibility of Consequences	
Simple	High	High	High	Maximum Efficiency*
Complex	Low	High	High	
Simple / Complex	Coupled (some org. components w/High; some w/Low)	High	High	

*Highest proportion of discounted present value of benefits to costs.

In the case of organizations or subunits with low task-environment complexity, our hypotheses are consistent with the hierarchical approach but inconsistent with the human-relations approach. With high complexity, our hypotheses are consistent with the human-relations approach but inconsistent with the hierarchical approach. We differ from both approaches in the hypothesized importance of visibility of consequences and the use of the concept of organizational coupling. The latter concept allows us to distinguish between a professional component (high complexity, collegial control) and a nonprofessional component (low complexity, hierarchical control).

PART II:

THE EMPIRICAL EVIDENCE

Introduction

The evidence from two comparative field studies collected in order to test the model of organizational efficiency consisted of data from not-for-profit organizations (community general hospitals) and for-profit organizations (insurance companies).

THE COMMUNITY GENERAL HOSPITAL

The hospitals studied were 30 medium-sized, short-term, general, not-for-profit community hospitals in the Greater Chicago area. *Medium-sized* refers to hospitals with a 100-500 bed capacity. The 100-bed minimum was chosen because experience has taught us that in still smaller institutions the management style differs sharply.[1] The distribution of the sample hospitals by size, as measured by the number of beds, is as follows:

"Short-term" refers to a hospital where the average length of patient stay (ALOS) is less than thirty days. The distribution of average length of stay is as follows:

TABLE I-1

Hospital Size

No. of Beds	No. of Hospitals
100	9
200	8
300	7
400	2
500	4
TOTAL	30

TABLE I-2

Average Length of Patient Stay in Days

Days	7	8	9	10	11	12+	Total
No. of Hospitals	4	5	10	6	2	3	30

General hospitals, unlike special hospitals such as children's or eye-and-ear hospitals, admit patients with a wide range of ill-nesses.

Not-for-profit hospitals as defined in the *Hospital* "Guide Issue" do not encompass proprietary, city, county, state, or fed-eral hospitals.

Community hospitals have as their primary goal good patient care, as compared with hospitals affiliated with medical schools, which expend a great part of their resources and efforts in teach-ing medical students, interns, and residents, and on research. This limitation excludes the largest Chicago hospitals. However, some of the hospitals in this sample have comparatively modest resi-dency programs, usually staffed by foreign medical-school gradu-ates.

This sample of hospitals is fairly typical of not-for-profit community general hospitals. In 1969, there were 7,144 hospitals of all types in the United States. Excluding government and pro-prietary hospitals, there were 3,428 voluntary not-for-profit, short-term general, and other special hospitals. Of these, 28 were psychiatric and 137 special hospitals. Thus, there were 3,291 not-for-profit, short-term community general hospitals, including be-tween 300 and 500 major teaching hospitals.[2]

As can be seen from Table I-3, the mean size of our hospital is larger than it is in the universe, but similar in occupancy rate, average length of stay, and per-diem costs. Because we excluded small hospitals, the sample differs from the universe on size (308.5 beds to 172 beds). Adjusting for the exclusion of hospitals with fewer than 100 beds, the size distribution for the universe and our sample are similar.

By selecting organizations with these characteristics, we have controlled for major differences in technology, in treatment styles

TABLE I-3

Comparison of Sample and Universe

	All U.S. Voluntary Not-for-Profit Short-term General Hospitals	Our Sample
Number of Hospitals	3,291	27[3]
Mean Size (beds)	172	308.5
Occupancy	81.1	82.04
Average Length of Stay	8.3	9.7
Per-diem Cost	$65.49	$68.96

and types of patients, in size, and for differences in organizational goals as well as in market characteristics. Because these hospitals are in one contiguous area, their quality of care can be evaluated by physicians who are familiar with many of them, variance in costs due to regional differences in salaries and wages and costs of supplies are minimized, and the impact, if any, of state and city laws is uniform.

Finally, 26 of the 30 hospitals participated in the Hospital Administration Services (HAS) data-collection program. Hospitals may voluntarily subscribe to HAS, a subsidiary of the American Hospital Association, for a modest fee, and over half the hospitals in Chicago do. Each participating hospital, using standardized definitions, submits a monthly cost, man-hour, and statistical report to HAS, which compiles statistics for each hospital and averages for various categories of hospitals. These monthly reports are then sent to each participating hospital. In this way, the hospital is provided with basic statistics and a comparison with other hospitals of the same size and in the same region. We chose HAS hospitals to obtain cost, man-hour, and output figures based on the same standardized definitions.

The hospitals in our sample, as is usually the case in general hospitals in the U.S., are organized as complex, coupled organizations. The nonprofessional component is headed by the hospital administrator, who, it is presumed, specifies procedures for his staff. The professional component, to which the administration is coupled, is headed by a medical chief of staff and, again presumably, is coordinated in a relatively collegial fashion. We make these presumptions because the worker in the professional component, the doctor treating his patient, apparently has relatively more discretion over his work than does, for instance, the worker in the laundry section of the administrative component.

In general hospitals, the most complex task-environment is the treatment of the patient. The wide range of diseases and wide age-span of the patients call for different types of treatment.[4] Treatment procedures are frequently difficult to specify and are never specified for more than one patient at a time. This complexity is reflected by the long period of training required of physicians and the extensive medical literature.

In sharp contrast to the complexity of the medical departments is the low complexity of the task-environment of the housekeeping, laundry, stores, and purchasing units. Here production activities are comparatively simple, routine, and stable. Consistent with the Entrepreneurial Theory, these departments fall under the hierarchical control of the hospital administrator, while physicians are given considerably more autonomy.

Because the hospitals are divided into two components, in order to test our hypotheses we must have measures of specification of production procedures, specification of visibility procedures, and visibility of consequences and goal attainment for each component. Operationalizations of the variables, and the assumptions underlying each of the measures will be discussed in Chapter VII, which offers data on the administrative component, and Chapter VIII, which is devoted to the professional component.

THE INSURANCE COMPANIES

The insurance companies studied, comprising 15 of the 31 companies located in Venezuela, had to meet the following criteria:

a. Their headquarters and main line of operations had to be in the capital city of Caracas. (This condition was established in an effort to hold the environment constant. Twenty-six of the 31 companies listed in the directory of the Camara de Asaguaradores de Venezuela were found to meet this requirement.)

b. Every company selected had to offer basically the same type of coverage—fire, life, etc. Twenty of the companies fulfilling (a) also fulfilled (b).

c. During the period covered by the financial data—1968-70 —the companies were not to have undergone changes in ownership or major changes in management. This criterion eliminated two of the companies. Thus, cooperation was solicited from either the top operating executive or the second-highest executive in the hierarchy of the remaining 18 companies.

Fifteen of the 18 companies agreed to cooperate. The three noncooperating companies do not seem markedly different from those which did. One company was 5th in size and second in profitability, one was 10th in size and 18th in profitability, and the third was 15th in size and 13th in profitability. The cooperating companies were distributed in size as follows: in millions of Bolivares (1 B equals c. 22¢) one each at 17, 20, 24, 28, 36, 50, 58, 64, 72, 82, 117, 123, 192, and two at 19.

Because it was assumed that the insurance companies, unlike the hospital organizations, were simple complete bureaucracies with executive authority patterns, they will not be divided into components; the hypotheses, methodology, assumptions, and data will be presented in Chapter XI.

CHAPTER 7

The Hospital
Organization Study:
THE ADMINISTRATIVE COMPONENT—
LOW COMPLEXITY TASK-ENVIRONMENT

For this component of the organization we have hypothesized that specification of production procedures, specification of
procedures to increase C_V, and C_V itself are all positively related to
efficiency. Measurements of each of these variables were obtained
in the nonmedical (nonphysician) segment of 27 community general hospitals.

MEASUREMENT OF THE VARIABLES*

Efficiency. Five separate measures of efficiency were obtained:
   1. A *cost index* ($), based on the cost in each hospital of
providing one standardized day of patient care. The higher the
cost index, the less efficient the hospital.
   2. A *man-hour index* (MH), based on the number of employee man-hours in each hospital used to provide the same standardized day of patient care. The higher the man-hour index, the
less efficient the hospital.
   Both of these indexes are based on the per-unit costs of seven
departments: dietary, housekeeping, laundry, medical records,
pharmacy, laboratory, and radiology. Nursing was excluded because no adequate output measures were available. The per-unit
cost and man-hour figures were obtained primarily from the HAS
data or comparable sources. These data were checked for errors,
and, where possible, verified by comparison with other hospital
records.

The mean number of units of output per patient day for each of the seven departments was obtained for the 27 hospitals. The cost index was obtained for each hospital by multiplying that hospital's per-unit cost with the average level of output per patient day for each department and summing across the seven departments. The man-hour index was derived in the same way, but instead of using per-unit costs it used employee man-hours per unit of output.

3. *Mean expert evaluation index* (EE). Seven experts in health management with extensive knowledge of some or all of the hospitals in this sample were asked to evaluate these hospitals on a 5-point scale. None of these experts was employed by any of these hospitals. They each made their ratings independently. Although they undoubtedly used somewhat different perspectives to make their evaluations, their ratings reflected some similarities: the interrater reliability was +0.50. To obtain the over-all EE index, the experts' ratings were adjusted to give each the same mean value and then an average was obtained for each hospital. The higher the mean expert evaluation index, the more efficient the hospital.

4. *The Joint Commission on Accreditation of Hospitals Evaluation Index* (JCAH). The Joint Commission is an independent organization which systematically and periodically evaluates the performance of U.S. hospitals with emphasis on adherence to minimum standards of excellence such as completion of medical records, fire safety, and condition of the physical plant. This is a voluntary effort, but nearly all U.S. general hospitals seek accreditation as a sign of excellence, and often because reimbursement from Blue Cross and Medicare is dependent on accreditation. All the hospitals in our sample are accredited, as are more than 90 percent of all general hospitals. As a rule, a hospital is inspected every year or two by a physician-evaluator employed by the JCAH who evaluates up to 20 different areas of the hospital. Six of these areas relate primarily to the nonmedical component; an index based on these ratings has been developed here using a 5-point scale, from acceptable to unacceptable. Unacceptable was scored as 1; the three acceptable categories were scored 3, 4, and 5. The scores were summed over the six areas to form this index. The higher the JCAH index, the higher the efficiency.

5. *Occupancy rate* $(\emptyset)$. This is the proportion of hospital beds filled with patients on an average day over a year's period of time. This was included as an *ex post facto* measure, because it was found to be strongly correlated with the other measures of efficiency. Theoretical justification for the use of this measure of efficiency is given by Hage.[1] The higher the occupancy, the higher the efficiency.

To the degree that these measures reflect the identical factor—i.e., efficiency—they should be correlated with one another. These correlations cannot be perfect, because the separate measures focus on different aspects of efficiency which may not themselves be perfectly correlated. Table VIII-1 shows the results. As noted, the cost and man-hour indexes vary inversely with efficiency, while the JCAH evaluation, expert evaluation, and occupancy-rate measures vary directly with efficiency. As expected, then, cost and man-hour indexes are positively related to each other and negatively related to the other measures of efficiency. (See Table VIII-1.)

All the correlations are in the expected direction, and 9 out of 10 are statistically significant. Based on this matrix of correlations, we feel reasonably certain that the five measures are tapping a common factor, which we define as efficiency.

Specification-of-Production Procedures. Five different measures of specification-of-production procedures were obtained. The first is a perceptual measure; the rest are based on the existence of various formal controls.

1. *Perceived specification-of-production procedures* (P_p). An index based on responses by department heads to three items on a questionnaire concerning the degree to which work activities of those subordinate to them were defined by them or others in the managerial hierarchy. The department heads asked were generally those in charge of dietetics, laundry, housekeeping, medical records, pharmaceutics, and personnel. This is a continuous but truncated variable with a potential range of 2 to 12. The mean for the 27 hospitals is 9.17.

2. *Use or nonuse of budget by the hospital.* The budget is presumed to be a device for controlling operating costs[2] by centralizing and defining decisions on expenditures. Twenty out of

TABLE VIII-1

Correlations Between the Five Different Measures
of Administrative Efficiency
(Nonmedical Component, n = 27)[a]

	Cost Index ($)	Man-hour Index (MH)	JCAH Evaluation (JCAH)	Occupancy Rate ($\emptyset$)
Average Expert Evaluation (EE)	−.542** (−.605)	−.568** (−.547)	+.398* (.453)	+.663** (+.686)
Cost Index ($)		+.632** (+.648)	−.505** (−.445)	−.445** (−.467)
Man-Hour Index (MH)			−.313 (−.369)	−.502** (−.525)
JCAH				+.523** (+.612)

*p < .05.

**p < .005.

[a]In this and other tables, Pearson product moment correlations are shown without parentheses. Immediately below them, Spearman rank order correlations are shown in parentheses. Here are in the following tables, statistical significance levels are shown only for the product moment correlations for clarity of of presentation. Statistical significance levels here and elsewhere for Pearson r's are from H. Walker and J. Lev, *Statistical Inference* (New York: Holt, Rinehart and Winston, 1953), Table XI, p. 470.

the 27 hospitals in this sample used budgets. This is a dichotomous variable.

3. *Use of position control.* This is a system for limiting the number of employees in each department in each job classification. Sixteen hospitals used a position control. This is a dichotomous variable.

4. *Use of a salary control system that defines starting salaries and periodic salary increments for each type of hospital employee.* Twenty-five hospitals have salary control systems. This is a dichotomous variable.

5. *Use of written job descriptions to define the tasks performed by individual employees* (P_j). In 13 of the hospitals, all

hospital personnel are covered by job descriptions. This is measured by the percentage of employees covered by job descriptions and, therefore, varies from 0 to 100.

Of these measures, those which more accurately operationalize the theoretical concept of specification-of-production procedures are perceived specification of procedures (P_p) and the percentage of employees covered by job descriptions (P_j). This is the case because both measures reflect perception of, or actual hierarchically imposed constraints on, job performance of workers.

The correlations of all five measures of this variable are shown in Table VIII-2. The different measures of specification-of-production procedures are positively correlated with each other. The two preferred measures, (P_p) and (P_j), are correlated +.432.

Visibility of Consequences. This is measured by how accurately the administrator can compare his hospital with other similar hospitals in the area. The administrator was asked to compare, on a 5-point scale from low to much higher, his hospital to others of similar size in the Chicago area, on the following performance factors: occupancy, average length of stay, direct cost per meal, direct cost of 100 lbs. of laundry, per-diem costs of patient day, staffing ratio, and over-all operating efficiency. The actual figures were independently derived and the 27 hospitals were ranked from highest to lowest on each of these characteristics. The administrator's 5-point evaluations were correlated with the actual rank orders of the hospital. If the correlation was positive, the administrator had an accurate picture of where his hospital stood (high visibility of consequences). If the correlation was negative, then the administrator had an inaccurate picture (low visibility of consequences). This correlation is used as the measure of visibility of consequences (C_v). Using this measure, we assume that C_v consists of an administrator knowing how his department is performing, and that to judge whether the performance is good or bad he compares it to some standard, in this case, competing organizations, especially when such information is (partially) readily available from the JCAH and AHA. We feel that measuring C_v at this broad level is valid for the chief administrator and board chairmen, but that the content of the measure would be different at lower levels in the hierarchy.

TABLE VIII-2

Correlations Between Measures of Specification-
of-Production Procedures

	Budgets (2)	Position Control (3)	Salary Control (4)	Job Descriptions (5)
1. Perceived Worker P+	+.128 (+.302)	+.158 (+.158)	+.123 (+.360)	+.432* (+.670)
2. Budgets Used[a]		+.213 (+.429)	+.250 (+.440)	+.093 (−.011)
3. Position Control[a]			+.426* (+1.00)	+.378 (+.597)
4. Salary Control[a]				+.510** (+1.00)

[a]Yule and Kendall's Q correlations are shown in parentheses for the dichotomized variables.

*p < .05.

**p < .005.

In 17 of the hospitals (the Catholic hospitals were excluded) the chairman of the board was asked to complete the same questionnaire, and the board chairman's C_V score was derived in the same way. The Pearson correlation between the administrator's and the chairman's C_V scores was +.249. In these hospitals the mean visibility score for the administrators was +.401 (n = 17), while the mean visibility score for the chairmen was +.129. In the case of the administrators, 4 out of 17 had negative correlations, which indicates not merely lack of information but misinformation on how their hospital ranks. As to the chairmen, 7 out of 17 had negative correlations.

Specification of Procedures to Increase C_V. This is measured by an index based on the extent and frequency of performance reports being compiled in the hospital on a routine basis. If no report existed, the score was 0. If a report was compiled yearly, the score was 1; if semi-annually, 2; if quarterly, 3; and if monthly, 4. The reports covered operating expenses, capital, cash flow, manpower, overtime, turnover, absenteeism, disciplinary action, patient, personnel and physician-attitude questionnaires. These scores for each type of report were then summed to form the index of specification of procedures to increase C_v (PC_v).

Tests of Hypothesis

Specification-of-Production Procedures. We have hypothesized that specification-of-production procedures (P_p) is positively correlated with efficiency. Operationally the (P_p) measures should be negatively correlated with the cost and man-hour indexes and positively with the JCAH evaluation, the mean expert evaluation, and occupancy rate. The results are shown in Table VIII-3. Of the 25 correlations, 23 are in the predicted direction, and 13 of these are significant at the .05 level or better. Note that the strongest correlations are for perceived specification of procedures and for the proportion of employees covered by job descriptions, the two operationalizations of specification-of-production procedures that we feel best reflect the theoretical concept.

It was interesting to see the department heads' comments when they filled out the questionnaire on perceived specification of procedures. Several of the department heads, in laundry, dietetics, and housekeeping, became somewhat disturbed by the two questions on specification-of-worker procedures. They had heard a great deal about "participation," "letting the workers set their own work pace," and "letting them work without close supervision." But apparently their efforts to apply these methods had not been successful. They found that they had "to tell their workers what to do," and "to keep an eye on things," or nothing would get done. Some of them were rather upset about what to them seemed a discrepancy between theory and practice. It is quite consistent with the Entrepreneurial Theory that this conflict was felt most strongly in dietetics, housekeeping, and laundry, which have the least complex tasks and the lowest-ranking professional workers, rather than in medical records and pharmaceutics, where the workers are relatively more skilled and the tasks somewhat more complex.

TABLE VIII-3

Efficiency and Specification-of-Production Procedures
(Nonmedical Component)[a]
(n = 27)

	Measures of Efficiency				
	Cost Index (1)	Man-hour Index (2)	Expert Evaluation (3)	JCAH Index (4)	Occupancy (5)
Perceived Worker P+ (1)	-.469* ((-.494))	-.483* ((-.399))	+.371* ((+.339))	+.364* ((+.406))	+.540* ((+.469))
Budget (2)	-.024 (-.111)	+.214 (+.231)	+.064 (.000)	+.151 (+.302)	+.174 (+.200)
Position Control (3)	-.340* (-.633)	-.658** (-.841)	+.257 (+.333)	+.163 (+.158)	+.141 (-.018)
Salary Control (4)	-.120 (-.333)	-.210 (-.538)	+.362* (+.474)	+.021 (+.143)	-.011 (-.082)
Job Description (5)	-.565** (-.714)	-.495** (-.474)	+.504** (+.692)	+.462* (+.600)	+.348* (+.339)

(n = 27)
*p < .05.
**p < .005.

[a]Three of the (P+) variables are dichotomous (Budget, Position Control, Salary Control). For these three variables, in addition to the Pearson product moment correlations, Yule and Kendall's Q's are shown in single parentheses. These Q's were obtained by dichotomizing the efficiency variables at the mean. Rank-order correlations shown in double parentheses were appropriate. For clarity of presentation, statistical significance levels are indicated only for the product moment correlations in this and the following tables.

In the model of organizational efficiency, no distinctions were made between personnel at different levels of the hierarchy. This assumes that while department heads, for instance, may have fewer specified procedures than their workers, in low-complexity organizations the more efficient department heads will have a higher proportion of procedures specified for them. That this is a false assumption becomes obvious from the responses made by the department heads when asked to what extent they felt their own procedures were specified for them. Correlating perceived department-head specification of procedures with the five measures of efficiency, we find four of the five correlations to be negative, including the two that reach the .05 level of significance (see Table VIII-4).

Even though this was an unpredicted finding, it is not a surprising one. In the Entrepreneurial Theory, Becker and Gordon state, "Not only does the uniqueness of skills increase as one moves from the lowest to the highest administrative levels, but the responsibility for coordination and planning also increases."[3] Our inability to predict was based on our ignorance of how "high up" in the hierarchy a department head stood. We did not know the degree of complexity of a department head's task: Ought he to be

TABLE VIII-4

Correlations Between Perceived Department-Head Specification-of-Production Procedures and Efficiency

Efficiency Measure	Correlations Product Moment	Rank Order
Cost Index (1)	+.285	(+.212)
Man-hour Index (2)	−.065	(−.161)
Expert Evaluation (3)	−.384*	(−.328)
JCAH Evaluation (4)	−.224*	(−.154)
Occupancy	−.113	(−.063)

*$p < .05$.

treated like a professional or like a highly skilled technician? (Perhaps if we compared heads of the laundry and the pharmaceutical departments we might find differences in the way perceived specifications of department-head procedures relate to efficiency.)

At any rate, based on our data, it seems that the good administrator hires "professional" department heads who know their job, can function autonomously, and will specify procedures for their subordinates.

Specification of Procedures to Increase C_V *and* C_V. We have hypothesized that both these variables are positively related to organizational efficiency. Based on the data in Table VIII-5, we claim support for our hypotheses, although the relationships for PC_V are not as strong as are those for specification-of-production procedures. PC_V is positively related to the expert evaluation and the JCAH index, while all the other correlations have the proper signs but are not statistically significant. Also, the correlations of the administrators' C_V scores with efficiency are not statistically significant even though they have all the predicted signs. The chairman of the board's C_V score for 17 hospitals all point in the right direction, and four of the five are statistically significant.

We claim support for the hypotheses despite the number of "nonsignificant" correlations for two reasons. One, and less important, is that the signs of all the correlations point in the predicted direction; second, two correlations between PC_V and efficiency reach the .05 level and one, the .10 level, and four of the five correlations between board chairman C_V and efficiency are significant. In the Entrepreneurial Theory, C_V is determined, first, by the owner's, in this case the board members', awareness of how outcomes relate to goal achievement. Consequently, the five nonsignificant correlations involving the administrator, while food for reflection, are not damaging to the theory or to the test of the hypothesis. Rather, we suggest that the administrator, unlike the board chairman, probably knows the cost of a patient meal, whether it is higher or lower than last year's, but the board chairman knows how the cost of that patient meal compares with that of other hospitals. In other words, the administrators' standards are more likely to involve internal organizational matters while the board chairmen's focus on external problems. Clearly, the board chairmen play an important role in promoting hospital efficiency.

TABLE VIII-5

Correlations Between Efficiency, Specification-of-Visibility Procedures, and Visibility of Consequences (Nonmedical Component)

	Measures of Efficiency[a]					
	Cost Index (1)	Man-hour Index (2)	Mean Expert Evaluation (3)	JCAH Index (4)	Occupancy (5)	(n)
Specification-of-Visibility Procedures (Reports) (PC_V^+)	−.320 (−.249)	−.298 (−.307)	+.390* (+.452)	+.391* (+.325)	+.237 (+.278)	(27)
Visibility of Consequences (Administrator) (C_V)	−.122 (−.080)	−.180 (−.033)	+.037 (−.020)	+.233 (+.203)	+.133 (+.052)	(27)
Visibility of Consequences (Administrator) (C_V)	−.116 (−.058)	−.235 (−.085)	+.195 (+.039)	+.011 (−.164)	+.045 (−.070)	(17)
Visibility of Consequences (Board Chairman) (C_V)	−.670** (−.659)	−.483* (−.431)	+.492* (+.426)	+.382 (+.214)	+.460* (+.466)	(17)

*p < .05.
**p < .005.
[a]Pearson product moment correlations shown without parentheses; rank order correlations shown within parentheses.

Differences in Complexity. Compared with the medical component, the nonmedical component of the hospital has a low level of task-environment complexity. However, there are differences in task-environments in these low-complexity, nonmedical components. The nonmedical components were divided into high- and low-complexity groups, based on how many of 15 different types of technical personnel were employed in the nonmedical component of each hospital. We assumed that the wider the range of different types of personnel, the wider the range of tasks performed, and the higher the complexity.

We have hypothesized that a higher proportion of specified production procedures will be associated with efficiency in lower-complexity units than in higher ones. The cost index was used as the measure of efficiency,[4] and the results of this test are shown in Table VIII-6.

We can claim partial support from the data in Table VIII-6. In the low-complexity nonmedical components, the higher the specification-of-production procedures, the higher the efficiency (as measured by a lower cost index). This is true for both measures of specification-of-production procedures. In the high-complexity nonmedical components, the higher the specification-of-production procedures, the lower the efficiency (as measured by a higher cost index), although this relationship is not significant.

Using the same method to control for complexity, there appears to be no modification in the positive relationship between specification-of-visibility procedures (PC_V), visibility of consequences (C_V), and efficiency.[5] This, too, is consistent with our model of organizational efficiency.

The final hypothesis to be tested with this segment of the organization is whether specification-of-production procedures, specification of procedures to increase C_V, and C_V, have positive and additive effects on efficiency. That is to say, each of the independent variables will explain some of the variance in efficiency when their effects are examined simultaneously. Multiple regression techniques were used to test this hypothesis. In these equations, four different measures of efficiency are used: the cost index, the man-hour index, the average expert evaluation, and occupancy.[6] Two measures of specification-of-production procedures are used: perceived worker specification of procedures (P_p) and the index

TABLE VIII-6

**The Relationship Between Specification-of-Production
Procedures and Efficiency Controlling for Complexity
in the Nonmedical Component of the Hospital (n = 27)**

		Lower-Complexity Components (Cx)[a]		High-Complexity Components (Cx)[a]	
		Cost Index ($)		Cost Index ($)	
		Low	High	Low	High
Perceived Worker P+	Low	0	6	3	1
(P_p^+)	High	6	3	4	4
		Q = −1.00		Q = +.40	
		p < .02		NS	
Extent of Job Descriptions	Low	0	8	3	1
(P_j^+)	High	6	1	4	4
		Q = −1.00		Q = +.40	
		p < .001		NS	

[a]The Q is Yule and Kendall's Q coefficient of correlation. Significance is based on χ^2 test from D. J. Finney *et al.*, *Tables for Testing Significance in a 2 X 2 Contingency Table* (Cambridge: Cambridge University Press, 1963). Complexity here refers only to the nonmedical component.

based on the proportion of employees covered by job descriptions (P_j). Two additional control variables were added: hospital size and complexity.

In some previous studies[8] it was concluded that hospital size is positively correlated with efficiency, and therefore it is appropriate to control for size. Theoretically, economies of scale exist only when some indivisibilities make small size relatively inefficient, but once a hospital is large enough so that indivisibilities have no effect, there should be no economies of scale. If this is correct, then the relationship between efficiency and size is nonlinear and may be approximated by the reciprocal of size.

In our model of efficiency we state that complexity influences the effect of management activities on efficiency, so it is appropriate to control for this variable, too. Another reason for including complexity as an independent variable was to see if the cost and man-hour indexes were affected by the scope of services being provided by the hospital. To avoid the problem of collinearity, only one of the two (P+) variables and only one of the control variables are used in each equation. The efficiency variables are the dependent variables, and each equation has four independent variables.

This results in the 16 different regression equations shown in Table VIII-9. Tables VIII-7 and VIII-8 list the variables used, their theoretical definitions, operational measures, means, standard deviations, and theoretical ranges.

In every equation, for every dependent variable entered, the results support the hypothesis. Both measures of specification-of-production procedures (P_p, P_j), visibility of consequences (C_v), and specification-of-visibility procedures (PC_v) are negatively related to the cost and man-hour indexes and positively related to occupancy and the mean expert evaluation. In addition, the reciprocal of size is positively related to cost and man-hours, showing the existence of economies of scale over the size range observed. The relationships are all in the predicted direction, and the cumulative r's are all statistically significant.

Note that the cost index of efficiency seems almost complexity-free, in that complexity enters last in both equations where used to predict the cost index. This is not the case for the expert-evaluation and occupancy measures of efficiency. The cost and man-hour indexes were designed so as to be minimally influenced by complexity. The complexity measure is always positively related to efficiency. This is probably so in part because it picks up the size effect to which it is so closely related.

These regressions explain from 28% to 60% of the variance in the efficiency of the nonmedical component. At best, these equations explain 43% of the variance in the cost index, 60% in the man-hour index, 47% in occupancy, and 52% in the mean expert evaluation. This appears to be a substantial improvement over previous studies of the impact of managerial behavior on organizational performance. According to Dubin and Homans, in their

TABLE VIII-7

Multiple-Regression Equations Predicting Efficiency with
Specification-of-Production Procedures, Specification-of-
Visibility Procedures, Visibility of Consequences,
Organization Size, and Complexity

Symbol	Theoretical Name	Operational Measure
$	Efficiency	Cost Index
MH	Efficiency	Man-hour Index
EE	Efficiency	Mean Expert Evaluation
$\emptyset$	Efficiency	Percent Occupancy
P_p^+	Specification-of-Production Procedures	Perceived Worker P+
P_j^+	Specification-of-Production Procedures	Percent of Employees Covered by Job Descriptions
C_v	Visibility of Consequences	Administrator Awareness
PC_v^+	Specification-of-Visibility Procedures	Reports Index
S	Organizational Size	Number of Beds
C_x	Organizational Complexity	Index of Number of Different Technical Personnel in Hospital

Stepwise multiple regression is used (BM34T Computer Program). Directly below each independent variable the t values are shown. If $t > 1.96$ then $p < .05$. In all equations n = 27.

reviews of studies of leadership and productivity,[9] differences in the quality of supervision have accounted for at best 20% and an average of 10% of the variance in performance. Considerable explanatory power seems to have been gained by the use of our model of organizational efficiency.

*Greater detail on any of the measures is available from the authors on request.

TABLE VIII-8

Means, Standard Deviations, and Maximum Ranges of the Variables (n = 27)

Variable Symbol	Variable Name	Mean
$	Cost Index	23.25
MH	Man-hour Index	4.74
EE	Expert Evaluation	3.19
$\emptyset$	Occupancy	82.04
P_p^+	Perceived Worker P+	9.17
P_j^+	Job Descriptions	61.11
C_v	Visibility of Consequences (Admin.)	0.384
PC_v^+	Reports Index	22.33
S	Size	308.5
C_x	Complexity	10.81
1/S	Reciprocal of Size	3.79×10^{-3}

[a]These indicate the extreme maximum values which these variless than 0 and no more than 100% of all employees can be covered

Standard Deviation	Maximum Possible Range[a]
3.42	$0 > \$$
0.70	$0 > MH$
0.73	$1 > EE \leqslant 5$
6.61	$0 \geqslant \emptyset$
0.83	$2 \geqslant P_p^+ \leqslant 12$
43.18	$0 \geqslant P_j^+ \leqslant 100$
0.50	$-1.00 \geqslant C_v \leqslant +1.00$
6.78	$0 \geqslant PC_v^+ \leqslant 44$
123.5	$100 \geqslant S \leqslant 530$
2.45	$1 \geqslant C_x \leqslant 15$
1.55×10^{-3}	

ables can take in theory. For example, for P_j^+, no
by job descriptions.

TABLE VIII-9

Multiple-Regression Equations Predicting Efficiency for the Nonmedical Component[a]

Dependent Variable	Constant	Independent Variables		
		P_p^+	P_j^+	C_v
$	+36.17	−1.25	. . .	−1.22
	(4.50)	(1.58)	. . .	(1.00)
$	+24.71	. . .	−.036	−1.34
	(10.10)	. . .	(−2.42)	(1.18)
$	+28.00	. . .	−.040	−1.06
	(8.07)	. . .	(2.43)	(0.86)
$	+42.00	−1.70	. . .	−0.91
	(6.19)	(2.01)	. . .	(0.70)
MH	+ 6.05	−0.16	. . .	−0.41
	(4.42)	(1.19)	. . .	(1.96)
MH	+ 4.58	. . .	−.005	−0.42
	(10.88)	. . .	(1.96)	(2.15)
MH	+ 6.70	. . .	−.005	−.041
	(10.00)	. . .	(1.46)	(1.72)
MH	+ 8.60	−0.22	. . .	−0.39
	(6.66)	(1.40)	. . .	(1.59)
φ	+52.04	+3.19	. . .	+1.96
	(3.40)	(2.10)	. . .	(0.84)
φ	+82.09	. . .	+0.32	+2.59
	(15.39)	. . .	(0.99)	(1.04)
φ	+60.50	. . .	+0.01	+3.44
	(9.57)	. . .	(0.35)	(1.52)
φ	+43.20	+2.36	. . .	+2.82
	(3.77)	(1.67)	. . .	(1.30)
EE	+ 2.43	+0.08	. . .	+0.23
	(1.54)	(0.50)	. . .	(0.96)
EE	+ 3.10	. . .	+.005	+0.22
	(6.43)	. . .	(1.68)	(1.00)
EE	+ 1.15	. . .	+.005	+0.22
	(1.62)	. . .	(1.32)	(0.86)
EE	+ .002	+0.12	. . .	+0.22
	(0.0001)	(0.70)	. . .	(0.84)

[a]Regression coefficients shown without parentheses; t values

PC$_v^+$	1/S	C$_x$	Cumulative		
			r	r^2	P
−0.14 (1.57)	+569 (1.34)	. . . . . .	.59	.35	< .005
−0.58 (0.63)	+667 (1.81)	. . . . . .	.66	.43	< .005
−.050 (0.49)	. . . . . .	−.05 (0.20)	.59	.35	< .005
−.14 (1.47)	. . . . . .	−.0015 (0.05)	.55	.30	< .005
−.027 (1.82)	+249 (3.44)	. . . . . .	.75	.56	< .0005
−.016 (0.99)	+259 (4.08)	. . . . . .	.77	.60	< .0005
−.013 (0.68)	. . . . . .	−0.11 (2.17)	.65	.42	< .0005
−.023 (1.31)	. . . . . .	−0.10 (1.89)	.64	.41	< .0005
+0.17 (1.01)	−1017 (1.25)	. . . . . .	.61	.37	< .0005
+0.14 (0.67)	−1589 (1.98)	. . . . . .	.53	.28	< .0005
+0.12 (0.68)	. . . . . .	+1.50 (3.13)	.64	.41	< .0005
+0.13 (0.81)	. . . . . .	+1.22 (2.49)	.69	.47	< .0005
+.039 (2.24)	−241 (2.90)	. . . . . .	.68	.46	< .0005
+.026 (1.42)	−233 (3.21)	. . . . . .	.72	.52	< .0005
+.023 (1.15)	. . . . . .	+0.11 (1.91)	.63	.39	< .0005
+.034 (1.79)	. . . . . .	+0.11 (1.88)	.60	.36	< .005

shown within parentheses. P refers to the cumulative r.

CHAPTER 8

The Hospital Organization Study:

THE PROFESSIONAL COMPONENT— HIGH COMPLEXITY

We hypothesized that specification-of-production procedures (P_p) is negatively related to efficiency in an organization having a highly complex interaction with its environment, while both specification of procedures to increase visibility of consequences (PC_v) and visibility of consequences (C_v) are positively related to efficiency. To test this hypothesis, measures of P_p, PC_v, C_v, and efficiency are necessary. In the hospital organization the staff of physicians and the tasks they perform define the complex component whose subgoal is high-quality patient care.

Measurement of Efficiency

Given quality medical care as the goal, efficiency must be defined as the degree to which high-quality patient care is achieved. (Partly because physicians are not paid by the hospital, costs of quality care play a considerably smaller role than does quality of care itself.) Measurement of quality of medical care is extremely difficult and several yardsticks have been proposed. We evaluated efficiency with four of the most widely used measures.

1. *Mean Expert Evaluation Index* (EE). Five experts, all physicians not connected with the hospitals in this sample, used a 5-point scale to evaluate the quality of care in these hospitals, in line with the study of Denton *et al.*[1] The mean interrater reliability between these experts was high at +.738, which testifies to a considerable amount of agreement among the raters. The Expert Evaluation Index was arrived at by recalibrating each rater's scores to give them a standardized mean value and then obtaining an

average evaluation for each hospital. The higher the Expert Evaluation Index, the greater the efficiency of the professional component of the organization.

2. *The Joint Commission on Accreditation of Hospitals
Quality Index* (JCAH). The physician evaluator of the JCAH
scored 20 hospital areas on an acceptable/unacceptable basis. Six
of these areas were used for the nonmedical efficiency index. The
remaining 14 are here used as the basis for the quality index. The
following scoring was used for each of these 14 areas:[2]

Unacceptable or Absent 1

Present, Unacceptable/Acceptable
   (halfway in-between) 2

Present, Acceptable, but with
   major problems noted 3

Present, Acceptable, no major
   problems noted 4

The JCAH Quality Index was obtained by summing the
scores across the areas. The higher the index, the greater the efficiency of the professional component of the organization.

3. *Physician-Qualifications Quality Index.* There is some evidence to suggest that, on the average, board-certified specialists
provide higher-quality care than do general practitioners,[3] although these findings might be hotly contested by general practitioners. If, however, these findings are accurate and generalizations
can be made, then the higher the proportion of board-certified
specialists, the higher the quality of care. We took the percentage
of board-certified specialists on the active (voting) staff of the
hospital as a measure of efficiency.[4]

4. *Death Rate Adjusted for Severity of Illness as a Measure
of Quality of Care* (SADR). This measure was developed by
Roemer *et al.*[5] It is based on the percentage of patients who died
in the hospital, adjusting for the average severity of illness. Severity of illness is approximated by difference in the average length
of stay, which in turn is modified by differences in demand ("pressure") for beds. Admittedly, this is an approximate measure of
quality, but it is one of the few "hard" output measures available.
The higher the SADR, the lower the quality of care.

Each of the four measures can logically be related to quality of care. Consequently, they should be correlated with one another (see Table IX-1). Four of the six correlations reach the .05 level of significance. The two correlations which might have occurred by chance are those involving the percentage of board-certified specialists. Being an input rather than an output measure, percentage of board specialists also seems to reflect something other than quality of care and therefore will not be used as a measure of efficiency.

Measurement of Specification of Procedures to Increase Visibility of Consequences (PC_v)

Two measures of this variable were obtained in the medical component of the hospital. They are:

1. *PC_v is measured by an index based on the extent and frequency of statistical reports on medical staff activities.* The index is determined by whether and how frequently the hospital

TABLE IX-1

Correlations Between the Measures of Quality of Care

	Percent of Board-Certified Specialists	JCAH Evaluation	SADR
Mean Expert Evaluation (EE)	+.557** (+.489)	+.528** (+.714)	−.456** (−.372)
Percent of Board-Certified Specialists		+.214 (+.369)	−.270 (−.293)
JCAH Evaluation			−.364* (−.323)

*p < .05.

**p < .005.

Expert evaluation (n = 30), % Specialists (n = 26), JCAH evaluation (n = 29), SADR (n = 29), Pearson Product Moment Correlations are shown without parentheses and rank order correlations are shown within parentheses. Here and in the rest of the tables in this chapter, significance levels are shown only for the former.

compiles data on incomplete medical records, percentage of normal tissue removed, consultative rates, postoperative deaths, anesthesia deaths, admissions per physician per year, and physician attendance at staff meetings. The higher the index score, the higher the specification-of-visibility procedures.

2. *The second PC_v measure for the medical component is the hospital's autopsy rate, i.e., the proportion of autopsies performed on all patients who died in the hospital.* The autopsy is the definitive technique for ascertaining the cause of death, and therefore points the way to evaluating the effects of medical treatment. It is a method of making the effects of procedures visible. Thus, the higher the autopsy rate, the higher the specification-of-visibility procedures.

The two measures purportedly tap the same variable and so should be related. They are, in fact, significantly correlated, r = .39; p < .05.

Visibility of Consequences (C_V) for the Medical Component

The visibility-of-consequences measures for the medical component were obtained in exactly the same way as for the nonmedical component and by the use of the same questionnaire. The administrator and the chairman of the board were asked, using a 5-point scale, to rate their hospital above or below other similar hospitals in the Chicago area on a number of variables relating to quality of care.

Both the administrator's and board chairman's ratings were then correlated with his hospital's actual standing (rank order) on these four characteristics. This correlation between the evaluations and the hospital's rank order was used as a measure of visibility of consequences. The higher this correlation, the higher the visibility of consequences.[6]

Both the administrators and chairmen of the board of 17 non-Catholic hospitals filled out this questionnaire. In these hospitals the correlation between the administrator's C_V score and the chairman's C_V score was +.841.[7] The mean C_V score for the 27 administrators was +.136, and that for the 17 board chairmen +.160. The fact that these means are greater than zero would suggest that on the average these respondents had an accurate idea of their hospitals' relative performance.

Specification-of-Production Procedures (P_p) for the Medical Component

Although there are many rules physicians must follow—e.g., required consultations prior to performing certain procedures—the sense of the variable specified procedures is that they are imposed by the owner or his agent, the board of directors, or the chief administrative officer. In hospitals, two such measures are available:

1. *Use of a formulary.* This limits the range of drugs which a physician can prescribe in the hospital,[8] in contrast to hospitals which allow the physician to prescribe any drug he wishes. This measure was scored on a yes/no basis. (28% of the hospitals use a formulary.)

2. *Suspension of admitting privileges in case of excessive number of incomplete medical records.* Such a rule is indicative of the willingness of the hospital administration to invoke sanctions against individual physicians to enforce hospital rules concerning the completion of such records. This measure was scored on a yes/no basis. (88% of hospitals suspend privileges for incomplete records.)

A third, less concrete, measure of specification of procedures also was obtained:

3. Physicians' influence in the hospital as perceived by the chief or president of the medical staff, who rated physician influence on a 6-point scale. The higher the score, the higher the perceived influence and, presumably, the lower the specification of procedures. (Mean value = 4.38.)

The correlations between these three measures of specification of procedures are shown in Table IX-2. The measures are neither strongly nor systematically related to one another. We expected the measure of perceived physician influence to be negatively related to the other P_p measures, but we find a (nonsignificant) positive correlation with use of a formulary. For purposes of hypothesis testing, it is hoped that the absence of a relationship[9] among these measures reflects the multidimensional character of the variable rather than a lack of validity of our measures.

TABLE IX-2

Correlations Between the Measures of Specification-
of-Production Procedures (P+) for the
Medical Component[a]

	Suspension of Privileges	Perceived MD Influence
1. Formulary used	−.237 (−.714)	+.244 (+.059)
2. Suspension of admitting privileges		−.105 (−.043)

[a]Pearson Product Moment Correlation shown without parentheses; Yule and Kendall's Q shown within parentheses.

Tests of the Hypotheses Concerning the Medical Component of the Hospital

We have hypothesized that specification of procedures to increase C_V, PC_V, and visibility of consequences (C_V) are positively related to efficiency. The correlations between PC_V, C_V, and efficiency (quality of care) are shown in Table IX-3. The results are all in the predicted direction and are statistically significant for 7 of the 12 correlations. Both high C_V and high PC_V are positively correlated with the mean expert and the JCAH evaluation and negatively correlated with the severity-adjusted death rate. As with the nonmedical component, board C_V is a better predictor of efficiency than is administrator C_V.

We have also hypothesized that, given high complexity, specification-of-production procedures will be negatively related to efficiency. This hypothesis is tested by correlating our three measures of quality of care with the three measures of specification-of-production procedures for the medical component of the hospital. The results are shown in Table IX-4, along with the predicted direction of these relationships. Of the nine relationships shown in this table, all but one are in the predicted direction, and of these, three are statistically significant at the .05 level. This provides only modest support for the hypothesis.

TABLE IX-3

Correlations Between Specification-of-Visibility Procedures
(PC_v^+), Visibility of Consequences (C_v), and Efficiency
(Quality of Care) for the Medical Component of the Hospital

	Quality of Care		
	Mean Expert Evaluation	JCAH Evaluation	SADR Adjusted Death Rate
PC_v^+			
Reports index	+.514**	+.308	−.107
Autopsy rate	+.495**	+.502**	−.443*
C_v			
Administrator	+.468*	+.183	−.231
Board (n = 17)	+.753**	+.424*	−.158

*p < .05
**p < .005

TABLE IX-4

Specification-of-Production Procedures (P+) and
Efficiency (Quality of Care) for the
Medical Component of the Hospital

	Mean Expert Evaluation	JCAH Index	Adjusted Death Rate
Predicted Direction of Relationships Based on Hypothesis VI			
1. Formulary used	−	−	+
2. Suspension of privileges	−	−	+
3. Perceived MD influence	+	+	−
Observed Relationships			
1. Formulary used	−.294	−.325*	+.124
2. Suspension of privileges	−.381*	+.016	+.228
3. Perceived MD influence	+.276	+.286	−.326*

*p < .05.

Because of the ambiguity of these results we sought further evidence. A new index was developed to provide a better measure of the degree to which physicians participated in specifying their own procedures. The rationale underlying the index is as follows:

If a proportionately large number of physicians serve on the board of the hospital or if the physicians can meet with the board frequently in a joint conference committee (JCC), then it is assumed that the board is less likely to impose rules upon the professionals without their participation and consent. In the absence of physician membership on the governing board, the next best thing is having the professionals confer frequently with the board. In hospitals, the usual vehicle for such meetings is the joint conference committee, in which chiefs of the medical staff meet with the executive board. Although decisions of the JCC are not binding on the board, they tend to carry great weight.[10] Using this reasoning the following scale was developed:

(P–) > 10% of board are MDs and JCC meets frequently . .1

≤ 10% of board are MDs and JCC meets frequently
> 10% of board are MDs and JCC meets infrequently ²

≤ 10% of board are MDs and JCC meets infrequently 3

No MDs on board and JCC meets frequently 4

(P+) No MDs on board and JCC meets infrequently 5

If the joint conference committee meets six or more times a year, it is defined as "frequently"; if it meets less than six times, "infrequently." The higher the scale number here, the higher the specification of procedures.

Based on our hypothesis, we predict that this index is negatively correlated with the expert evaluation of quality of care and with the JCAH rating of quality, and positively correlated with the adjusted death rate. The results, shown in Table IX-5, are in the predicted direction, and two of the relationships are significant at the .05 level. This provides considerably better support for the hypothesized relationship between efficiency and specification-of-production procedures in the complex component of the organization.

This hypothesis can be further tested by subdividing these

TABLE IX-5

Correlations Between Specification-of-Procedures Index and Measures of Quality of Care

	Quality of Care Measures		
	Expert Evaluation	JCAH	Adjusted Death Rate
P+ Index	−.092	−.449*	+.435*

*$p < .05$.

medical components into high and low complexity. To do this we used a complexity index based on whether or not 11 different surgical operations were performed in the last year, the use of cardiac monitors, and the availability of a premature nursery. The higher the complexity index, the more complex the medical component. The negative relationship between P_p and quality of care should be greater in the high-complexity medical components. The results are shown in Table IX-6.

TABLE IX-6

Complexity, Quality of Care, and (P+) for the Medical Component

		Low Complexity				High Complexity			
		Report Evaluation		SADR		Report Evaluation		SADR	
		Low	High	Low	High	Low	High	Low	High
7. P+ Index	Low	3	2	3	2	3	2	7	2
	High	3	1	1	3	5	2	2	4
		Q = −.333		Q = +.636		Q = −.667		Q = +.750	

　The JCAH 17 Index did not divide evenly enough between high and low complexity to allow for this type of analysis. Qs are Yule and Kendall's Q: a measure of association. None of these 2 x 2 tables are statistically significant by themselves using χ^2 as the test of significance. The variables shown here have been dichotomized at the mean.

Because of the very small sample sizes involved, these results are not statistically significant and should be viewed cautiously. For both high- and low-complexity groups, the higher the specification-of-production procedures the lower the expert's evaluation of the quality of care and the higher the death-rate index. In the high-complexity groups, these associations (as measured by the larger Q's) are slightly stronger. This is consistent with the hypothesis.

According to the model of organizational efficiency, the effects of P_p, PC_V, and C_V are unrelated, and so we should be able to demonstrate that their effects on efficiency are additive. This hypothesis will be tested by the use of multiple-regression equations to predict efficiency (quality of care) in exactly the same way as was done with the nonmedical component in Chapter VII.

Three measures of quality of care are used: the mean expert evaluation (EE), the Joint Commission on the Accreditation of Hospitals (JCAH) evaluation score, and the severity-adjusted death rate (SADR), which is negatively related to quality of care.

Two measures of specification of procedures to increase C_V are used: the reports index and the autopsy rate. Because they both measure the same theoretical concept, these two measures will not be used in the same regression equation.

The specification-of-production-procedures index used is the one developed retrospectively in this chapter.

Two additional control variables have been entered: the natural log of hospital size, and medical-component complexity. The log of size is used because the first-order correlations between log of size and quality-of-care measures are stronger than for linear size. Unlike the cost indexes of nonmedical efficiency, there is no compelling theoretical reason for choosing one particular form of size measure over any other. To avoid the problem of collinearity between these two independent variables, complexity and log size were not used in the same regression equations. As a result, we arrived at 12 separate equations, shown in Table IX-7. These results support the hypothesis, with the partial exception of one of the two specification of procedures to increase C_V measures.

As predicted, the P_p measure is negatively related to the expert-evaluation and JCAH indexes, and positively to the SADR index. That is to say, the more specified the procedures, the lower the quality of care.

TABLE IX-7

Specification-of-Production Procedures (P+), Visibility of Consequences (C_V), and Specification-of-Visibility Procedures (PC_V^+)

P+ Measure	Predicted Direction of Relationship*	(PC_V^+) Reports Index	(PC_V^+) Autopsy Rate	Administrator C_V	Board C_V (n = 17)
1. Formulary used	−	+.082	−.174	+.210	+.116
2. Privileges suspended	−	−.186	−.043	−.361	−.163
4. P+ Index	−	−.434*	−.355*	+.012	−.212
3. Perceived MD influence	+	+.021	+.190	+.345*	+.258

*p < .05. For explanation, see text.

As predicted, visibility of consequences is positively related to the quality of care.

Consistent with the findings of Denton et al.,[11] size and complexity are positively related to the quality of care.

With respect to the relationship between quality of care and specification of procedures to increase C_v, the autopsy-rate measure is consistently in the predicted direction. The reports-index measure is in the predicted direction in three out of the six equations in which it is used. It is not in the predicted direction in the three equations with the lowest r^2s. In three of four matched comparisons, the r^2s are higher where the autopsy rate rather than the reports index is used.

The r^2s for these equations tend to be higher than for the nonmedical component. At best, we can explain 66% of the variance in the mean expert evaluation, 76% of the JCAH evaluation, and 43% of the death rate index.

To further test the hypothesis that specification-of-production procedures should be negatively related to quality of care, the perceived measure of specification-of-production procedures was used in place of the P_p index in the regressions equations. This measures the degree of perceived physician influence in the hospital. The higher the score, the greater the physician influence and the lower the specification of procedures. Therefore, it is predicted that this perceived P_p measure (P_p) should be positively correlated with the expert-evaluation (EE) and JCAH index, and negatively with the SADR index. The results are shown in Table IX-11. Instead of showing all possible regression equations, only three, one for each different measure of quality of care, are shown. The equations chosen are those with the highest r^2 and F values obtained. The results shown in Table IX-12 are consistent with the hypothesis. The greater the physician influence, the higher the expert evaluation and JCAH index and the lower the severity-adjusted death rate. The visibility variables enter with the expected signs, with the single exception of C_v in the JCAH equation.

The hypotheses derived from our model of organizational efficiency as applied to the complex component of the hospital seem to be well supported by the cumulative weight of the evidence presented in this chapter.

TABLE IX-8

**Multiple-Regression Equations Predicting
Quality of Medical Care**

Symbol	Theoretical Name	Operational Measure
EE	Quality of care	Mean expert evaluation
JCAH	Quality of care	Joint Commission on the Accreditation of Hospitals Index
SADR	Quality of care	Severity-adjusted death rate
C_x	Complexity	Index of operations performed
log S	Size	Log of the number of hospital beds
PC_v^+	Specification-of-visibility procedures	Reports index
A	Specification-of-production procedures	Autopsy rate
P+	Specification-of-visibility procedures	Index of physician participation in decision-making
C_v	Visibility of consequences	Administrator awareness

TABLE IX-10

Multiple-Regression Equations Predicting Quality of Care for the Medical Component[a]

Dependent Variable	Constant	P+	C_v	PC_v	A	log S	C_x	r	r^2
EE	-4.56 (2.42)	-0.10 (1.08)	+0.21 (1.02)	+0.04 (1.71)	...	+1.28 (4.17)	...	.81	.66
EE	-3.38 (1.88)	-0.14 (1.55)	+0.35 (1.75)	...	+0.013 (1.24)	+1.12 (3.42)	...	.80	.64
EE	+1.32 (1.22)	-0.12 (0.99)	+0.48 (1.92)	+0.025 (0.86)	...	...	+0.15 (2.02)	.67	.45
EE	+0.91 (0.92)	-0.11 (1.05)	+0.51 (2.33)	...	+0.021 (1.76)	...	+0.14 (2.08)	.72	.52
JCAH	-8.22 (0.69)	-1.62 (2.73)	+0.40 (0.30)	+0.069 (0.47)	...	+9.94 (5.12)	...	.84	.70
JCAH	-6.69 (0.68)	-1.41 (2.82)	+0.52 (0.48)	...	+0.12 (2.06)	+8.88 (4.91)	...	.87	.76
JCAH	+37.45 (5.01)	-1.75 (2.13)	+2.46 (1.42)	-0.045 (0.23)	...	...	+1.13 (2.23)	.65	.43
JCAH	+28.25 (4.46)	-1.16 (1.75)	+1.84 (1.32)	...	+0.18 (2.41)	...	+1.06 (2.38)	.75	.57
SADR	+5.99	+0.059	-0.65	+0.61	...	-0.88	...		

								r	r^2
	(1.24)	(2.43)	(1.21)	(1.01)		(1.11)		.58	.34
SADR	+8.14 (1.96)	+0.34 (1.60)	−0.38 (0.82)	...	−0.049 (1.98)	−0.58 (0.77)	...	.65	.43
SADR	+1.91 (0.85)	+0.60 (2.43)	−0.83 (1.61)	+0.071 (1.16)	...	...	−0.096 (0.63)	.56	.31
SADR	+5.79 (2.88)	+0.32 (1.51)	−0.46 (1.05)	...	−0.053 (2.19)	...	−0.065 (0.46)	.64	.42

[a] Regression coefficients shown without parentheses, t values within parentheses. For all equations n = 23.

TABLE IX-11

Multiple-Regression Equations Predicting Quality of Care Using the Perceived Measure of Specification-of-Production Procedures (P_p^+)[a]

Dependent Variable	Constants	P_p^+	C_v	PC_v	A	log S	C_v	r	r^2
EE	−5.21 (3.03)	+0.027 (0.23)	+0.16 (0.78)	+0.052 (2.60)	...	+1.29 (4.24)	...	.80	.65
JCAH	−18.69 (1.19)	+0.91 (0.87)	−1.72 (0.94)	+0.34 (1.89)	...	+9.35 (3.38)	...	.69	.47
SADR	+6.42 (3.21)	−0.34 (1.11)	−0.27 (0.54)	...	−0.049 (1.94)	...	+0.93 (0.65)	.51	.26

[a] Regression coefficients shown without parentheses, t values within parentheses.

TABLE IX-9

**Means, Standard Deviations, and
Maximum Ranges of the Variables**

Variable Symbol	Variable Name	Mean	Standard Deviation	Maximum Possible Range
EE	Expert evaluation	3.04	0.85	$1 \leqslant EE \geqslant 5$
JCAH	JCAH index	43.87	5.73	$0 \leqslant JCAH \geqslant 50$
SADR	Death rate	3.87	1.57	
C_X	Complexity	11.00	2.02	$0 \leqslant C_X \geqslant 13$
log S	Log size	5.62	0.40	
PC_V^+	Reports index	16.91	6.12	$0 \leqslant PC_V^+ \geqslant 28$
A	Autopsy rate	40.74	12.43	$0 \leqslant A \geqslant 100$
P+	Specification of procedures	3.87	1.57	$1 \leqslant P+ \geqslant 5$
C_V	Administrator awareness	+.047	0.65	$-1.00 \leqslant C_V \geqslant +1.00$

CHAPTER 9

The Hospital
Organization Study:
THE THREE MISSING OBSERVATIONS—
CASE STUDIES

Three of the 30 hospitals in the sample were unable or unwilling to provide much information. These hospitals, however, are sufficiently different from the others that descriptions of them, even at a primarily anecdotal level, provide data consistent with our model of organizational efficiency.

Because of the lack of information the only measures of efficiency available to us are the experts' ratings. Let us keep in mind that experts' ratings of administrative efficiency were strongly correlated with all other measures of efficiency (Table VIII-1), and that experts' ratings of quality of care were strongly related to other measures of quality of care (Table IX-1). The low-complexity components of these hospitals ranked 23rd, 27th, and 30th in efficiency, while the medical staffs, or high-complexity components, ranked 25th, 26th and 30th on quality-of-medical-care efficiency. Clearly, these three hospitals are among the lowest in efficiency.

Low-efficiency organizations, according to the model, should be characterized by low visibility of consequences, low specification-of-visibility procedures, and in the high-complex units relatively high specification-of-production procedures and in the low-complex units relatively low specification-of-production procedures.

In the low-complex units, visibility of consequences depends, among other things, on high specification-of-visibility procedures, on procedures designed to produce measures of a number of operating characteristics. In two of these three hospitals, no financial information was produced in the six months prior to the study. Their only financial information was their bank balances, and in one case this was not reconciled with canceled checks, so there was no verification of its accuracy. This hospital had absolutely no idea of its financial position, even though it had little in the way of cash reserves and no endowment. Needless to say, these two hospitals had not contributed financial data to the HAS data-collection service for over a year although they were paying for this service.

The arsenal of managerial practices of one of these administrators includes the refusal to answer his telephone and eating all his meals alone in his office. Such behavior hardly makes for maximum visibility. His unfeeling attitude toward the community in which the hospital is located testifies to his utter lack of awareness. He was amazed to learn that the interviewer had taken a bus to the hospital, for the bus route goes through a poor neighborhood. That, in his opinion, made travel by bus unsafe, a remarkable observation in view of the fact that a great many of the hospital clients and of its employees live there and take that bus. The personnel director did not know how many people were employed by the hospital. The panel of expert evaluators concluded that the administration of this hospital showed very little concern for its community.

The administrators of two of the three hospitals had been with their organizations for some time yet were not at all involved in any professional activities. They neither attended seminars nor served on external committees nor wrote for professional journals. In other words, they shielded themselves against learning about the rest of the hospital world. They appeared to be concerned only with their own hospital, making little effort to find out what others were doing. The lack of financial and other operative data, as well as the behavior and attitudes of the administrators, lead to the conclusion that the three administrative units were low on specification-of-visibility procedures and low on visibility of consequences.

We could claim complete consistency with our model if the low-complexity unit also showed low specification-of-production procedures. None of the three used budgets, and two did not have position controls. None of the three had job descriptions. The low-complex units conform to the model.

A departure from the model was discussed in Chapter VII, wherein we showed that in more efficient administrations, department heads were given greater leeway in carrying out their jobs. This was certainly not the case in one of these three hospitals, as the following incident suggests.

A new head dietician had spent eighty hours working out a two-week menu cycle, a demanding task involving the proper balancing of calories, menu variety, and the use of leftovers. After having drawn up the menu, the dietician was told by the administrator that the price of lamb chops was too high and that they and certain other foods could not be purchased. This invalidated her entire menu cycle, and she was very upset when the interviewer arrived at her office. In no other hospital in this sample did the administrator specify detailed procedures for his department heads. In the better-managed hospitals the administrator made an effort to get competent "professional" department heads and allowed them to specify production procedures in their departments, although visibility procedures were specified by the administrator. The detailed supervision in this hospital was reflected by the fact that it, compared with the other hospitals in the sample, had the second-highest score for perceived department head P+. In administering and specifying so many procedures, the administrator had to work exhausting, long hours because of his unwillingness to delegate responsibility.

In short, the low-complex administrative component of these three hospitals tended to have low P+ for workers, low C_V, low PC_V, and high P+ for department heads. Based on the model and on the empirical evidence in Chapter VII, these are all the wrong preconditions for efficient functioning.

Now let us turn to the high-complexity medical component. With respect to the use of reports on medical-staff activities (PC_V^+), these hospitals were below average. Two of them did not maintain the disease and operations indexes required by the Joint Commission on Accreditation of Hospitals. At the turn of the century, it

was very common for hospitals to evaluate the care they provided
by indicating whether the patient left the hospital improved, the
same, or worse than when he was admitted, or whether he died in
the hospital. One of these hospitals still uses this system. Looking
at their figures for a year's period of time, every patient either left
"improved" or died, the logic behind this being that if a patient
had not improved, why discharge him? If he is not improved or
worse, he would not be discharged. The usefulness of this approach is rather doubtful. This is an example of a report (PC_V^+)
which does not measure much of anything. Even though the hospital collected this information it was never used. The medical-
record librarian said that this information had been entered into a
large ledger as long as she could remember and they just kept on
doing it. In addition, these hospitals had lower than average autopsy rates.

Visibility of consequences on the part of the administrator
was not particularly high. For example, one of these administrators had no idea whether the chiefs of his medical staff were
elected by the doctors or appointed by the board.

A unique and distinguishing feature of these hospitals is their
apparent practice of nepotism to fill the key medical staff positions. Given low visibility of consequences, the Entrepreneurial
Theory would predict that such important decisions would more
likely be made on grounds not relevant to achieving the organization's goals. In two of these hospitals the senior officer on the
medical staff was closely related to an influential board member.
Apparently these two key people specified procedures for the rest
of the medical staff. This would seem to be the opposite of collegial decision-making and suggests high specification of procedures for the medical staff as a whole.

In one of these hospitals, due to unusual pre-existing conditions and perpetuated by the incumbent management, a number
of the most active doctors responsible for about half of all admissions to the hospital were barred from becoming active (voting)
members of the medical staff. These physicians, as well qualified
professionally as the rest of the staff, were classified as temporary
(nonvoting) members of the medical staff even though some had
been admitting a substantial number of patients there for years.
Thus these doctors enjoyed no formal collegial rights to partici-

pate in medical-staff decisions. This may well be symbolic of high specification of procedures (P+) for this medical staff. At this same hospital one physician on the voting staff admitted 1,000 patients a year (100 admissions a year is about average). It seems that he employed a number of unlicensed foreign medical graduates who did all the work in order to cope with this staggering patient load. Needless to say, these doctors were not eligible to be voting colleagues on the medical staff.

In short, the medical components of these hospitals tended to be characterized by low PC_V^+, low C_V and high P+. Based on the model and on the empirical evidence in Chapter VIII, these conditions are negatively related to efficiency. It is consistent with the theory that these hospitals ranked last, fourth-from-last, and fifth-from-last on quality of medical care provided.

In summary, these three hospitals are poorly managed and relatively inefficient.[1] Visibility is low and procedures are specified in an inappropriate manner. These "case studies" provide further support for the hypotheses derived from our model of organizational efficiency.

CHAPTER 10

The Insurance Organization Study

(WITH JUAN A. BUSTILLO)[1]

HYPOTHESES

This study was conceived of as a major test of the explanatory power of the variable visibility of consequences. The major hypothesis being tested maintains that organizations with higher visibility of consequences will be more efficient than will those with lower visibility of consequences.

Because the organizations studied were owned and managed by Venezuelan nationals, other variables, some possibly reflecting cultural differences, were added to the study, one of them being the managerial "use of time" in the pre-decision-making process—evaluation of alternatives; and in the post-decision-making process—assessment of outcomes.

Culture and the Use of Time. Management can handle time in the pre- and post-decision-making process in three ways: (a) "rational" behavior, (b) impulsive behavior, and (c) postponing-neglectful behavior.

Behavior will be considered "rational" when available information related to the decision problem is taken into consideration in the pre- and post-decision-making stages of the process.

Impulsiveness, making a decision without evaluating available information, can be inherently valuable in the sense that management may put a high premium on reaching decisions quickly, or it may be related to the unwillingness to delay gratification. There are those who possibly equate decision-making with problem-solving. Developing and evaluating alternatives in the pre-decision-making process will delay problem-solving and hence gratification. It is this delay in expected gratification that can make management act in an impulsive manner. In the post-decision-making process, the assessment of the results achieved, an impulsive manager might avoid reviewing a decision because gratification has already been attained, or outcomes might be assessed using less "rational" criteria. (Assessment criteria will be discussed below.)

Postponing or neglecting a problem or decision can also be a source of gratification, since what might be a painful search and fact-facing process is put off or avoided. Postponing problem-solving can be gratifying because it avoids the possibly negative effects of a decision.

Both impulsive and postponing-neglectful use of time will be considered "nonrational" and will affect visibility of consequences in the following way. Visibility of consequences includes the ability to evaluate the outcomes of procedure-resource interactions as well as the making of such evaluations (the degree to which the owner or his surrogate *can* and *does* evaluate the costs of reaching a given level of goal attainment from a procedure-resource interaction). If within a firm there exists the capability for evaluating procedure-resource interactions, a capability that might be called managerial technology, and if management is nonrational in the decision-making process, then either the technology will be ignored or it will be utilized less than optimally (see discussion of assessment criteria below). Hence we could find high potential visibility of consequences with low actual visibility of consequences and relatively low efficiency.

Potential Visibility of Consequences (C_{vp}). The ability to evaluate procedure-resource interactions depends on management's awareness and comprehension of the various managerial tools or technology available in the environment. The making of such judgments is related to the motivation to do so. Hence C_{vp} is defined as a function of managerial attitudes toward the use of various management technologies and managerial awareness and comprehension of how these technologies work and the probable results of their application. When C_{vp} is high, and given "rational" use of time, C_v will be high. However, given "nonrational" use of time, even with high C_{vp}, actual C_v may be low when the technology either is ignored or used with inappropriate criteria for assessment of outcomes.

Assessment Criteria. Two kinds of criteria can be used to assess organizational actions according to J. Thompson:[2] (a) instrumental, and (b) economic. Instrumental assessment asks the question whether the specified actions do, in fact, produce the desired outcomes, while economic assessment questions whether the desired results are obtained with the least necessary expenditure of resources. It can be argued, based on observation and anecdotal evidence, that some Venezuelan organizations score well on instrumental but not on economic tests. The job gets done, but resources are not employed to their fullest capacity; some are employed at cross-purposes.

Managers with low C_{vp} will of necessity use more instrumental criteria in assessing their actions. With high C_{vp}, management will use economic assessment criteria if they are more "rational" in the treatment of time. However, a managerial component high on impulsiveness in the pre- or post-decision-making process will use instrumental criteria for assessment, despite higher levels of C_{vp}. This will occur because instrumental criteria typically can be applied more rapidly and so provide information for further rapid decision making, or more rapid gratification from knowledge of results. Likewise, high levels of postponing-neglectful behavior in the pre- or post-decision-making process will also predispose toward use of instrumental criteria, despite high levels of C_{vp}. This is so because, with high levels of postponing-neglectful behavior, the evaluating-assessing process will be constrained by a lack of time. Use of available information will require too much time, and hence instrumental-assessment criteria will be utilized.

With the addition of the variables use of time, potential visibility of consequences, and assessment criteria, the following propositions were investigated:

1. Organizations with higher actual visibility of consequences (C_V) will be more efficient than organizations with lower actual visibility of consequences.

2. Potential visibility of consequences (C_{vp}) is positively related to actual visibility of consequences.

3. With C_{vp} held constant, managerial components given to more "rational" treatment of time in the pre- and post-decision-making process will use economic criteria in the assessment of organizational actions and will have higher actual C_V, while less "rational" use of time in the decision-making process will be associated with instrumental-assessment criteria and hence lower actual C_V.

MEASUREMENT OF THE VARIABLES

In order to test the hypotheses detailed above, it is necessary to measure the dependent variable organizational efficiency, and the independent variables C_V, C_{vp}, use of time, and assessment criteria.

Organizational Efficiency. We have defined efficiency as:

$$\text{Efficiency} = \frac{\text{output and discounted future output}}{\text{inputs}}$$

Venezuelan insurance companies are for-profit organizations and hence have economic goals. A measure of efficiency could be:

$$\text{Efficiency} = \frac{\text{profits}}{\text{assets}}$$

However, such a measure ignores future profits. It is extremely difficult to arrive at an accurate estimate of future profits or to calculate their current worth. Our approximation of future earnings is based on the assumption that the current attitudes of important customers of the insurance organizations are indicators of intent to continue to do business with them. To that end, eight insurance brokers prominent in the industry served as a panel of experts. The experts were asked to rate the insurance companies from most efficient to least efficient, keeping in mind the following criteria: (1) speed and accuracy with which policies are processed; (2) length of time between claim and reimbursement; (3) accuracy of company's accounting systems; (4) time needed to indemnify broker's client; and (5) general satisfaction with and confidence in the firm. The reliability of the experts' rankings was quite high, Kendall's coefficient of concordance, w = .724.

Financial data for the years 1968, 1969, and 1970 were available from the office of the Superintendent of Insurance Companies, which is part of the government system regulating the insurance industry. Data for earlier years were lost in two fires. The law compels each company to file a complete annual report, which is made available to the public. The ratio of profits to assets, averaged over three years, constituted one measure of efficiency. The brokers' ranking constituted a second measure; and a third index was developed by combining the profitability ranking and the brokers' ranking, equally weighted, into one index.

Visibility of Consequences. Operationalization of C_V was carried out in the top two hierarchic levels in each company. By means of a highly structured interview, C_V scores were obtained for the chief executive and five department heads in each of the 15 companies. The interview with the chief executive was designed to elicit the degree of knowledge he had regarding each functional area in the company and its contribution to over-all goal attainment. When the chief executive indicated he had some degree of knowledge about any given functional area, he was asked how he had acquired it. If reports, either verbal, written, or statistical, formed the basis of his opinion, the frequency of those reports was established. The quality of the report and the degree of detail in it were also ascertained by probing questions about the exact nature of the report and what specifically he remembered from the last report.

The chief executive was questioned about the following areas: (1) profitability of each department and its function and role in goal achievement; (2) contributions and costs of certain staff functions (legal, personnel, etc.); (3) costs and benefits of the time required to process information in the organizations; (4) costs and benefits from purely insurance business and from its investment efforts; and (5) relative ranking vis-à-vis other companies on all of the above. Immediately after the interview, the interviewer, evaluating the responses to these questions, rated each executive on a scale ranging from 1 to 200.

The department heads were questioned on their knowledge of their departments' variable costs and the effects of these costs on their departmental and organizational goals and also how they had acquired that knowledge. Probing elicited information regarding the nature and detail of the reports. Based on these responses, the interviewer graded each department head on a scale from 1 to 100. The scores of the five department heads were averaged to obtain C_V for level two of the organization. Level one and average level two scores were summed to obtain overall C_V. This procedure gives twice as much weight to level one scores (1-200) than to level two scores (1-100).

The variable costs about which each department head was questioned follow:

Technical Department

1. Future costs and benefits of issuing of a policy.
2. Variable costs and benefits of an existing portfolio (commissions, administrative costs, etc.).
3. Variable costs and benefits of a given reinsurance policy as a function of capital, volume of free reserves, future revenues, portfolio consistency, etc.

Treasury Department

1. Variable costs and benefits of investment policy.
2. Changes in an enterprise's solvency as a consequence of amount of new businesses and future premiums.

Production Department

1. Variable costs and benefits of training new agents.
2. Variable costs and benefits of a given expansion policy (branches, agencies).
3. Variable costs and benefits of current and potential marketing policies.

4. Variable costs and benefits of applying a given rate to a given risk.

5. Variable costs and benefits of a given technical department policy.

Damage Department

1. Variable costs and benefits of processing claims (accuracy, time constraints, etc.).

2. Variable costs of technical and production departments' policies.

Administrative Services Department

1. Variable costs and benefits of control systems.
2. Variable costs and benefits of electronic data-processing.
3. Variable costs and benefits of auditing.
4. Variable costs and benefits of collection policy.

Potential visibility of consequences, use of time, and assessment criteria all were measured by means of a questionnaire. The questionnaire was pretested in two companies excluded from the study because of changes in ownership and lines of business during the period for which we had financial information.

In each company, questionnaires were addressed to every top- and middle-level management member, together with a covering letter explaining the study and guaranteeing anonymity. One person was then contacted in each company who, we felt, because of his hierarchical position and his interest in the study, could best elicit cooperation from organizational members. This person was made responsible for the distribution of the questionnaires, the follow-up, and once completed, their collection in sealed envelopes. We found that the higher the person was in the hierarchy, the faster he returned the completed questionnaires, and the higher the percentage of respondents. Return rates are shown in Table XI-1. The questionnaire (translated into English) is shown in Appendix B.

Potential Visibility of Consequences. The first section of the questionnaire measured the respondent's attitudes toward managerial technology through a set of Likert-type scales.

TABLE XI-1

Respondents by Company and Managerial Level

Company	Top Executive Officials			Middle Management		
	Sent	Returned	%	Sent	Returned	%
A	2	2	100	15	8	53
B	4	3	75	7	4	57
C	2	1	50	7	3	42
D	2	2	100	9	7	77
E	4	2	50	16	9	56
F	2	2	100	11	6	54
G	2	2	100	5	4	80
H	5	2	40	12	8	66
I	3	2	66	8	3	37
J	3	1	33	6	4	66
K	6	4	66	17	12	70
L	3	2	66	5	3	60
M	2	2	100	8	5	62
N	2	2	100	12	7	58
O	3	1	33	8	6	75
TOTAL	45	28	62	132	89	67

Percentage of Questionnaires Returned: 66.

The statements were very broad in scope: the effect of the techniques upon general administration; the hiring of personnel to implement managerial technology; the effectiveness of such procedures in a country like Venezuela; the use of outside consultants; the value of being an innovator in the use of managerial technology; the value of broadening the knowledge of management through formal courses in new managerial techniques.

The second section measured managers' awareness and comprehension of managerial technology as well as the company's ability to make use of these techniques in conducting its operations. Measured was knowledge of: (a) forecasting; (b) game theory; (c) regression and correlation analysis; (d) statistical decision theory; (e) statistical sampling; (f) PERT.

Respondents' level of sophistication with regard to these topics was assessed by low-level sophistication questions on accounting, budgeting, and cash flows, as well as higher-level sophistication questions on concepts such as break-even analysis, elasticity of demand, marginal cost-analysis, correlation analysis, PERT, cost-benefit analysis, and the use of the computer and programming. A company's score was based on the top management's and department heads' attitudes, knowledge, and the number of techniques available within the company. The mean of the managers' scores within a company constituted the company score.

It is worth noting that the number of techniques available within the company constitutes a rough measure of procedures designed to increase visibility of consequences, P_{cv}, in the hospital study. Many of the techniques involve data-processing, aggregation and summarizing, forecasting, and comparison of outcomes with forecasts, etc. All these feedback mechanisms, if specified (if available and used within the company), constitute procedures to increase visibility of consequences. If we were to consider this variable a rough proxy for P_{cv}, then it could serve as a test of the model and should be positively related to C_v and efficiency.

Culture and the Use of Time. This variable was measured by a number of questions ranging from impulsive behavior in decision-making, as in:

(23) "The efficient manager can be recognized by the speed with which he makes decisions";

to postponing-neglectful behavior in decision-making, as in:

(26) "The mere postponement of an administrative problem can lead to a satisfactory solution to that problem."

Search behavior in decision-making was also emphasized:

(22) "When you must make a relatively complex decision, your colleagues consider your involvement in the gathering and processing of pertinent information as:"

Companies were ranked from most rational to least rational, according to how close they were to the mean of the distribution, which we took to signify neither impulsive nor postponing.

Assessment Criteria. Respondents were asked to rank in order of importance, from 4 (most important) to 1 (least important), the following qualities of an efficient manager:

a. The effort to utilize personnel for the function for which they are best suited.

b. A belief that obtaining results was the most important consideration.

c. Weighing a variety of alternative actions in order to select the one most beneficial.

d. Considering costs and benefits as a whole in decision-making, but not considering it necessary to calculate specific details.

The manager with economically oriented assessment criteria will value those characteristics (items) more highly that imply primary concern for efficiency and maximum benefit—that is, he will rank the above items (c) and (a) in positions 4 and 3, respectively. The manager with a high degree of instrumentality will value "just getting the job done" and being concerned only with overall functioning more highly. Hence, he will tend to give higher ranking to items (b) and (d), respectively. Based on such rankings, it is possible to develop a 24-point economic to instrumental scale.

RESULTS

The major hypothesis, that actual visibility of consequences is positively correlated with efficiency, was upheld. The product-moment coefficient of correlation between C_V and profits/assets was $r=.66$; between C_V and panel ranking of efficiency, $r=.73$; and between C_V and the composite index, $r=.82$.

The second hypothesis, relating actual visibility of consequences and potential visibility of consequences, also was upheld. The correlation between C_V and C_{vp} was $r=.74$.

The third hypothesis specified that rational use of time would be associated with use of economic criteria of assessment, which would lead to high visibility of consequences. This hypothesis was partly upheld. Rationality and use of economic-assessment criteria correlated $r_s=.30$, while rationality and C_v were not correlated, and economic assessment criteria and C_v correlated .38.

Testing each hypothesis separately does not allow us to assess each variable's power to explain variability in efficiency. Regression analysis gives us that information. Two stepwise regression analyses were performed, with efficiency as the dependent variable. The measure of efficiency in the first analysis was the index composed of the expert rankings and profits/assets; in the second, only profits/assets was used. Assessment criteria, potential visibility of consequences, size (as a control), use of time, and visibility of consequences were independent variables that were allowed to enter the equation according to how much variance was explained in the dependent variable. The results are shown in Tables XI-2 and XI-3.

In terms of explaining variance in the index measure of efficiency, neither size nor use of time was powerful enough to enter the equation in the presence of the other three variables. Visibility of consequences obviously is the most powerful explanatory variable of the three making up the best fit equation.

A relatively similar picture emerges when profits/assets is the measure of efficiency. Visibility of consequences is the most powerful variable, although size explains enough variance to enter the equation. Perhaps the reason for this is that the experts' rankings of the companies' ability to provide various services correlated positively with size, so when the ranking is included in the dependent variable, no further variance can be explained by size and it does not enter the equation.

Based on the correlational relationships and the regression analyses, the conclusion seems inescapable that the model of organizational efficiency provides a good description of reality. The description is a good one not because of the amount of variance explained, but because the model predicts that visibility of consequences should emerge as the most powerful explanatory variable.

TABLE XI-2

Multiple Regression of Efficiency Index on Its Best Predictors

Independent Variable	Regression Coefficient	t-Value	One-tail p Value
Actual Visibility of Consequences	.62	2.17	< .025
Potential Visibility of Consequences	.33	1.22	> .10
Economic Assessment Criteria	.25	1.57	.10 > p > .05

$R^2 = .87$; Adjusted $R^2 = .83$
Standard error of residuals = 2.45

TABLE XI-3

Multiple Regression of Profits/Assets on Its Best Predictors

Independent Variable	Regression Coefficient	t-Value	One-tail p Value
Actual Visibility of Consequences	1.01	3.82	< .005
Size	−.49	−1.99	< .05
Economic Assessment Criteria	.36	1.58	.10 > p > .05

$R^2 = .76$; Adjusted $R^2 = .68$
Standard error of residuals = 1.01

CHAPTER 11

Discussion and Evaluation

At this point it seems necessary and useful to summarize our findings, compare them to the relevant literatures, and evaluate the model of organizational efficiency. The basic model and the hypotheses drawn from it are relatively simple. We hypothesized that visibility of consequences (C_v) and specification of procedures to increase visibility of consequences (P_{cv}) would be positively related to efficiency, regardless of the level of complexity of the organization's interaction with its environment. We also hypothesized that specification-of-production procedures (P_p) would be positively related to efficiency in organizational components having low complexity, and negatively to efficiency in components having high complexity.

THE HOSPITAL STUDY

In the administrative component of the hospital, the one we characterized as having a less complex interaction with its environment than the medical component, we found, as predicted, that specification-of-production procedures for the workers, specification of procedures to increase visibility of consequences, and visibility of consequences all were positively related to efficiency. This conclusion was validated by both simple correlations and regression analyses. In the regression analysis, size and complexity were added to the independent variables P_p, P_{cv}, and C_v. Economies of scale were observed, and together the independent variables explained from 30 to 60 percent of the variance in efficiency.

159

One finding not predicted by the model was that specification-of-production procedures for department heads in the administrative component were negatively related to efficiency. Apparently, department heads are sufficiently high in the hierarchy to function like professionals, though perhaps one should not generalize on the basis of this finding. Foremen in some industries probably function most efficiently when their procedures are specified for them, while in other industries the opposite may be the case. What seems to be generally valid is the assumption that the more complex the task of the foreman or department head, either in an information-processing, response-selecting sense, or in the sense of skill or difficulty of performance, the less efficient it would be to specify production procedures for that person.

In the medical component, the more complex component, specification-of-production procedures for the workers (physicians) was, as predicted, negatively related to efficiency, while specification of procedures to increase visibility of consequences and visibility of consequences as predicted were positively related to efficiency. This conclusion also can be substantiated by either simple correlations or by the use of multiple regressions. Again, size and complexity were entered in the multiple-regression analyses, and economies of scale were observed. The independent variables together explained from 26 to 76 percent of the variance in efficiency (quality of care).

Relevant Research. By and large, previous studies of economies of scale in hospitals of the size and range found in our sample have observed that costs standardized for complexity have declined with size. Our data support this. The studies of quality of care by Denton et al.[1] and Roemer et al.[2] have been repeated with very similar results. Like Denton et al., we found a high degree of interrater reliability between expert evaluators of quality of care and a strong and positive relation between mean expert evaluation and hospital size. Like Roemer et al., we found that the severity-adjusted death rate is negatively related to other measures of quality of care.

To the extent that they overlap, our findings are consistent with those of Georgopoulos and Mann. They found that hierarchically imposed rules were positively related to efficiency in their hospitals. Because they were looking at the nonmedical component of the hospital, these findings are consistent with ours. Georgopoulos and Mann sum up their findings by saying:

> Advance planning and formal organizational rules and regulations are essential to organizational functioning and coordination, but they are not enough in and of themselves. Effective day to day communication between superiors and subordinates about the work process and work problems provides an additional key mechanism for coordination.[3]

This conclusion is very similar to our findings for the nonmedical component, that P_p, P_{cv}, and C_v have an additive, positive effect on efficiency. Their concept of communication is akin to visibility of consequences and specification of procedures to increase visibility of consequences.

Our study goes beyond that of Georgopoulos and Mann, since we also examined the medical component and found that specification of procedures was negatively related to quality of care, a conclusion which apparently conflicts with a very recent study completed by Milton Roemer and Jay Friedman.[4] They looked at medical-staff structure and quality of care in 10 general hospitals. Table XII-1 may be considered a summary of their findings. Unlike we in our own study, Roemer and Friedman observed a wide range of sizes (from 42 to 1,500 beds) and of ownership, including proprietary, local, and federal government ownership. Their SADR index of quality of care is the same as used by us and is inversely related to quality of care.

The uniqueness of this empirical study of medical-staff structure warrants some discussion. Their general conclusion is that the more structured the medical staff, the higher the quality of care.

Their analysis of the degree of medical-staff organization (MSO) takes into account the rules and regulations governing the medical staff, the amount of documentation, the rigorousness of the selection criteria for admission to the staff, the jurisdiction of control committees, etc.[5] The extent of committee control is one of seven subcomponents of the MSO score.

We attempted to construct an index of physician participation based on the descriptions presented by Roemer and Friedman. The index is similar to the one used in our study. It includes

TABLE XII-1

Roemer and Friedman's Medical Staff and Structural Characteristics of 10 Hospitals

Name of Hospital	Number of Beds	Index of Degree of Medical Staff Organization (MSO)	Severity-Adjusted Death Rate (SADR)	Physician Participation	Index Extent of Committee Control
Kenter	42	25	4.71	MDs own the hospital	3
Hillside	76	28	2.32	2 of the 7 owners of this proprietary hospital are MDs	6
View	141	36	2.98	MDs own the hospital	6
Midland	230	56	3.62	No data	9
Pebble	447	60	0.97	6 of the 15 board members are MDs	12
St. Martins	265	62	2.12	No MDs on board of this Catholic hospital, but active joint conference committee exists	12
Scopus	490	71	1.45	No MDs on board but active joint conference committee exists	12
Medical Group	346	80	1.63	Not clear	6
Public	729	82	5.33	Owned by local government; 65 employed MDs subject to government administrative code	6
Veterans	1,500	84	1.31	Owned by federal government; no MD ownership; low MD participation	6

such factors as the presence of physicians on the governing board, the relative importance of joint conference committees, and the degree to which the physicians as a group exert control over medical-component procedures. Because the available data for their Midland and Medical Group hospitals were insufficient, they were excluded. The Roemer veterans' hospital also was eliminated because of its low staffing ratio.[6] The severity-adjusted death-rate measure is liable to distortion by major differences in efficiency, and thus should be excluded from the analysis that follows.[7]

Our theory and data suggest that hierarchical specification of procedures—low physician participation and control—is an inappropriate managerial style for the professional medical staff and should lead to lower-quality medical care. If Roemer and Friedman are correct, then minimal physician participation and control should lead to highest-quality medical care.

As can be seen in Table XII-2, the hospital with the highest P_p has low MD participation, low collective control, and a high degree of medical-staff structure. Kenter, Hillside, and View, the three smallest hospitals, all have MDs on the governing board, but have the lowest collective control, least structured medical-staff organization. Although St. Martins and Scopus have no MDs on the governing body, they are reported to have active joint conference committees and strong collective control. Pebble, the hospital with the lowest P_p, has high MD participation and strong collective control, as reflected by the committee control index. Based on the SADR index it seems clear that high MD participation combined with strong collective control (lowest P_p) is most conducive to high-quality care, highest P_p the least conducive, and high participation with weak collective control and medium participation with strong collective control fall in-between. This is consistent with our findings in Chapter VIII, in which we demonstrate that when structure is imposed by the colleagues themselves, it is associated with high quality, but when imposed hierarchically, quality declines.

THE INSURANCE STUDY

Guided by Professor Bustillo's superior perceptions of and knowledge of Venezuelan managers and the Venezuelan insurance

TABLE XII-2

Reconstruction of the Roemer and Friedman Study of Hospital Medical-Staff Structure

	Low MD Participation, Weak Collective Control Highest (P_p)	High MD Participation, Weak Collective Control Less (P_p)	Medium MD Participation, Strong Collective Control Less (P_p)	High MD Participation, Strong Collective Control Lowest (P_p)
Hospitals	Public	Kenter Hillside View	St. Martins Scopus	Pebble
Mean SADR Index of quality of care	5.33	3.33	1.84	0.97
Mean Committee Control Index	6	5	12	12
Mean size (beds)	729	86	328	447
Mean MSO Index	82	30	67	60

industry, we did not test the model in its entirety, and added some variables extraneous to it. He felt there would be little variability in a measure of specification-of-production procedures, and also that potential visibility of consequences as well as assessment criteria and external use of time all should be measured. Hence the hypotheses were slightly different from those in the hospital study.

We hypothesized that visibility of consequences was positively related to efficiency, and that potential visibility was positively related to actual visibility. We also hypothesized that rational use of time would be related to use of economic assessment criteria, which in turn would be related to visibility of consequences. All these hypotheses were substantiated by simple correlation analyses. In the regression analysis, almost 79% of the variance in efficiency was explained by visibility of consequences, use of economic assessment criteria, and potential visibility of consequences.

Relevant Research. Astonishingly, there is almost no research in which the dependent variable profitability and/or future profitability is related to the kinds of structural and managerial organization variables in which we are interested. Lawrence and Lorsch[8] related efficiency to degrees of differentiation and integration, but they were unable to obtain rates of return for the subsidiaries they studied and so were forced to use changes in net profit as their measure of efficiency. In addition, they used changes in net profit as an independent rather than an output variable.

Woodward[9] found that for a particular type of technology— unit, mass, or process—firms which deviated from the average structure were less profitable. This implies that for each type of technology there is an optimal form of organizational structure. (In this context, structure basically means span of control.)

Seashore and Yuchtman[10] collected data from 75 life insurance sales agencies over the period 1952-1962. They factor analyzed 76 performance variables and came up with 10 factors, all of which are probably related to rate of return and future rate of return; unfortunately, however, they did not have data on profitability.

Lieberson and O'Connor[11] found that changes in leadership, after an appropriate time lag, explained more variance in profit margin than did industry or company effects. This was not the case for sales or net income, however. Our finding neither corroborates nor contradicts this conclusion.

Hirsch[12] investigated a number of firms in different industries and found that environmental and industry effects overwhelmed intraorganizational structural effects in explaining profitability and product innovation.

Again, this is not contradictory to our findings. In both the hospital and insurance studies, we held environmental factors constant as nearly as possible, in order to determine the effect of internal structural variables.

EVALUATION OF THE MODEL

To accept our findings as proof positive that the model of organization efficiency is *the* model assumes that the studies have no flaws, that all variables were reliably and validly measured, that no operationalizations can be questioned. Certainly we cannot and would not want to make such far-reaching claims. For instance, in measuring efficiency in the hospital organizations, we utilized five measures in the administrative component and four others (later discarding one) for quality of care. In neither instance did we measure discounted present value of future efficiency. (The formal definition of efficiency was developed after the study was completed.) We (probably erroneously) utilized the same measure of visibility of consequences for the hospital administrator and the board member, an error we avoided in the insurance study. In that study, however, we were forced to combine in an arbitrary fashion measures of visibility of consequences derived from different levels of the hierarchy in order to obtain a measure of C_V for the entire organization.

Obviously, these, and probably all other empirical studies, are not perfect. The relevant question is, was what was done sufficient so that we may assume that the data, and hence the model, more or less reflect reality. In our opinion it was. The consistency of the relationships across all variables in the hospital study, plus the fact that the same relationships were observed in the insurance industry, lead to our positive conclusion. The model is applicable not only to not-for-profit and for-profit industries, but cross-culturally as well.

Comparison with Other Contingency Theories. In a paper exploring current theories of formal organization, Shortell[13] evaluates the Thompson, Perrow[14] and the Entrepreneurial Theory approaches on the following criteria: formalism, closure, simplicity, generality, ability to predict, and realism. Shortell rates Thompson's work high on simplicity, generality, and closure, but relatively low on formalism in that ". . . the logical form of the propositions are not spelled out in operational terms. . . ." Shortell notes, however, that others, like Lawrence and Lorsch, have successfully utilized Thompson's ideas of "integration" and "environment." He also criticizes Thompson's lack of conceptual clarity in his treatment of the three types of uncertainties faced by organizations.

Shortell characterizes Perrow's work as typology rather than a theory, and hence does not apply those same criteria for evaluation. Based on Shortell's questions about the clarity and specificity of the typology and of some of Perrow's assumptions about interdependence and power, one might conclude that Perrow's work (in Shortell's terms) lacks generality, realism, and closure as well as operationality.

Shortell does not evaluate Galbraith's[15] work, but we can do so, using Shortell's criteria. Galbraith's work is high on closure, simplicity, and generality. It is difficult to judge its ability to predict, since no specific predictions are made concerning the four possible strategies to be used when more information needs to be processed. He simply states that one or more of the four strategies will be adopted, or that by default the one of slack resources will be applied. The only operationalization he proposes is for the creation of lateral-relations strategy, and that by way of citation of the Lawrence and Lorsch work.

Shortell rates the Entrepreneurial Theory as good on closure, simplicity, and generality, and cites the two studies reported here as evidence of its ability to predict. He questions the realism of the theory because of the importance assigned to the goals of the owner of the organization. He notes as a special plus the fact that the variables in the theory are stated in operational terms.

What emerges from this comparison is that the E.T. and Thompson's work constitute the most highly developed "theories." Shortell cites four empirical works that specifically test portions of Thompson's formulation, so that both Thompson and the E.T. have received empirical support. Which of the two theories is superior (or whether with greater precision and implementation Galbraith's will emerge as a better explanatory device) awaits further empirical work.

Implications of the Model. There are only three parts to the problem of organizational efficiency: *coordination* and *control* over resources for achievement of some *goal*. The discussion in Chapter I details how the concept of the owner in the Entrepreneurial Theory aids in solving the problem of whose goal is the relevant one, a necessary first step in the measurement of organizational efficiency. The empirical studies address themselves to the other parts of the problem, coordination and control.

In looking at problems of control and coordination, some theorists will concentrate on organizational structure, on the problems of communication, distribution of power, centralization, etc. Others will look at technology, substitution of capital for labor, man-machine relationships, etc. Still others will look at the human factor, managerial style, morale, motivation, role definition, etc. In our model we deal with structure and managerial style and view them as the same variable—e.g., degree to which specified procedures determine not only authority patterns but structural patterns as well. The various patterns and the conditions under which they are optimal, including the complex decentralized forms of coupling, are elaborated in the Entrepreneurial Theory.

What is clear from our model of organizational efficiency, from the Entrepreneurial Theory, from our empirical data, from the work of Burns and Stalker and of Lawrence and Lorsch, is that under some rigidly specified conditions, nonparticipative managership is most effective. Further, it is clear that in complex organizations both styles of supervision (and their implied differences in structure) are necessary for efficient functioning.

The complex, coupled nature of the hospital organization has long been seen as an incomprehensible anomaly when viewed from a classical Weberian bureaucratic ideal. Charles Perrow in his review of the literature says:

> The most important insight or perspective which has influenced the study of general hospitals is the way in which they deviate from the standard bureaucratic model of large scale organizations. This has probably been the most basic underlying concern in the significant studies of general hospitals.[16]

It is true that most hospitals deviate from a "standard" bureaucracy. To us it is not surprising that the coupled structure is so persistent and widespread among hospitals, for, according to our model, it is rational to do so.

One further readily apparent implication is the importance and ubiquity of the variable visibility of consequences. Regardless of the nature of the organizations under consideration, whether not-for-profit or for-profit, visibility of consequences is positively related to efficiency. The lessons for owners and managers seem self-evident.

APPENDIX A

THE HOSPITAL STUDY: MEASURING INSTRUMENTS

NONMEDICAL COMPONENT

Perceived Specification of Production Procedures for Workers

Most of the time there are rules which define what people (employees) around here are supposed to do. (Check one.)[a]

____ Very strongly agree   ____ Mildly disagree
____ Strongly agree   ____ Strongly disagree
____ Mildly agree   ____ Very strongly disagree

How things are done here is left up to the employee doing the work. (Check one.)[b]

____ Very strongly agree   ____ Mildly disagree
____ Strongly agree   ____ Strongly disagree
____ Mildly agree   ____ Very strongly disagree

Perceived Specification-of-Production Procedures for Department Heads

How much does your job give you a chance to do things the way you want to? (Check one.)[c]

____ An excellent chance   ____ A good chance
____ A very good chance   ____ A fair chance
    ____ Little chance

On the job, how free do you feel to set your own work pace? (Check one.)[c]

____ Completely free   ____ Some freedom
____ Quite a bit of freedom   ____ Little freedom

If you have a suggestion for improving the work or changing the set-up in some way, how easy is it for you to get your ideas across to your superiors? (Check one.)[c]

____ Very difficult   ____ Not too easy
____ Rather difficult   ____ Fairly easy
    ____ Very easy

[a] Adapted from Georgopoulos and Mann, *Community General Hospital*, pp. 642-646.
[b] Adapted from Michael Aiken and Jerald Hage, "Organizational Alienation: A Comparative Analysis," *American Sociological Review*, XXXI (August, 1966), 497.
[c] These questions are adapted from Georgopoulos and Mann, *op. cit.*, pp. 642-646, and Aiken and Hage, *op. cit.* p. 497.

APPENDIX B

THE INSURANCE STUDY:
MEASURING INSTRUMENTS

Lately controversy has arisen between managers with respect to the usefulness of certain *approaches* to administrative problems. One group of managers considers these *approaches* to have a negative or, at best, a neutral effect upon the operations of their firm. Whereas others believe that these *approaches* to administrative problems make a direct and substantial contribution toward increasing the efficiency of their firm.

ATTITUDES TOWARD MANAGERIAL TECHNOLOGY*

Because the insurance industry is an essential part of the nation's economy, we would like to know your opinion on how the uses of the following *approaches* to administrative problems would affect or do affect the operations of your department.

a) Program budgeting
b) Cash flows
c) Break-even analysis
d) Correlation analysis
e) Linear programming
f) PERT
g) The use of the computer for nonroutine functions

Place an X in front of the answer which best describes your opinion.

01. The over-all effect of the use of the *approaches* upon the administration of this department would be valuable.

___ Totally agree
___ Agree
___ Undecided
___ Disagree
___ Totally disagree

02. The employment of permanent personnel for the introduction and implementation of the *approaches* would *not* be of benefit to this department.

___ Totally agree
___ Agree
___ Undecided
___ Disagree
___ Totally disagree

---

*Headings were not used on original questionnaires but are shown here merely to identify the various parts of the questionnaire.

03.   The little effectiveness of the *approaches* is due to the peculiarities of
      our country.

      ___ Totally agree
      ___ Agree
      ___ Undecided
      ___ Disagree
      ___ Totally disagree

04.   This department will be better if we computerize all possible
      operations.

      ___ Totally agree
      ___ Agree
      ___ Undecided
      ___ Disagree
      ___ Totally disagree

05.   The efforts to establish the use of the *approaches* in this firm have
      found, or would find, *support* and *cooperation:*

      a. *from top management*

      ___ Totally agree
      ___ Agree
      ___ Undecided
      ___ Disagree
      ___ Totally disagree

      b. *from department heads*

      ___ Totally agree
      ___ Agree
      ___ Undecided
      ___ Disagree
      ___ Totally disagree

06.   The employment of an outside adviser is desirable to *study* and make
      recommendations about the functioning of my department.

      ___ Totally agree
      ___ Agree
      ___ Undecided
      ___ Disagree
      ___ Totally disagree

07.   The insurance company that makes the fastest and best use of the
      approaches will obtain a substantial advantage in profit over its
      competition.

      ___ Totally agree

___ Agree
___ Undecided
___ Disagree
___ Totally disagree

08. A successful manager will use his *intuition* to a high degree when making decisions.

___ Totally agree
___ Agree
___ Undecided
___ Disagree
___ Totally disagree

09. All managers should take courses to enlarge their knowledge of the administrative *approaches* in spite of the time and effort required.

___ Totally agree
___ Agree
___ Undecided
___ Disagree
___ Totally disagree

AWARENESS AND COMPREHENSION OF MANAGERIAL TECHNOLOGY

The administrative *approaches* and *concepts* mentioned above have been integrated into the world's insurance industry to varying degrees. We would like to know which of the *approaches* or *concepts* presented below are being used or have been used in your company and with what specific objective.

10. *Accounting*

___ Is not used   ___ Is being used   ___ Has been used but is not being used at the present time

Accounting is used, or has been used, basically as:

___ a. the best method of managerial control.
___ b. an instrument that permits the manager to know the consequences of his decisions through the effect of those decisions upon the financial statements of the firm.
___ c. a financial summary of the past operations of the firm.

Please indicate which of the uses specified above you consider makes a positive contribution to the efficient operation of the firm and add any other uses you consider beneficial for the administration of the firm.

___ a.   ___ b.   ___ c.

Other:

11. *Budgeting*

     ___ Is not used   ___ Is being used   ___ Has been used but is not being used at the present time.

It is used or has been used with the specific objective of:

     ___ a. obtaining a larger volume of sales by quantitative analysis of all administrative operation.
     ___ b. controlling the activities of the business in such a way that operating costs are as low as possible.
     ___ c. finding the most profitable way to direct the firm's efforts in order to achieve its primary goals.

Please indicate which of the uses specified above seems appropriate and indicate any other use you consider suitable.

     ___ a.   ___ b.   ___ c.

Other:

12. *Cash-flows*

     ___ Is not used   ___ Is being used   ___ Has been used but is not being used at the present time

It is used, or has been used, with the specific objective of:

     ___ a. anticipating future cash needs.
     ___ b. knowing the sources and uses of funds.
     ___ c. projecting the balance sheet.

Please indicate which of the specific uses mentioned above you consider makes a positive contribution to the efficient operation of the firm and add any other use that you consider beneficial for the administration of the business.

     ___ a.   ___ b.   ___ c.

Other:

13. *Break-even Analysis*

     ___ Is not used   ___ Is being used   ___ Has been used but is not being used at the present time

It is used, or has been used, with the specific objective of:

____ a. knowing to what level of production total costs will equal total revenue.

____ b. knowing to what level of production profit is maximized.

____ c. knowing how efficient are the operations of the firm.

Please indicate which of the specified uses mentioned above you consider makes a positive contribution to the efficient operation of the firm and add any other use that you consider beneficial for the administration of the business.

____ a.   ____ b.   ____ c.

Other:

14. *Elasticity of Demand*

____ Is not used   ____ Is being used   ____ Has been used but is not being used at the present time

It is used, or has been used, with the specific objective of:

____ a. knowing the incremental change that will occur in the number of policies sold with varying rates.

____ b. determining the ability to which the firm may vary its rates (excluding governmental regulation)

____ c. knowing the maximum level at which the firm may establish rates for maintaining the present level of production.

Please indicate which of the specified uses mentioned above you consider makes a positive contribution to the efficient operation of the firm and add any other use that you consider beneficial for the administration of the business.

____ a.   ____ b.   ____ c.

Other:

15. *Marginal Income and Cost Analysis*

____ Is not used   ____ Is being used   ____ Has been used but is not being used at the present time

It is used, or has been used, with the specific objective of:

—— a. knowing the incremental change in total income or cost each time the firm issues a new policy
—— b. knowing the income or cost of the last policy issued.
—— c. knowing the average income or cost of each policy issued.

Please indicate which of the specified uses mentioned above you consider makes a positive contribution to the efficient operation of the firm and add any other use that you consider beneficial for the administration of the business.

—— a.   —— b.   —— c.

Other:

16. *Cost-Benefit Analysis*

—— Is not used   —— Is being used   —— Has been used but is not being used at the present time

It is used, or has been used, with the specific objective of:

—— a. evaluating the consequences of different courses of action.
—— b. selecting resources such as equipment before they become available.
—— c. deciding about investments that require large sums of money.

Please indicate which of the uses specified above you consider makes a positive contribution to the efficient operation of the firm and add any other use that you consider beneficial for the administration of the business.

—— a.   —— b.   —— c.

Other:

17. *The Computer*

—— Is not used   —— Is being used   —— Has been used but is not being used at the present time

It is used, or has been used, with the specific objective of:

—— a. registering accounting operations
—— b. budgeting control
—— c. preparation of payment orders

___ d. account statements of agents and brokers
___ e. preparation of the financial statements of the firm
___ f. payroll
___ g. investment strategy

Please indicate which of the specified uses mentioned above you consider makes a positive contribution to the efficient operation of the firm and add any other use that you consider beneficial for the administration of the business.

___ a.   ___ b.   ___ c.   ___ d.   ___ e.   ___ f.   ___ g.

Other:

18. *Program*

___ Is not used   ___ Is being used   ___ Has been used but is not being used at the present time

It is used, or has been used, with the specific objective of:

___ a. deciding the most profitable use of the firm's resources.
___ b. determining personnel needs.
___ c. assuring solvency of the firm in the future.

Please indicate which uses specified above you consider makes a positive contribution to the efficient operation of the firm and add any other use you consider *beneficial* for the administration of the firm.

___ a.   ___ b.   ___ c.

Other:

ASSESSMENT CRITERIA

19. Rank in order of importance (most important number 4 to the least important number 1) the following characteristics with respect to what you consider an efficient manager.

___ a. One who makes the effort to utilize personnel for the function that they are best suited for.
___ b. One who considers obtaining results as most important.
___ c. One who considers a variety of alternative actions in order to select the one that is most beneficial.
___ d. One who considers costs and benefits as a whole in decision making, but does not consider it necessary to calculate the specific details.

USE OF TIME IN DECISION-MAKING

Please place an X in front of the answer which best describes your opinion.

20. When you must make a *relatively complex decision,* your colleagues consider that you get

    ____ Too much
    ____ Much
    ____ Average
    ____ Little
    ____ Too little

    involved in the *gathering and processing* of pertinent information.

21. The efficient manager can be recognized by the speed with which he makes decisions

    ____ Totally agree
    ____ Agree
    ____ Undecided
    ____ Disagree
    ____ Totally disagree

22. Even though one has the necessary information for making a decision about a complex problem, it is generally better to postpone making the decision because something new may occur that will facilitate the decision.

    ____ Always
    ____ Frequently
    ____ Sometimes
    ____ Rarely
    ____ Never

23. When you believe that you have the answer to problems, what percentage of these problems require a sufficiently long period of consideration before a decision is made.

    0%   25%   50%   75%   100%

24. The mere postponement of an administrative problem can lead to a satisfactory solution of that problem.

    ____ Always
    ____ Frequently
    ____ At times
    ____ Rarely
    ____ Never

25. When one is presented with an administrative decision that requires time for searching for and processing of pertinent information, it is better to make the decision immediately rather than postpone it.

_____ Always
_____ Frequently
_____ At times
_____ Rarely
_____ Never

Please place an X next to the group which represents your present age.

1. 21-30 ( )	6. 49-52 ( )
2. 31-34 ( )	7. 53-55 ( )
3. 35-40 ( )	8. 56-60 ( )
4. 41-44 ( )	9. 61-64 ( )
5. 45-48 ( )	10. 65 + ( )

Place of birth _____

Number of years in residence in this country _____

Level of education

1. High school   _____ years
2. Attendance at a university   _____ years
   Major _____
3. Degree obtained at the university _____
4. Postgraduate study   _____ years
   Major field of specialization _____
5. Special courses attended   ( ) yes   ( ) no

How many years of experience have you had in the insurance industry?

_____ years
_____ months

How many years have you worked for this company?

_____ years
_____ months

How long have you been in this or a similar position?

_____ years
_____ months

Visibility of Consequences (Top Level Managers)

A.   Will you enumerate the relative contributions of each sector (fire, life, casualty, etc.) as it pertains to the profits of the company.

1. _____   2. _____   3. _____

In what percentage (approximately)?

1. _____%   2. _____%   3. _____%

How often do you receive this information and in what form do you receive it?

Monthly   Quarterly   Annually

_____

_____

B.   Considering the insurance industry as a whole, which sector is the most profitable?

1. _____   2. _____   3. _____

C.   What is the present position of your firm in the industry with regard to each of these sectors?

1. _____   2. _____   3. _____

. . . in general _____

_____

D.   What do you suspect will be the position of each sector in the near future (short and medium run)?

1. _____   2. _____   3. _____

E.   Your information about the market is obtained through:

1. reading of magazines and reports
2. conversations with colleagues
3. other

F.   What criteria do you have for the development of new life insurance policies and new covering of risks?

_____

_____

_____

G.   The profits of an insurance company are probably divided between investment returns and returns from policies. What percentage of your company's profits are distributed between returns from investments and returns from insurance policies?

Insurance _____%

Investment _____%

Do you believe this to be a proper distribution?

_____

H. How do you obtain this information and how often do you receive it?

_____

_____

I. What is the average time it takes your firm to process a policy and what does it depend upon?

_____

_____

_____

J. How long does it take your firm to process a claim and what does it depend upon?

_____

_____

K. Are you notified when the normal time for processing a claim has elapsed?

_____

L. How does the use of the computer help to facilitate the processing procedures of claims?

_____

_____

M. Is there conflict or friction in the company, and if so, what are you doing about it?

_____

_____

_____

N. Who establishes the long- and short-run objectives of your firm, and how is it done?

_____

_____

O. Do you believe that the established objectives of the firm become distorted at low levels of the firm's organization?

_____

_____

P. What percentage of the firm's income from premiums comes from direct business, brokers, and agents?

      Direct business   _____
      Brokers   _____
      Agents   _____

Q. How have these proportions varied in the last year, and why?

_____

_____

R. Do you have any idea of the contribution the legal and personnel functions make to net profit in respect to their costs?

_____

_____

    How do you obtain this information? _____

S. What criteria do you base your plans upon for opening new branches and employing new agents?

_____

_____

T. What kind of information would you require in order to obtain a better understanding of the firm?

_____

_____

U. Do you have more information than time to study it?

_____

_____

_____

Visibility of Consequences (Middle-Level Managers)

Technical Department

A.   Does information exist about the effect of a new policy upon the profits of the business?

_____

_____

B.   What proportion of the firm's total profit for the past fiscal year does your department contribute, and what do you expect its contribution will be this year? Why?

_____

_____

C.   What were the percentages of administrative costs, commissions, etc., and profit with respect to your portfolio income?

_____

_____

D.   What criteria do you base your department's policy for reinsurance upon?
     1. Volume of free reserves
     2. Future income
     3. Portfolio consistency

Production

A.   What is the estimated cost for the training of a new agent and how long does it take to recuperate this cost through his production?

       Cost   _____
       Recuperation time   _____

B.   What percentages of the firm's income from premiums come from direct business, brokers and agents?

       Direct business   _____
       Brokers   _____
       Agents   _____

How have these proportions varied in the last year, and why?

_____

_____

C.   What was the relationship between costs and profits for the past fiscal
       year with respect to the branches, and what do you expect the
       relationship will be this year?

       _____

       _____

D.   How do you decide to apply a rate to a given risk (excluding regulation
       by the superintendent)?

       _____

       _____

E.   How long does it take for you to receive information from the claims
       department?

       _____

       _____

Claims Department

A.   Does information exist about the cost to process a claim and do you
       know what this cost is before the actual processing procedure begins?

       _____

       _____

B.   Do you have information about the relationship between costs and
       benefits for the use of a claims adjuster in your department?

       _____

       _____

C.   Do you have information about the cost of collecting premiums?

       _____

       _____

CRITERIA PROVIDED PANEL OF EXPERTS
FOR RANKING COMPANIES

Dear Sir:

At this time, we would like to complete our study of the insurance industry. The variables we are studying are organizational in nature, such as perceived control, management's criteria for the evaluation of the firm, visibility of consequences of the policies of management, etc. Because this is the first time in any country that some of these variables are to be studied in the private sector, we believe that it will have great benefit for the insurance industry as a whole.

It will be necessary for us to measure the efficiency of each company. However, because there is no agreement upon how to measure efficiency, we must rely upon the experience and knowledge of independent brokers to rank the insurance companies with respect to efficiency. We understand that providing these classifications might become a problem of professional ethics. In order to remove this problem, we have required that ranking of the companies be totally anonymous. Furthermore, we have guaranteed the insurance companies that the data will be used in aggregate form. Moreover, because the objective of this study is clearly scientific, IESA has guaranteed not to divulge the data provided.

On the attached piece of paper you will find an example of the manner in which we wish you to prepare the data.

The basic criterion should be present and future profitability; however, there are other criteria that must be considered. In order to make your task easier, we have selected various criteria that may be used as a base for your ranking.

Please remember that you are ranking the firm and not any specific person in that firm.

  a) Your satisfaction with the situation of the firm.

  b) The speed and accuracy in which policies are processed.

  c) Time it takes in order to receive reimbursement for a casualty.

  d) The statements of account with the company are up to date.

  e) The time it takes to provide service to the client.

  f) The level of confidence the company inspires in the client.

It is important to remember that all these factors must be considered as a whole in order to obtain an accurate ranking.

Please do not try and rank any company in which you are not familiar.

We suggest that you do not postpone this task and complete it as soon as possible because we anxiously await the results.

We greatly appreciate your time and consideration with regard to this matter.

Sincerely yours,

Juan A. Bustillo

JAB:ih

Notes

NOTES TO INTRODUCTION, PART I

(Pp. 3-38)

1. P. M. Blau and R. A. Schoenherr, *The Structure of Organization* (New York: Basic Books, 1971); D. McFarland, "A Dynamic Theory of the Growth and Structure of Organization," *American Sociological Review* (forthcoming); M. Meyer, "Size and the Structure of Organizations," *American Sociological Review*, XXXVII (1972), pp. 434-41.
2. Richard H. Hall, *Organizations* (Englewood Cliffs, N.J.: Prentice-Hall, 1972), p. 97.
3. S. W. Becker and G. Gordon, "An Entrepreneurial Theory of Formal Organizations," reprinted from *Administrative Science Quarterly*, XI, No. 3 (December, 1966), pp. 315-44.
4. Peter M. Blau and Scott W. Richard, *Formal Organizations* (San Francisco: Chandler Publishing Co., 1962), p. 1.
5. Chester I. Barnard, *The Functions of the Executive* (Cambridge, Mass.: Harvard University Press, 1951), p. 73.
6. For a discussion of the nature and types of multiple ownership, *see* Robin M. Williams, Jr., *American Economic Institutions* (New York: Alfred A. Knopf, 1960).
7. Kingsley Davis, *Human Society* (New York: Macmillan Co., 1949), p. 452.
8. *Ibid.*, p. 455.
9. *Ibid.*, p. 457. Similar views are also expressed by Williams, *op. cit.*, p. 188.
10. *Ibid.*, p. 463. A similar distinction can be inferred from Williams' discussion of control and beneficial rights; Williams, *op. cit.*, p. 189.
11. *Ibid.*, p. 465.
12. Simon writes ". . . a primary function of organization is to enforce the conformity of the individual to norms laid down by the group, or by its authority wielding members"; H. Simon, "Decision-Making and Administrative Organization," *Public Administration Review*, IV (Winter, 1944), p. 18. We see the right to demand certain kinds of behavior as the distinguishing feature between property rights and social norm, for the social norm is the right to expect a certain kind of behavior.
13. This definition of "professional" differs from many commonly accepted definitions. *See*, for example, Talcott Parsons, "The Professions and Social Structure," *Social Forces*, XVII (May, 1939); E. C. Hughes, *Men and Their Work* (Glencoe, Ill.: The Free Press, 1958); E. Greenwood, "Attributes of a Profession," in S. Nosow and W. H. Form (eds.), *Man, Work and Society* (New York, Basic Books, 1962). Most of these definitions combine role prerequisites and social evaluations of the role as determinants of professionalism. Since modern society is characterized by rapid

technological and social change, social evaluations of roles frequently neglect changes in the role demands. Our definition bases increasing or decreasing professionalism on functions within the organization and thereby avoids cultural lag in role evaluations.

14. Our definition and use of resources was influenced by James Thompson and Frederick L. Bates, "Technology, Organization and Administration," *Administrative Science Quarterly*, 1957, pp. 325-43.

15. Our use of specified procedure is akin to March and Simon's concept of programmed activity; James G. March and Herbert A. Simon, *Organizations* (New York: John Wiley and Sons, 1958).

16. Max Weber, "The Essentials of Bureaucratic Organization: An Ideal-Type Construction," in R. Merton, A. Gray, B. Hockey and H. Selvin (eds.), *Reader in Bureaucracy* (Glencoe, Ill.: The Free Press, 1952), p. 21.

17. *Ibid.*, p. 24.

18. Frank Knight, *The Economic Organization* (Chicago: University of Chicago Press, 1933), pp. 5-10.

19. Simon Marcson, "Organization and Authority in Industrial Research," *Social Forces*, XL, No. 1 (October, 1961), p. 73.

20. This statement holds true especially for short-term rather than for long-term leases.

21. Thomas L. Whisler, "Measuring Centralization of Control in Business Organizations," in W. Cooper, H. Leavitt, and M. W. Shelly (eds.), *New Perspectives in Organization Research* (New York: John Wiley and Sons, 1964).

22. Our thinking on the Truncated Bureaucracy was greatly influenced by Arthur L. Stinchcombe, "Bureaucratic and Craft Administration of Production," *Administrative Science Quarterly*, IV (1959).

23. Where the managerial skills required are very simple and hence in ample supply, the managerial functions are performed by temporary employees. In terms of its dynamics, this type of organization acts like a complete bureaucracy.

24. Marcson has defined this authority pattern as a "system of control in which authority is shared by all members of the working group. Authority is deemed to rest in the group rather than in an individual." Simon Marcson, "Decision-Making in a University Physics Department," *American Behavioral Scientist*, VI, No. 4 (December, 1962), p. 38.

25. *Time* Magazine, January 13, 1961.

26. Our development of optimal forms of organization, as well as our later treatment of decentralization, relies heavily on March and Simon's discussion of the relationship between complex environments and organizational search behavior; March and Simon, *op. cit.*

27. If, for instance, a single standardized part is needed by all the autonomous units, then purchase of enough parts for all the units by the central bureaucracy can result in savings.

28. The colleagues would be autonomous rather than forming a single bureaucratic structure if each had a proportionate share of the organiza-

tion's resources to do with as he wished. Generally, the colleagues jointly decide on the conversion of general resources to specific ones, i.e., they form a single bureaucratic structure in order to coordinate. Similarly, partners in a law firm would be completely autonomous if no resources were controlled by the partnership *sui generis*.

29. Use of general resources/total resources makes it possible to develop measures of the extent of decentralization, i.e., which level has discretion and which does not. Measures of the distribution of power or discretion at an individual level also could be determined with the help of these concepts.
30. The material on this variable is taken from an unpublished paper, "The Entrepreneurial Theory of Formal Organizations, Part II: Functioning of Formal Organizations," by Gerald Gordon and Selwyn W. Becker.
31. Becker and Gordon, *op. cit.*, p. 318.
32. Oswald Hall, "The Informal Organization of the Medical Profession," *Canadian Journal of Economics and Political Science*, XII (February, 1946).
33. Ritualization can and does occur in truncated bureaucracies. Procedures are ritualized by the external authority and formally accepted by the internal authority and thus cannot be considered usurpation.
34. Etzioni confines this relationship to worker-management relations rather than to operator-owner relations; *see* Amitai Etzioni, *A Comparative Analysis of Organizations* (New York: The Free Press, 1961).
35. *Ibid.*

NOTES TO CHAPTER I

(Pp. 39-50)

1. Martin Feldstein, *Economic Analysis for Health Services Efficiency* (Amsterdam: North Holland Publishing Co., 1967); Jerald Hage, "An Axiomatic Theory of Organizations," *Administrative Science Quarterly*, X (1965), pp. 289-320; Ralph Berry, "Competition and Efficiency in the Market of Hospital Services: The Structure of the American Hospital Industry" (unpublished Ph.D. dissertation, Harvard University, 1965). Also, Peter M. Blau, Wolf V. Heydebrand, Robert E. Stauffer, "The Structure of Small Bureaucracies," *American Sociological Review*, XXXI, No. 2 (April, 1966), pp. 179-91; Thomas R. Hefty, "Return to Scale in Hospitals: A Critical Review of Recent Research," *Health Services Research* (Winter, 1969), pp. 267-80; Mary Lee Ingbar and Lester D. Taylor, *Hospital Costs in Massachusetts* (Cambridge, Mass.: Harvard University Press, 1968); Kong Kyun Ro, "A Statistical Study of Factors Affect-

ing the Unit Costs of Short Term Hospital Care" (Ph.D. dissertation, Yale University, 1966 [mimeographed]); Melvin E. Horton, "An Economic Analysis of Progress in the Medical Care of the United States Navy and Marine Corps Personnel" (unpublished Ph.D. dissertation, University of Washington, 1966).

2. Although there exists an extensive literature on differences in quality of care in hospitals, none of the studies conceptualize quality as a ratio, thereby controlling for differences in inputs. See, for example, D. Neuhauser and F. Turcotte, "Costs and Quality of Care in Different Types of Hospitals," *The Annals of the American Academy of Political and Social Science* (January, 1972); Isidore Altman, Alice J. Anderson, Kathleen Barker, *Methodology in Evaluating the Quality of Medical Care* (Pittsburgh: University of Pittsburgh Press, 1969); J. A. H. I ə, S. L. Morrison, J. N. Morris, "Fatality from Three Common Surgical Conditions in Teaching and Non-teaching Hospitals," *The Lancet* (October 19, 1957), pp. 785-90; Jean Carroll, "The Structure of Teaching Hospitals" (unpublished Ph.D. dissertation, Department of Sociology, University of Chicago, 1969).

3. For example, Dan Eldor, "An Empirical Investigation of Hospital Output, Input, and Productivity" (unpublished Ph.D. dissertation, Department of Economics, New York University, February, 1969); Solomon Fabricant, "Productivity," in *International Encyclopedia of the Social Sciences* (New York: Macmillan Co. and the Free Press, 1968), XII, pp. 523-25; U.S. Bureau of Labor Statistics, *Productivity: A Bibliography* (Washington, D.C.: U.S. Government Printing Office), July, 1966, Bulletin No. 1514; John W. Kendrick, *Productivity Trends in the United States* (Princeton, N.J.: Princeton University Press, 1961); Seymour Melman, *Dynamic Factors in Industrial Productivity* (New York: John Wiley and Sons, 1956).

4. Robert Dubin, George C. Homans, Floyd C. Mann, and Delbert C. Miller, *Leadership and Productivity* (San Francisco: Chandler Publishing Co., 1965); Robert A. Sutermeister, *People and Productivity* (2d ed.; New York: McGraw-Hill, 1969); Daniel Katz, Nathan Maccoby, and Nancy C. Morse, *Productivity, Supervision and Morale in an Office Situation, Part I* (Ann Arbor: Survey Research Center, Institute for Social Research, University of Michigan, December, 1950); Alan C. Kerckhoff, "The Need for a Systematic Theory of Worker Productivity," *Social Forces*, XXXVIII (December, 1959), pp. 115-18; Abraham Zaleznik, *The Motivation, Productivity and Satisfaction of Workers* (Cambridge, Mass.: Harvard University, Graduate School of Business, 1958); Hans B. Thorelli, "The Tantalizing Concept of Productivity," *The American Behavioral Scientist*, IV (November, 1960), pp. 6-11.

5. Paul Wasserman, *Measurement and Evaluation of Organizational Performance* (Ithaca, N.Y.: Graduate School of Business and Public Administration, Cornell University, 1959 [A McKinsey Foundation Annotated Bibliography]).

6. Theodore Caplow, "The Criteria of Organization Success," *Social Forces*, XXXII (October, 1953), pp. 1-9; A. M. Woodruff and T. G. Alexander, *Success and Failure in Small Manufacturing: A Study of 20 Small Manufacturing Concerns* (Pittsburgh, Pa.: University of Pittsburgh Press, 1958).

7. Stanley Seashore, "Criteria of Organizational Effectiveness," *Michigan Business Review* (July, 1965), pp. 26-30. Amitai Etzioni, *Modern Organizations* (Englewood Cliffs, N.J.: Prentice-Hall, 1964), p. 8, defines effectiveness as the degree of goal achievement. James L. Price, *Organizational Effectiveness* (Homewood, Ill.: Richard D. Irwin, 1968), follows Etzioni's lead: "For example a prison, which has a custodial goal, and which has a low escape rate among its inmates, would be considered an effective organization. Or, again, a mental hospital, which has a therapeutic goal, and which successfully releases a high proportion of its inmates into the community would be considered an effective organization" (p. 3). Basil Georgopoulos and Arnold S. Tannenbaum, "A Study of Organization Effectiveness," *American Sociological Review*, XXII, No. 5 (October, 1957), pp. 534-40.

8. Etzioni, "Two Approaches to Organizational Analysis: A Critique and a Suggestion," *Administrative Science Quarterly*, V (1960), p. 257. Etzioni rejects the goal model for the systems model of effectiveness. A. L. Comrey *et al.*, "Factors Influencing Organizational Effectiveness," Parts 1-8, *Personal Psychology*, V (1952), p. 307; Chris Argyris, *Interpersonal Competence and Organizational Effectiveness* (Homewood, Ill.: Dorsey Press, 1962); Etzioni, "Authority Structure and Organizational Effectiveness," *Administrative Science Quarterly*, IV (June, 1959), pp. 43-67; Seymour Warkov, "Irregular Discharge from Veterans Administration Tuberculosis Hospitals: A Problem of Organizational Effectiveness" (unpublished Ph.D. dissertation, Yale University, 1959); James L. Price, "The Study of Organizational Effectiveness" (University of Iowa, Department of Sociology, October 30, 1970; mimeographed); Argyris in "Effectiveness and Planning of Change," *International Encyclopedia of the Social Sciences* (New York: Macmillan Co. and The Free Press, 1968), II, pp. 311-19, states "Concepts of organizational effectiveness typically focus on the degree to which the organization accomplishes its objectives."

9. Daniel Katz and Robert L. Kahn, *The Social Psychology of Organizations* (New York: John Wiley and Sons, 1966).

10. Problems related to goal displacement are discussed in David L. Sills, *The Volunteers: Means and Ends in a National Organization* (Glencoe, Ill.: The Free Press, 1957), esp. pp. 253-65; Mayer N. Zald and Patricia Denton, "From Evangelism to General Service: The Transformation of the YMCA," *Administrative Science Quarterly*, VIII, 1963, pp. 214-34; Sheldon L. Messinger, "Organizational Transformation: A Case Study of a Declining Social Movement," *American Sociological Review*, XX (1955), pp. 3-10. Discussion of a more general nature can be found in James K. Dent, "Organizational Correlates of the Goals of Business Man-

agement," *Personnel Psychology*, XII (1959), pp. 365-93; Herbert Simon, "On the Concept of Organizational Goal," *Administrative Quarterly*, IX (1964), pp. 1-22; Charles Perrow, "The Analysis of Goals in Complex Organizations," *American Sociological Review*, XXVI (1961), pp. 854-66; Perrow, "Organizational Goals," in *International Encyclopedia of the Social Sciences* (New York: Macmillan Co. and The Free Press, 1968), II, pp. 305-11; James D. Thompson and William J. McEwen, "Organizational Goals and Environment: Goal-setting as an Interaction Process," *American Sociological Review*, XXIII (1958), pp. 23-31; Zald, "Comparative Analysis and Measurement of Organizational Goals: The Case of Correctional Institutions for Delinquents," *Sociological Quarterly*, IV (1963), pp. 206-30.

11. Although it might be poor strategy in studies of efficiency, inferring goals from behavior may be appropriate in studies of goal conflict or goal change or any other study where the possible tautology does not matter greatly.

12. For an exception, see Warren W. Etcheson, *A Study of Business Terminations* (Seattle: University of Washington, December, 1962), and Woodruff and Alexander, *op. cit.*

13. Talcott Parsons, *Structure and Process in Modern Societies* (New York: The Free Press, 1960).

14. T. Caplow, *Principles of Organization* (New York: Harcourt, Brace & World, 1964), p. 121.

15. Katz and Kahn, *op. cit.*, chap. vii.

16. This reaction is reflected in Rensis Likert's call for human-assets accounting in organizations to reflect the level of worker morale, goodwill, and similar factors which are not accurately reflected in the cost and financial reports; Likert, *The Human Organization* (New York: McGraw-Hill, 1967).

17. S. Becker and G. Gordon, "An Entrepreneurial Theory of Formal Organizations," *Administrative Science Quarterly*, XI, No. 3 (December, 1966), 315-44.

18. For one of many introductory descriptions of this approach, see C. Horngren, *Cost Accounting: A Managerial Emphasis* (2d ed.; Englewood Cliffs, N.J.: Prentice-Hall, 1972).

NOTES TO CHAPTER II

(Pp. 51-68)

1. D. J. Hickson, "Convergence in Organization Theory," *Administrative Science Quarterly*, XI (1966-67).

2. *Ibid.*, p. 227. References to Hickson's Table are: Max Weber, *The Theory of Social and Economic Organization*, trans. A. M. Henderson and T. Parsons (Glencoe, Ill.: The Free Press, 1947). T. Burns and G. M. Stalker, *The Management of Innovation* (London: Tavistock, 1961). T. Barnes, "Industry in a New Age," *New Society*, XVIII (January, 1963), pp. 17-20. William Foote Whyte, "Incentives for Productivity: The Bundy Tubing Company Case," *Applied Anthropology*, VII (1948), pp. 1-16. Jerald Hage, "An Axiomatic Theory of Organizations," *Administrative Science Quarterly*, X (December, 1965), pp. 289-320, esp. 295. M. Crozier, *The Bureaucratic Phenomenon* (London: Tavistock, 1964). G. Gordon and S. Becker, "Changes in Medical Practice Bring Shifts in the Patterns of Power," *The Modern Hospital*, CII (February, 1964), pp. 89-91. V. A. Thompson, "Bureaucracy and Innovation," *Administrative Science Quarterly*, X (June, 1965), pp. 1-20. E. Litwak, "Models of Bureaucracy which Permit Conflict," *American Journal of Sociology*, LXVII (1961), pp. 177-84. M. Janowitz, "Changing Patterns of Organizational Authority: The Military Establishment," *Administrative Science Quarterly*, III (March, 1959), pp. 473-93. A. Gunder Frank, "Administrative Role Definition and Social Changes," *Human Organization*, XXII (Winter, 1963-64), pp. 238-42. H. A. Simon, *The New Science of Management Decisions* (New York: Harper, 1960). R. V. Presthus, "Toward a Theory of Organizational Behavior," *Administrative Science Quarterly*, III (June, 1958), pp. 48-72. Warren G. Bennis, "Leadership Theory and Administrative Behavior: The Problem of Authority," *Administrative Science Quarterly*, IV (December, 1959), pp. 259-301. F. W. Taylor, *Scientific Management* (New York: Harper, 1947). H. Fayol, *General and Industrial Management* (London: Pitman, 1949). L. F. Urwick, *The Elements of Administration* (London: Pitman, 1947). E. F. I. Brech, *Organization: The Framework of Management* (London: Longmans Green, 1957). W. Brown, *Exploration in Management* (London: Heinemann, 1960). Rensis Likert, *New Patterns of Management* (New York: McGraw-Hill, 1961). Douglas McGregor, *The Human Side of Enterprise* (New York: McGraw-Hill, 1960). Christopher Argyris, *Understanding Organizational Behavior* (Homewood, Ill.: Dorsey Press, 1960), and *Integrating the Individual and the Organization* (London: Tavistock, 1964).

3. S. W. Becker and G. Gordon, "An Entrepreneurial Theory of Formal Organizations," *Administrative Science Quarterly*, XI, No. 3 (December, 1966), pp. 315-44.

4. *Ibid.*

5. *Ibid.*

6. Hickson, *op. cit.*

7. See E. A. Fleishman, E. H. Harris, H. E. Burtt, "Leadership and Supervision in Industry," *Ohio State Business Educational Research Monograph*, No. 33 (1955).

8. See L. K. Williams, L. R. Hoffman, F. C. Mann, "An Investigation of the Control Graph: Influence in a Staff Organization," *Social Forces*, XXXVII, No. 3 (1959).

9. M. M. Rosner, "An Analysis of Organizational Influences on Hospital Adoption of New Drugs" (unpublished Ph.D. dissertation, University of Chicago, 1965).

10. Hage, *op. cit.*

11. Winston W. Hill and Wendell L. French, "Perceptions of the Power of Department Chairmen by Professors," *Administrative Science Quarterly*, XI (1965).

12. Brech, *op. cit.*

13. E. Jacques, *Equitable Payment* (London: Heinemann, 1961) and *Time Span Handbook* (London: Heinemann, 1964).

14. Hage, *op cit.*

15. Thomas L. Whisler, Harold Meyer, Bernard H. Baum, Peter F. Sorenson, Jr., "Centralization of Organizational Control: An Empirical Study of Its Meaning and Measurement," *The Journal of Business*, XL, No. 1 (January, 1967), pp. 10-26.

16. Joan Woodward, *Industrial Organization, Theory and Practice* (London: Oxford University Press, 1965), pp. 189-91.

17. Thomas L. Whisler, "Measuring Centralization of Control in Business Organizations," in W. W. Cooper, H. J. Leavitt, and M. W. Shelly (eds.), *New Perspectives in Organization Research* (New York: John Wiley and Sons, 1964).

18. Whisler *et al.*, *op. cit.*

19. A. S. Tannenbaum, *Control in Organizations* (New York: McGraw-Hill, 1968).

20. Whisler *et al.*, *op. cit.*

21. Hickson, *op. cit.*, p. 232.

22. Weber, *op. cit.*

23. Fayol, "General Principles of Management," in H. F. Merrill (ed.), *Classics in Management* (New York: American Management Association, 1960), p. 217.

24. F. W. Taylor, "The Principles of Scientific Management," in Merrill, *ibid.*, p. 113.

25. L. Urwick, *A Dictionary of Industrial Administration*, ed. John Lee (London: Isaac Pitman & Sons, 1928). Webster Robinson, *Fundamentals of Business Organization* (New York: McGraw-Hill, 1925). Brech, *op. cit.*

26. Hage, *op. cit.*, p. 297.

27. John M. Pfiffner, "The Effective Superior," *Personnel* (May, 1955), pp. 530-40.

28. Arnold Lowin, "Participative Decision Making: A Model Critique, and Prescriptions for Research," *Organizational Behavior and Human Performance*, III (1968), p. 89.

29. R. M. Stogdill and A. E. Coons (eds.), *Leadership and Behavior, Its Description and Measurement* (Columbus: Ohio State University Press, 1957). B. S. Georgopoulos and Floyd C. Mann, *The Community General Hospital* (New York: Macmillan Co., 1967).

30. Georgopoulos and Mann, *ibid.*, p. 363.

31. *Ibid.*, p. 7.
32. *Ibid.*, pp. 8-12.
33. *Ibid.*, p. 490.
34. Ray Brown, Seminar at the Center for Health Administration Studies, University of Chicago, May 23, 1968. H. L. Smith, "Two Lines of Authority Are One Too Many," *Modern Hospital*, LXXXIV (March, 1955), pp. 59-64. Everett A. Johnson and V. Laurio, "A Method for the Qualitative Analysis of Hospital Performance," *Graduate Program in Hospital Administration* (Chicago: University of Chicago, 1960), p. 7.
35. B. E. Noltingk, *The Human Element in Research Management* (Amsterdam: Elsevier, 1959), p. 35.
36. Roger K. Merton, *Social Theory and Social Structure* (Glencoe, Ill.: The Free Press, 1957), p. 199.
37. A. W. Gouldner, *Patterns of Industrial Bureaucracy* (Glencoe, Ill.: The Free Press, 1954).
38. R. White and R. Lippit, "Leader Behavior and Member Reaction in Three 'Social Climates,' " in Dorwin Cartwright and Alvin Zander (eds.), *Group Dynamics* (2d ed.; Evanston, Ill.: Row, Peterson and Company, 1962).
39. H. Baumgartel, "Leadership Style as a Variable in Research Administration," *Administrative Science Quarterly*, II (1957), pp. 344-60.
40. P. Blau and W. R. Scott, *Formal Organizations* (San Francisco: Chandler Publishing Company, 1962), p. 148.
41. Harold Leavitt, *Managerial Psychology* (rev. ed.; Chicago: University of Chicago Press, 1964), p. 166.
42. Stephen M. Sales, "Supervisory Style and Productivity: Review and Theory," *Personnel Psychology*, XIX, No. 3 (1966), pp. 275-86.
43. *Ibid.*
44. Daniel Katz and Robert L. Kahn, *The Social Psychology of Organizations* (New York: John Wiley and Sons, 1966), p. 332.
45. McGregor, "The Human Side of Enterprise," in Harold J. Leavitt and L. R. Pondy (eds.), *Readings in Management Psychology* (Chicago: University of Chicago Press, 1964), p. 267. Likert, *op. cit.*, pp. 99-100.
46. Argyris, *op. cit.*, pp. 15, 18.
47. Whyte, *Money and Motivation* (New York: Harper and Bros., 1955), p. 94.
48. Katz and Kahn, *op. cit.*, p. 373. Fleishman, Harris, and Burtt, *op. cit.*
49. A. Maslow, *Motivation and Personality* (New York: Harper and Bros., 1954).
50. D. Katz, N. Maccoby, and N. C. Morse, *Productivity, Supervision and Morale in an Office Situation* (Ann Arbor: University of Michigan, Survey Research Center, 1950).
51. Katz and Kahn, *op. cit.*, p. 373.
52. D. T. Campbell, *Leadership and Its Effects upon the Group* (Columbus: Ohio State University Press, 1956). A. S. Tannenbaum and B. S. Georgopoulos, "The Distribution of Control in Formal Organizations," *Social Forces*, XXXVI (1957), pp. 44-50.

53. R. R. Blake and J. S. Mouton, "The Intergroup Dynamics of Win-Lose Conflict and Problem-Solving Collaboration in Union-Management Relations," in M. Sherif (ed.), *Intergroup Relations and Leadership* (New York: John Wiley and Sons, 1962), pp. 94-140.

54. D. Pelz and F. Andrews, *Scientists in Organizations* (New York: John Wiley and Sons, 1966), pp. 32-35.

55. Lowin, *op. cit.*

56. Blau and Scott, *op. cit.*, p. 187.

57. J. R. P. French, Jr., I. C. Ross, S. Kirby, J. R. Nelson, P. Smyth, "Employee Participation in a Program of Industrial Change," *Personnel*, XXXV (1958), pp. 16-29.

58. Taylor, *op. cit.* Likert, *op. cit.*, pp. 99-100.

59. N. Morse and E. Reimer, "The Experimental Change of a Major Organizational Variable," *Journal of Abnormal and Social Psychology*, LII (1956), p. 120.

60. Likert, *op. cit.*, pp. 99-100.

61. V. I. Lenin, *Selected Works* (New York: International Publishers), pp. 322-33.

62. H. Koontz and C. O'Donnell, *Principles of Management* (2d ed.; New York: McGraw-Hill, 1959), p. 418.

63. R. Tannenbaum and W. H. Schmidt, "How to Choose a Leadership Pattern," *Harvard Business Review*, XXXVI (1958), pp. 95-101.

64. Pelz and Andrews, *op. cit.*

65. Edgar H. Schein, *Organizational Psychology* (Englewood Cliffs, N.J.: Prentice-Hall, 1965), pp. 60-61.

66. W. Kornhauser, *Scientists in Industry* (Berkeley: University of California Press, 1962). Simon Marcson, The Scientist in American Industry (Princeton, N.J., Industrial Relations Section, Princeton University, 1960). Blau and Scott, *op. cit.* Amitai Etzioni, *Modern Organizations* (Englewood Cliffs, N.J.: Prentice Hall, 1964), chap. 8.

67. L. Meltzer, "Scientific Productivity in Organizational Settings," *Journal of Social Issues*, XII, No. 2 (1956), pp. 32-40. R. Gerard, "Mirror to Physiology . . . A Self-Survey of Physiological Science" (Washington, D.C.: *American Physiological Society*, 1958). Pelz and Andrews, *op. cit.*, pp. 32-35.

68. D. C. Pelz, "Motivation of Engineering and Research Specialists," American Management Association, *General Management Series*, No. 186 (1957), pp. 25-46.

69. V. H. Vroom and F. C. Mann, "Leader Authoritarianism and Employee Attitudes," *Personnel Psychology*, XIII (1960), pp. 125-40.

70. Becker and Gordon, *op. cit.*, pp. 315-44.

71. Blau and Scott, *op. cit.*, p. 185.

72. Katz and Kahn, *op. cit.*, p. 347.

73. *Ibid.* Tannenbaum and Schmidt, *op. cit.*, pp. 95-101. Lowin, *op. cit.*, pp. 68-106.

74. P. R. Lawrence and J. W. Lorsch, *Organization and Environment* (Boston: Harvard University, Division of Research, Graduate School of Business Administration, 1967).

75. Woodward, *op. cit.*

76. Burns and Stalker, *op. cit.*

77. Lawrence and Lorsch, *op. cit.*, p. 27. Their concept of environment is very similar to Woodward's technology and our use of "task-environment" (*see* Chapter V). Lawrence and Lorsch say they "have chosen to conceive of the physical machinery, the non-human aspect of production, as part of the environment. . . . Readers . . . may prefer . . . the production task 'rather than the techno-economic environment' " (*ibid.*).

78. *Ibid.*

79. *Ibid.*

80. Schein, *op. cit.*, pp. 60-61. F. E. Fiedler, *A Theory of Leadership Effectiveness* (New York: McGraw-Hill, 1967). Harold Leavitt agrees that it is new, but misses the ideological fervor evident in the early days of the human-relations studies; Leavitt, "Organizational Behavior" (unpublished paper; Stanford University, 1969).

NOTES TO CHAPTER III

(Pp. 69-76)

1. G. D. Bell, "Formalization versus Flexibility in Complex Organizations: A Comparative Investigation within a Hospital" (unpublished Ph.D. dissertation. Yale University, 1965), p. 6.

2. Joan Woodward, *Industrial Organization, Theory and Practice* (London: Oxford University Press, 1965).

3. P. R. Lawrence and J. W. Lorsch, *Organization and Environment* (Boston: Harvard University, Division of Research, Graduate School of Business Administration, 1967), p. 27. "The use of this term [environment] in relation to production" (*ibid.*) illustrates another difference in definitions. They are referring to the production (line) departments of an organization in contrast to staff or maintenance departments. In economics the production process often includes both line and staff maintenance activities. This difference parallels the effectiveness-efficiency debate presented in Chapter I.

4. Peter O. Steiner, "Markets and Industries," *International Encyclopedia of the Social Sciences* (New York: Macmillan Co. and The Free Press, 1968), IX, pp. 575-81.

5. Selwyn W. Becker and G. Gordon, "An Entrepreneurial Theory of Formal Organizations," *Administrative Science Quarterly*, XI, No. 3 (December, 1966), pp. 315-44.

6. Theodore Anderson and Seymour Warkov, "Organizational Size and Functional Complexity," *American Sociological Review*, XXVI, No. 1 (February, 1961). W. Heydebrand, "Bureaucracy in Hospitals" (unpublished Ph.D. dissertation, University of Chicago, 1965). B. S. Georgopoulos and Floyd C. Mann, *The Community General Hospital* (New York: Macmillan Co., 1967). Jerald Hage, "An Axiomatic Theory of Organizations," *Administrative Science Quarterly*, X (1965), pp. 289-320. Victor A. Thompson, *Modern Organization* (New York: Alfred A. Knopf, 1965), p. 13. B. M. Bass, *Leadership, Psychology and Organizational Behavior* (New York: Harper & Row, 1960), p. 343. S. H. Udy, Jr., "Technical and Institutional Factors in Productive Organizations: A Preliminary Model," *American Journal of Sociology*, LVII (1961), pp. 247-54. For additional somewhat similar concepts, see George F. Weiland, "Complexity and Coordination in Organizations" (unpublished Ph.D. dissertation, University of Michigan, 1965). Richard Morrill, "A Principle Components Analysis and Classification of Chicago Area Hospitals" (Chicago: Hospital Planning Council, Chicago Regional Hospital Study Paper 19, May, 1967 [mimeographed]). Gerald D. Bell, "Determinants of Span of Control," *American Journal of Sociology*, LXXIII, No. 1 (July, 1967), pp. 100-09.

7. Lawrence and Lorsch, *op. cit.*

8. Jay Galbraith, *Designing Complex Organizations* (Reading, Mass.: Addison-Wesley, 1973), p. 15.

9. If adding computers or assistants requires conversion of general resources to specific ones, then a structural change in the direction of increased bureaucratization has occurred.

10. James D. Thompson, *Organizations in Action* (New York: McGraw-Hill, 1967). Charles Perrow, "A Framework for the Comparative Analysis of Organizations," *American Sociological Review*, XXXII (April, 1967), pp. 194-208.

11. Thompson, *ibid.*, p. 15.

NOTES TO CHAPTER IV

(Pp. 77-84)

1. G. Gordon and S. W. Becker, unpublished, *op. cit.*

2. J. G. March and H. A. Simon, *Organizations* (New York: John Wiley and Sons, 1958).

3. D. Pelz and F. Andrews, *Scientists in Organizations* (New York: John Wiley and Sons, 1966). G. Gordon and S. Marquis, "Freedom, Visibility

of Consequences, and Scientific Innovation," *American Journal of Sociology*, LXXII (September, 1966), pp. 195-202. M. M. Rosner, "An Analysis of Organization Influences on Hospital Adoption of New Drugs" (unpublished Ph.D. dissertation, University of Chicago, 1965).

4. The concept visibility of consequences has been called tautologous presumably because it is thought that knowledge of how procedure-resource interactions affect goal attainment is identical with actual goal attainment. Such errors arise because the transformation process is overlooked. Understanding the transformation process may be necessary to goal attainment, but it is not sufficient. Hence knowing the process is not synonymous with goal attainment.

5. L. Coch and J. R. French, "Overcoming Resistance to Change," *Human Relations*, I (1958), pp. 512-32. Pelz and Andrews, *op. cit.* D. Cook, "The Effect of Frequency of Feedback on Attitudes and Performance," in *Empirical Research in Accounting: Selected Studies, 1967* (Chicago: The Institute of Professional Accounting, 1968).

6. B. S. Georgopoulos and F. C. Mann, *The Community General Hospital* (New York: Macmillan Co., 1967).

7. Archibald M. Woodruff and T. G. Alexander, *Success and Failure in Small Manufacturing* (Pittsburgh: University of Pittsburgh Press, 1958). These firms ranged in size from 30 to 1,200 employees with a mean of 236 for the failed firms and 279 for the successful firms. Unfortunately, this is a retrospective analysis which mars an otherwise fine study.

NOTE TO CHAPTER V

(Pp. 85-90)

1. Robert A. Sutermeister, *People and Productivity* (2d ed.; New York: McGraw-Hill, 1970), frontispiece.

NOTES TO CHAPTER VI

(Pp. 91-95)

1. In the case of voluntary hospitals the owner is the corporation, represented by the Board of Trustees or equivalent group.

2. The hospital administrator fills the role of owner's agent.

NOTES TO INTRODUCTION, PART II

(Pp. 99-103)

1. Duncan Neuhauser, "Hospital Size and Structure," *Proceedings of the Ninth Annual Symposium on Hospital Affairs, December 1966* (Chicago: University of Chicago, Graduate Program in Hospital Administration, 1967).
2. Data for United States hospitals are from "The Guide Issue," *Hospitals, Journal of the American Hospital Association*, XLV, Part 2 (August 1, 1970). This report does not separate teaching hospitals, so they have had to be included in the following analysis.
3. It was impossible to collect sufficient information from three of the thirty hospitals, partly because their business offices were in difficulty. These three hospitals have been excluded from the body of the main analysis and are separately treated as brief case studies.
4. Commission on Professional and Hospital Activities, *Length of Stay in Short-term General Hospitals (1963-64)* (New York: McGraw-Hill, 1966).

NOTES TO CHAPTER VII

(Pp. 105-123)

1. Jerald Hage, "An Axiomatic Theory of Organizations," *Administrative Science Quarterly*, X (1965), pp. 289-320.
2. Joint Commission on Accreditation of Hospitals, *Proposed Standards for Accreditation of Hospitals* (Chicago: Joint Commission on Accreditation of Hospitals, July, 1969), p. 6.
3. Selwyn W. Becker and G. Gordon, "An Entrepreneurial Theory of Formal Organizations," *Administrative Science Quarterly*, XI, No. 3 (December, 1966), p. 327.
4. We only used this measure of efficiency because the other measures yielded cell sizes too small for meaningful comparison after the hospitals were divided into high- and low-complexity groups.
5. The large number of nonsignificant paired 2 X 2 tables in support of this conclusion have not been shown because of the space required.
6. The JCAH index was not used because it did not approximate a normal distribution.
7. Size is measured by the number of beds; complexity by an index based

on a checklist of 15 different categories of full-time technical hospital employees. The correlation between size and complexity here is +.724.

8. Duncan Neuhauser, "Hospital Size: A Selected Annotated Bibliography," in *Proceedings of the Ninth Annual Symposium on Hospital Affairs, (December, 1966)* (Chicago: University of Chicago, Program in Hospital Administration, 1967). Thomas R. Hefty, "Returns to Scale in Hospitals: A Critical Review of Recent Research," *Health Services Research* (Winter, 1969), pp. 267-80.

9. Robert Dubin, George C. Homans, Floyd C. Mann, and Delbert Miller, *Leadership and Productivity* (San Francisco: Chandler Publishing Co., 1965).

NOTES TO CHAPTER VIII

(Pp. 125-140)

1. John C. Denton *et al.*, "Predicting Judged Quality of Patient Care in General Hospitals," *Health Services Research* (Spring, 1967), pp. 26-33.

2. The assumption here is that a missing area is as bad as an unacceptable one. Other scoring systems not making this assumption were tried, but not being as highly correlated with the other quality measures, they were dropped.

3. In his widely cited study of the quality of medical practice of North Carolina physicians, Osler Peterson found a large variance in the performance levels of physicians. The best predictor of these differences was the level of medical training. The best physicians were those in the top half of their class in medical school and who trained as interns and residents in medical schools affiliated with hospitals while preparing for their specialties. Similar results were obtained by Clute in Canada. Osler L. Peterson, L. P. Andrews, R. S. Spain, B. G. Greenberg, "An Analytical Study of North Carolina General Practice 1953-54," *Journal of Medical Education*, XXXI, Part 2 (December, 1956). Kenneth Clute, *The General Practitioner: A Study of Medical Education and Practice in Ontario and Nova Scotia* (Toronto: University of Toronto Press, 1963). Also, Fremont J. Lyden, H. Jack Geiger, Osler L. Peterson, *The Training of Good Physicians* (Cambridge, Mass.: Harvard University Press, 1968). Osler Peterson, "Medical Care in the U.S.," *Scientific American*, CCIX, No. 2 (August, 1963), pp. 19-27. Milton C. Maloney, Ray E. Trussell, Jack Elinson, "Physicians Choose Medical Care: A Sociometric Approach to Quality Appraisal," *American Journal of Public Health*, L (1960), p. 1678. Ray E. Trussell *et al., A Study of the Quality of Hospital Care*

Secured by a Sample of Teamster Family Members in New York City (New York: Columbia University School of Public Health and Administrative Medicine, 1964).

4. We are indebted to Geoffrey Gibson and the Center for Health Administration Studies, University of Chicago, for these data.

5. Milton I. Roemer, A. T. Moustafa, C. E. Hopkins, "A Proposed Hospital Quality Index: Hospital Death Rates Adjusted for Case Severity," *Health Services Research* (Summer, 1968), pp. 96-118, and "Hospital Death Rates as a Quality Index," *Hospitals JAHA*, XLII, No. 1 (1968), 43.

6. An alternative approach would have been to ask this question of the chief of staff. This conceptually would have placed the chief of staff in the category of owner's agent, like the administrator. By not doing so, we conceptually put the chief of staff in the category of professional colleague.

7. (n = 17) Yule and Kendall's Q + .920.

8. Martin M. Rosner, "An Analysis of Organizational Influences on Hospital Adoption of New Drugs" (unpublished Ph.D. dissertation, University of Chicago, 1965).

9. These findings, or lack of them, are consistent with those of Thomas Whisler, H. Meyer, B. H. Baum, P. F. Sorensen, Jr., "Centralization of Organizational Control," *Journal of Business*, XL, No. 1 (January, 1967), pp. 10-26. They found that their three measures of centralization of control which are akin to our measures of specification-of-production procedures were highly interrelated in departments with highly programmed tasks (akin to our nonmedical component) and not interrelated for departments with nonprogrammed tasks (akin to our medical component).

10. Robert Meyers, "Organizing the Medical Staff," in Joseph Owen (ed.), *Modern Concepts of Hospital Administration* (Philadelphia: W. B. Saunders, 1962), pp. 196-97.

11. Denton *et al., op. cit.* They found that hospital size was the strongest prediction of expert evaluation of quality of care. Roemer *et al., op. cit.* also found that larger hospitals had a lower death-rate index.

NOTES TO CHAPTER IX

(Pp. 141-145)

1. This description of some relatively inefficient hospitals is not intended to reflect adversely on hospitals generally. The data presented here tell us absolutely nothing as to whether hospitals are on the average better- or

worse-managed than other organizations. There are also some very badly managed businesses. To look on these data as furnishing a basis for a blanket criticism of hospital administration would be an error.

NOTES TO CHAPTER X

(Pp. 147-158)

1. Professor Bustillo is a member of the faculty of the Instituto de Estudios Superiores de Administracion, Caracas, Venezuela. He conducted all the interviews and collected all the data.
2. J. D. Thompson, *Organizations in Action* (New York: McGraw-Hill, 1967).

NOTES TO CHAPTER XI

(Pp. 159-169)

1. John C. Denton *et al.*, "Predicting Judged Quality of Patient Care in General Hospitals," *Health Services Research* (Spring, 1967), pp. 26-33.
2. Milton I. Roemer, A. T. Moustafa, C. E. Hopkins, "A Proposed Hospital Quality Index: Hospital Death Rates Adjusted for Case Severity," *Health Services Research* (Summer, 1968), pp. 96-118, and "Hospital Death Rates as a Quality Index," *Hospitals JAHA*, XLII, No. 1 (1968), p. 43.
3. B. S. Georgopoulos and Floyd C. Mann, *The Community General Hospital* (New York: Macmillan Co., 1967), p. 497.
4. Milton I. Roemer and Jay W. Friedman, *Doctors in Hospitals: Medical Staff Organization and Hospital Performance* (Baltimore: Johns Hopkins Press, 1971). Reference to this work will provide the interested reader with more detail as well as with the authors' interpretation of their data.
5. *Ibid.*, pp. 87-95.
6. *Ibid.*, p. 256.
7. Intensity of care refers to length of hospital stay. The longer the period of time, the lower the cost per patient day and staffing ratio when complexity has been controlled for. The SADR is appropriate to the extent that ALOS reflects complexity of care and severity of illness, not intensity of care. A simple test for this exists, namely, if ALOS and the staffing ratios vary positively with each other, the predominant observed

effect is the complexity phenomenon. If, on the other hand, ALOS and the staffing ratios vary inversely, then the intensity effect predominates.

8. P. R. Lawrence and J. W. Lorsch, *Organization and Environment* (Cambridge, Mass.: Harvard University, Division of Research, Graduate School of Business Administration, 1967).

9. Joan Woodward, *Industrial Organization, Theory and Practice* (London: Oxford University Press, 1965).

10. S. E. Seashore and E. Yuchtman, "Factorial Analysis of Organizational Performance," *Administrative Science Quarterly* (December, 1967), pp. 337-95.

11. Paul N. Hirsch, "The Organization of Consumption: A Comparison of Organizational Effectiveness and Product Innovation in the Pharmaceutical and Recording Industries" (unpublished Ph.D. dissertation, University of Michigan, Ann Arbor, 1973).

12. S. Lieberson and J. F. O'Connor, "Leadership and Organizational Performance: A Study of Large Corporations," *American Sociological Review*, XXXVII (April, 1972), pp. 117-30.

13. Stephen Shortell, *Current Approaches to the Study of Formal Organizations: Framework for a Theory.* In preparation. School of Public Health, University of Washington.

14. See Chapter III for abbreviated discussions of Thompson and Perrow.

15. Jay Galbraith, *Designing Complex Organizations* (Reading, Mass.: Addison-Wesley, 1973), p. 15.

16. Charles Perrow, "Hospitals, Technology, Structure and Goals," James March (ed.), in *Handbook of Organizations* (Chicago: Rand McNally, 1965), p. 190. *Also see* J. A. Spencer, *Management in Hospitals* (London: Faber and Faber, 1967), pp. 38-39. H. L. Smith, "Two Lines of Authority Are One Too Many," *Modern Hospital*, LXXXIV (March, 1955), pp. 59-64. Hans O. Mauksch, "It Defies All Logic—But a Hospital Does Function," *Modern Hospital* (October, 1960), pp. 67-70, reprinted in James K. Skipper and Robert C. Leonard (eds.), *Social Interaction and Patient Care* (Philadelphia: J. B. Lippencott Co., 1965), pp. 251-65.

Bibliography

ALTMAN, I., ANDERSON, A. J., BARKER, K. *Methodology in Evaluating the Quality of Medical Care.* Pittsburgh: University of Pittsburgh Press, 1969.

ANDERSON, T., and WARKOV, S. "Organizational Size and Functional Complexity." *American Sociological Review*, XXVI, No. 1 (February, 1961).

ARGYRIS, C. "Effectiveness and Planning of Change," *International Encyclopedia of the Social Sciences*, Volume II. New York: Macmillan Company and The Free Press, 1968.

————. *Interpersonal Competence and Organizational Effectiveness.* Homewood, Illinois: Dorsey Press, 1962.

————. *Integrating the Individual and the Organization.* London: Tavistock, 1964.

————. *Understanding Organizational Behavior.* London: Tavistock, 1960.

BARNARD, CHESTER I. *The Functions of the Executive.* Cambridge, Mass.: Harvard University Press, 1951.

BARNES, T. "Industry in a New Age," *New Society*, XVIII (January, 1963).

BASS, B. M. *Leadership, Psychology and Organizational Behavior.* New York: Harper & Row, 1960.

BAUMGARTEL, H. "Leadership Style as a Variable in Research Administration," *Administrative Science Quarterly*, II (1957).

BECKER, SELWYN W., and GORDON, GERALD. "An Entrepreneurial Theory of Formal Organizations, Part I," *Administrative Science Quarterly*, XI, No. 3 (December, 1966).

————. "An Entrepreneurial Theory of Formal Organizations, Part II: Processes and Functioning of Formal Organizations." Chicago, 1971 (mimeographed).

BELL, G. D. "Formalization versus Flexibility in Complex Organizations: A Comparative Investigation within a Hospital." Unpublished Ph.D. dissertation, Yale University, 1965.

BENNIS, W. G. "Leadership Theory and Administrative Behavior: The Problem of Authority," *Administrative Science Quarterly*, IV (December, 1959).

BERRY, RALPH. "Competition and Efficiency in the Market of Hospital Services: The Structure of the American Hospital Industry." Unpublished Ph.D. dissertation, Harvard University, 1965.

BLAKE, R. R., and MOUTON, J. S. "The Intergroup Dynamics of Win-Lose Conflict and Problem-Solving Collaboration in Union-Management Relations," *Intergroup Relations and Leadership*, Ed. M. SHERIF. New York: John Wiley & Sons, 1962.

BLAU, P. M., and SCHOENHERR, R. A. *The Structure of Organizations.* New York: Basic Books, 1971.

————, and SCOTT, W. RICHARD. *Formal Organizations.* San Francisco: Chandler Publishing Company, 1962.

215

————, HEYDEBRAND, WOLF V., and STAUFFER, ROBERT E. "The Structure of Small Bureaucracies," *American Sociological Review*, XXXI, No. 2 (April, 1966).

BRECH, E. F. L. *Organization: The Framework of Management.* London, Longmans Green, 1957

BROWN, R. Seminar at the Center for Health Administration Studies, University of Chicago, May 23, 1968.

BROWN, W. *Exploration in Management.* London: Heinemann, 1960.

BURNS, T., and STALKER, G. M. *The Management of Innovation.* London: Tavistock, 1961.

CAMPBELL, D. T. *Leadership and Its Effects upon the Group.* Columbus, Ohio: Ohio State University Press, 1956.

CAPLOW, THEODORE. "The Criteria of Organization Success," *Social Forces*, XXXII (October, 1953).

————. *Principles of Organization.* New York: Harcourt, Brace & World, 1964.

CARROLL, JEAN. "The Structure of Teaching Hospitals." Unpublished Ph.D. dissertation, University of Chicago, 1969.

CLUTE, K. *The General Practitioner: A Study of Medical Education and Practice in Ontario and Nova Scotia.* Toronto: University of Toronto Press, 1963.

COCH, L., and FRENCH, J. R. "Overcoming Resistance to Change," *Human Relations*, I (1958).

COMMISSION ON PROFESSIONAL AND HOSPITAL ACTIVITIES. *Length of Stay in Short-Term General Hospitals (1963-64).* New York: McGraw-Hill, 1966.

COMREY, A. L., and others "Factors influencing Organizational Effectiveness, Parts I-VII," *Personnel Psychology*, V (1952).

COOK, D. "The Effect of Frequency of Feedback on Attitudes and Performance," *Empirical Research in Accounting: Selected Studies, 1967.* Chicago: Institute of Professional Accounting, 1968.

CROZIER, M. *The Bureaucratic Phenomenon.* London: Tavistock, 1964.

DAVIS, KINGSLEY. *Human Society.* New York: Macmillan Company, 1949.

DENT, JAMES K. "Organizational Correlates of the Goals of Business Management," *Personnel Psychology*, XII (1959).

DENTON, J. C., *et al.* "Predicting Judged Quality of Patient Care in General Hospitals," *Health Services Research*, Spring, 1967.

DUBIN, R., HOMANS, G. C., MANN, F. C., and MILLER, D. *Leadership and Productivity.* San Francisco: Chandler Publishing Company, 1965.

ELDOR, DAN. "An Empirical Investigation of Hospital Output, Input, and Productivity." Unpublished Ph.D. dissertation, New York University, February, 1969.

ETCHESON, WARREN W. *A Study of Business Terminations.* Seattle, Washington: University of Washington, December, 1962.

ETZIONI, AMITAI. "Authority Structure and Organizational Effectiveness," *Administrative Science Quarterly*, IV (June, 1959).

————. *A Comparative Analysis of Organizations.* New York: The Free Press, 1961.

————. *Modern Organizations.* Englewood Cliffs, N.J.: Prentice-Hall, 1964.

————. "Two Approaches to Organizational Analysis: A Critique and a Suggestion," *Administrative Science Quarterly,* V (1960).

FABRICANT, SOLOMON. "Productivity," *International Encyclopedia of the Social Sciences,* Vol. XII. New York: Macmillan Company and The Free Press, 1968.

FAYOL, H. "General Principles of Management," *Classics in Management,* Ed. H. F. MERRILL. New York: American Management Association, 1960.

————. *General and Industrial Management.* London: Pitman, 1949.

FELDSTEIN, MARTIN. *Economic Analysis for Health Services Efficiency.* Amsterdam: North Holland Publishing Company, 1967.

FIEDLER, F. E. *A Theory of Leadership Effectiveness.* New York: McGraw-Hill, 1967.

FLEISHMAN, E. A., HARRIS, E. H., and BURTT, H.W. "Leadership and Supervision in Industry," *Ohio State Business Educational Research Monograph,* No. 33, 1955.

FRANK, A. G. "Administrative Role Definition and Social Changes," *Human Organization,* XXII (Winter, 1963-64).

FRENCH, J. R. P., ROSS, I. C., KIRBY, S., NELSON, J. R., and SMYTH, P. "Employee Participation in a Program of Industrial Change," *Personnel,* XXXV (1958).

GALBRAITH, JAY. *Designing Complex Organizations.* Reading, Mass.: Addison-Wesley, 1973.

GEORGOPOULOS, B. S., and MANN, F.C. *The Community General Hospital.* New York, Macmillan Company, 1967.

————, and TANNENBAUM, ARNOLD S. "A Study of Organization Effectiveness," *American Sociological Review,* XXII, No. 5 (October, 1957).

GERARD, R. "Mirror to Physiology ... A Self-Survey of Physiological Science." Washington: American Physiological Society, 1958.

GORDON, GERALD, and BECKER, SELWYN W. "Changes in Medical Practice Bring Shifts in the Patterns of Power," *The Modern Hospital,* February, 1964.

————, and MARQUIS, S. "Freedom, Visibility of Consequences, and Scientific Innovation," *American Journal of Sociology,* LXII (September, 1966), pp. 195-202.

GOULDNER, A. W. *Patterns of Industrial Bureaucracy.* Glencoe, Ill.: The Free Press, 1954.

GREENWOOD, E. "Attributes of a Profession," *Man, Work, and Society,* Ed. S. NOSOW and W. H. FORM. New York: Basic Books, 1962.

HAGE, JERALD. "An Axiomatic Theory of Organizations," *Administrative Science Quarterly,* X (1965).

HALL, OSWALD. "The Informal Organization of the Medical Profession,"

Canadian Journal of Economics and Political Science, XII (February, 1946).

HALL, RICHARD H. *Organizations*. Englewood Cliffs, N. J.: Prentice-Hall, 1972.

HEFTY, T. R. "Return to Scale in Hospitals: A Critical Review of Recent Research," *Health Services Research*, Winter, 1969.

HEYDEBRAND, W. "Bureaucracy in Hospitals." Unpublished Ph.D. dissertation, University of Chicago, 1965.

HICKSON, D. J. "Convergence in Organization Theory," *Administrative Science Quarterly*, XI (1966).

HILL, W. W., and FRENCH, W. L. "Perceptions of the Power of Department Chairmen by Professors," *Administrative Science Quarterly*, XI (1966).

HIRSCH, PAUL. "The Organization of Consumption: A Comparison of Organizational Effectiveness and Product Innovation in the Pharmaceutical and Recording Industries." Unpublished Ph.D. dissertation, University of Michigan, Ann Arbor, Michigan.

HORNGREN, C. *Cost-Accounting: A Managerial Approach*. Englewood Cliffs, N.J.: Prentice-Hall, 1962.

HORTON, MELVIN E. "An Economic Analysis of Progress in the Medical Care of the United States Navy and Marine Corps Personnel." Unpublished Ph.D. dissertation, University of Washington, 1966.

HUGHES, E. C. *Men and Their Work*. Glencoe, Ill.: The Free Press, 1958.

INGBAR, MARY LEE, and TAYLOR, LESTER D. *Hospital Costs in Massachusetts*. Cambridge, Mass.: Harvard University Press, 1968.

JACQUES, E. *Equitable Payment*. London: Heinemann, 1961.

———. *Time Span Handbook*. London: Heinemann, 1964.

JANOWITZ, M. "Changing Patterns of Organizational Authority: The Military Establishment," *Administrative Science Quarterly*, III (March, 1959).

JOHNSON, E. A., and LAURIO, V. "A Method for the Qualitative Analysis of Hospital Performance." Graduate Program in Hospital Administration, University of Chicago, 1960.

JOINT COMMISSION ON ACCREDITATION OF HOSPITALS. *Proposed Standards for Accreditation of Hospitals*. Chicago: Joint Commission on Accreditation of Hospitals, July, 1969.

JOURNAL OF THE AMERICAN HOSPITALS ASSOCIATION. "The Guide Issue," *Hospitals*, XLV, Part II (August, 1970).

KAHN, ROBERT L., and KATZ, DANIEL. "Leadership Practices in Relation to Productivity and Morale," *Group Dynamics* (2d ed.), ed. D. CARTWRIGHT and A. ZANDER. Evanston, Ill.: Row, Peterson and Company, 1962.

KATZ, DANIEL, and KAHN, ROBERT L. *The Social Psychology of Organizations*. New York: John Wiley & Sons, 1966.

———, MACCOBY, N., and MORSE, N. C. *Productivity, Supervision and Morale in an Office Situation*. Ann Arbor: Survey Research Center, University of Michigan, 1950.

KENDRICK, JOHN W. *Productivity Trends in the United States*, Princeton, N. J.: Princeton University Press, 1961.

KERCKHOFF, ALAN C. "The Need for a Systematic Theory of Worker Productivity," *Social Forces*, XXXVIII (December, 1959).

KNIGHT, FRANK. *The Economic Organization*. Chicago: University of Chicago Press, 1933.

KOONTZ, H., and O'DONNELL, C. *Principles of Management* (2d ed.). New York: McGraw-Hill, 1959.

KORNHAUSER, W. *Scientist in Industry*. Berkeley: University of California Press, 1962.

LAWRENCE, P. R., and LORSCH, J. W. *Organization and Environment*. Boston: Division of Research, Graduate School of Business Administration, Harvard University, 1967.

LEAVITT, HAROLD. *Managerial Psychology* (rev. ed.). Chicago: University of Chicago Press, 1964.

————, and PONDY, L. *Readings in Management Psychology*. Chicago: University of Chicago Press, 1964.

LEE, J. A. H., MORRISON, S. L., and MORRIS, J. N. "Fatality from Three Common Surgical Conditions in Teaching and Non-Teaching Hospitals," *The Lancet*, October, 1957.

LENIN, V. I. *Selected Works*. New York: International Publishers, 1967.

LIEBERSON, S., and O'CONNOR, J. R. "Leadership and Organizational Performance: A Study of Large Corporations," *American Sociological Review*, XXXVII (April, 1972).

LIKERT, RENSIS. *The Human Organization*. New York: McGraw-Hill, 1967.

————. *New Patterns of Management*. New York: McGraw-Hill, 1961.

LITWAK, E. "Models of Bureaucracy Which Permit Conflict," *American Journal of Sociology*, LXVII (1961).

LOWIN, A. "Participative Decision Making: A Model Critique, and Prescriptions for Research," *Organizational Behavior and Human Performance*, III (1968).

LYDEN, F. J., GEIGER, H. J., and PETERSON, O. L. *The Training of Good Physicians*. Cambridge, Mass.: Harvard University Press, 1968.

McFARLAND, D. "A Dynamic Theory of the Growth and Structure of Organizations," *American Sociological Review*, forthcoming.

McGREGOR, D. "The Human Side of Enterprise," *Readings in Management Psychology*, ed. H. J. LEAVITT and L. R. PONDY. Chicago: University of Chicago Press, 1964.

————. *The Human Side of Enterprise*. New York: McGraw-Hill, 1960.

MALONEY, M. C., TRUSSELL, R. E., and ELINSON, J. "Physicians Choose Medical Care: A Sociometric Approach to Quality Appraisal," *American Journal of Public Health*, L (1960).

MASLOW, A. *Motivation and Personality*. New York: Harper & Bros., 1954.

MARCH, J. G., and SIMON, H. A. *Organizations*. New York: John Wiley & Sons, 1966.

MARCSON, SIMON. "Decision Making in a University Physics Department," *American Behavioral Scientist*, VI, No. 4 (December, 1962).
————. "Organization and Authority in Industrial Research," *Social Forces*, XL, No. 1 (October, 1961).
MAUKSCH, H. O. "It Defies All Logic—But a Hospital Does Function," *Modern Hospital*, October 1960. Reprinted in *Social Interaction and Patient Care*, ed. J. K. SKIPPER and R. C. LEONARD. Philadelphia: J. B. Lippincott Company, 1965.
MELMAN, SEYMOUR. *Dynamic Factors in Industrial Productivity*. New York: John Wiley & Sons, 1956.
MELTZER, L. "Scientific Productivity in Organizational Settings," *Journal of Social Issues*, XII, No. 2 (1956).
MERTON, R. K. *Social Theory and Social Structure*. Glencoe, Ill.: The Free Press, 1957.
MESSINGER, SHELDON L. "Organizational Transformation: A Case Study of a Declining Social Movement," *American Sociological Review*, XX (1955).
MEYER, M. "Size and the Structure of Organizations," *American Sociological Review*, XXXVII (1972).
MEYERS, R. "Organizing the Medical Staff," *Modern Concepts of Hospital Administration*, ed. JOSEPH OWEN. Philadelphia: W. B. Saunders, 1962.
MILLS, C. W. *The Power Elite*. New York: Oxford University Press, 1956.
MORSE, N., and REIMER, E. "The Experimental Change of a Major Organizational Variable," *Journal of Abnormal and Social Psychology*, LII (1956).
NEUHAUSER, DUNCAN. "Hospital Size and Structure," *Proceedings of the Ninth Annual Symposium on Hospital Affairs, December, 1966*. Chicago: Graduate Program in Hospital Administration, University of Chicago, 1967.
————. "Hospital Size: A Selected Annotated Bibliography," *Proceedings of the Ninth Annual Symposium on Hospital Affairs, December, 1966*. Chicago: Graduate Program in Hospital Administration, University of Chicago, 1967.
————, and TURCOTTE, F. "Costs and Quality of Care in Different Types of Hospitals," *The Annals of the American Academy of Political and Social Science*, January, 1972.
NOLTINGK, B. E. *The Human Element in Research Management*. Amsterdam: Elsevier, 1959.
PARSONS, TALCOTT. "The Professions and Social Structure," *Social Forces*, XVII (May, 1939).
————. *Structure and Process in Modern Societies*. New York: The Free Press, 1960.
PELZ, D. C. "Motivation of Engineering and Research Specialists." New York: American Management Association, *General Management Series*, No. 186. 1957.

————, and ANDREWS, F. *Scientists in Organizations.* New York: John Wiley & Sons, 1966.

PERROW, CHARLES. "The Analysis of Goals in Complex Organizations," *American Sociological Review*, XXVI (1961).

————. "A Framework for the Comparative Analysis of Organizations," *American Sociological Review*, XXXII (April, 1967).

————. "Hospitals, Technology, Structure and Goals," *Handbook of Organizations*, ed. J. MARCH. Chicago: Rand McNally, 1965.

————. "Organizational Goals," *International Encyclopedia of the Social Sciences.* New York: Macmillan Company and The Free Press, 1968.

PETERSON, O. "Medical Care in the U.S.," *Scientific American*, CCIX, No. 2 (August, 1963).

————, ANDREWS, L. P., SPAIN, R. S., and GREENBERG, B. G. "An Analytical Study of North Carolina General Practice 1953-54," *Journal of Medical Education*, XXXI, Part 2 (December, 1956).

PFIFFNER, J. M. "The Effective Superior," *Personnel*, May, 1955.

PRESTHUS, R. V. "Toward a Theory of Organizational Behavior," *Administrative Science Quarterly*, III (June, 1958).

PRICE, JAMES L. *Organizational Effectiveness.* Homewood, Ill.: Richard D. Irwin, 1968.

————. "The Study of Organizational Effectiveness." Unpublished paper, University of Iowa, 1970.

KONG KYUN RO. "A Statistical Study of Factors Affecting the Unit Costs of Short Term Hospital Care." Unpublished Ph.D. dissertation, Yale University, 1966.

ROBINSON, W. *Fundamentals of Business Organization.* New York: McGraw-Hill, 1925.

ROEMER, M. I., and FRIEDMAN, J. *Doctors in Hospitals: Medical Staff Organization and Hospital Performance.* Baltimore: Johns Hopkins Press, 1971.

————, MOUSTAFA, A. T., HOPKINS, C. E. "A Proposed Hospital Quality Index: Hospital Death Rates Adjusted for Case Severity," *Health Services Research*, Summer, 1968.

————. "Hospital Death Rates as a Quality Index," *Hospitals JAHA*, XLII, No. 1 (1968).

ROSNER, M. M. "An Analysis of Organization Influences on Hospital Adoption of New Drugs." Unpublished Ph.D. dissertation, University of Chicago, 1965.

SALES, S. M. "Supervisory Style and Productivity: Review and Theory," *Personnel Psychology*, XIX, No. 3, 1966.

SCHEIN, E. H. *Organizational Psychology.* Englewood Cliffs, N. J.: Prentice-Hall, 1965.

SEASHORE, STANLEY. "Criteria of Organizational Effectiveness," *Michigan Business Review*, July, 1965.

————, and YUCHTMAN, E. "Factorial Analysis of Organizational Performance," *Administrative Science Quarterly*, December, 1967.

SHORTELL, STEPHEN. "Current Approaches to the Study of Formal Organizations: Framework for a Theory." Unpublished paper, Seattle, University of Washington, 1974.

SILLS, DAVID L. *The Volunteers: Means and Ends in a National Organization.* Glencoe, Ill.: The Free Press, 1957.

SIMON, H. A. "Decision Making and Administrative Organization," *Public Administration Review*, IV (Winter, 1944).

————. *The New Science of Management Decisions.* New York: Harper, 1960.

————. "On the Concept of Organizational Goals," *Administrative Science Quarterly*, IX (1964).

SMITH, H. L. "Two Lines of Authority Are One Too Many," *Modern Hospital*, LXXXIV (March, 1955).

SPENCER, J. A. *Management in Hospitals.* London: Faber and Faber, 1967.

STEINER, P. O. "Markets and Industries," *International Encyclopedia of the Social Sciences.* New York: Macmillan Company, 1968.

STINCHCOMBE, ARTHUR L. "Bureaucratic and Craft Administration of Production," *Administrative Science Quarterly*, IV (1959).

STODGILL, R. M., and COONS, A. E. (eds.). *Leadership and Behavior, Its Description and Measurement.* Columbus, Ohio: Ohio State University Press, 1957.

SUTERMEISTER, R. A. *People and Productivity* (2d ed.). New York: McGraw-Hill, 1970.

TANNENBAUM, A. S. *Control in Organizations.* New York: McGraw-Hill, 1968.

————, and GEORGOPOULOS, B. S. "The Distribution of Control in Formal Organizations," *Social Forces*, XXXVI (1957).

————, and SCHMIDT, W. H. "How to Choose a Leadership Pattern," *Harvard Business Review*, XXXVI (1958).

TAYLOR, F. W. *Scientific Management.* New York: Harper, 1947.

THOMPSON, J. D. *Organizations in Action.* New York: McGraw-Hill, 1967.

————, and BATES, FREDERICK L. "Technology, Organization and Administration," *Administrative Science Quarterly*, II (1957).

————, and McEWEN, WILLIAM J. "Organizational Goals and Environment: Goal-Setting as an Interaction Process," *American Sociological Review*, XXIII (1958).

THOMPSON, V. A. "Bureaucracy and Innovation," *Administrative Science Quarterly*, X (June, 1965).

————. *Modern Organization.* New York: Alfred A. Knopf, 1965.

THORELLI, HANS B. "The Tantalizing Concept of Productivity," *The American Behavioral Scientist*, IV (November, 1960).

Time Magazine, January 13, 1961.

TRUSSELL, R. E., and others. "A Study of the Quality of Hospital Care Secured by a Sample of Teamster Family Members in New York City." New York: Columbia University School of Public Health and Administrative Medicine, 1964.

UDY, S. H., JR. "Technical and Institutional Factors in Productive Organizations: A Preliminary Model," *American Journal of Sociology*, LXVII (1961).

URWICK, L. F. *The Elements of Administration*. London: Pitman, 1947.

————. *A Dictionary of Industrial Administration*, ed. J. LEE. London: Isaac Pitman & Sons, 1928.

U. S. BUREAU OF LABOR STATISTICS. *Productivity: A Bibliography*. Bulletin No. 1514. Washington, D. C.: U. S. Government Printing Office, July, 1966.

VROOM, V. H., and MANN, F. C. "Leader Authoritarianism and Employee Attitudes," *Personnel Psychology*, XIII (1960).

WARKOV, SEYMOUR. "Irregular Discharge from Veterans Administration Tuberculosis Hospitals: A Problem of Organizational Effectiveness." Unpublished Ph.D. dissertation, Yale University, 1959.

WASSERMAN, PAUL. *Measurement and Evaluation of Organizational Performance*. Ithaca, N.Y.: Cornell University, Graduate School of Business and Public Administration, 1959 (A McKinsey Foundation Annotated Bibliography).

WEBER, MAX. "The Essentials of Bureaucratic Organization: An Ideal-Type Construction," *Reader in Bureaucracy*, ed. R. MERTON, A. GRAY, B. HOCKEY and H. SELVIN. Glencoe, Ill.: The Free Press, 1952.

————. *The Theory of Social and Economic Organization*. Translated by A. M. HENDERSON and T. PARSONS. Glencoe, Ill.: The Free Press, 1947.

WHISLER, THOMAS L. "Measuring Centralization of Control in Business Organizations," *New Perspectives in Organization Research*, ed. W. COOPER, H. LEAVITT and M. SHELLY. New York: John Wiley & Sons, 1964.

————, MEYER, H., BAUM, B. H., and SORENSON, P. F., JR. "Centralization of Organizational Control: An Empirical Study of Its Meaning and Measurement," *The Journal of Business*, XL, No. 1 (January, 1967).

WHITE, R., and LIPPETT, R. "Leader Behavior and Member Reaction in Three 'Social Climates,' " *Group Dynamics*, ed. D. CARTWRIGHT and A. ZANDER (2d ed.). Evanston, Ill.: Row, Peterson and Company, 1962.

WHYTE, WILLIAM FOOTE. *Money and Motivation*. New York: Harper & Bros., 1955.

WILLIAMS, L. K., HOFFMAN, L. RICHARD, and MANN, FLOYD C. "An Investigation of the Control Graph: Influence in a Staff Organization," *Social Forces*, XXXVII, No. 3 (1959).

WILLIAMS, ROBIN M., JR. *American Economic Institutions*. New York: Alfred A. Knopf, 1960.

WOODRUFF, A. M., and ALEXANDER, T. G. *Success and Failure in Small Manufacturing*. Pittsburgh, Pa.: University of Pittsburgh Press, 1958.

WOODWARD, JOAN. *Industrial Organization, Theory and Practice*. London: Oxford University Press, 1965.

ZALD, MAYER N. "Comparative Analysis and Measurement of Organizational Goals: The Case of Correctional Institutions for Delinquents," *Sociological Quarterly*, IV (1963).

———, and DENTON, PATRICIA. "From Evangelism to General Service: The Transformation of the YMCA," *Administrative Science Quarterly*, VIII (1963).

ZALEZNIK, ABRAHAM. *The Motivation, Productivity and Satisfaction of Workers.* Cambridge, Mass.: Harvard University, Graduate School of Business, 1958.

Index

AHA (American Hospital Association), 109

ALOS, see hospital, average length of stay

ability (knowledge, skill, education, experience training), 88

adaptation, see change

administrative ratio (see managerial component), 3,4

alcoholism, 88

Aiken, Michael, and Hage, Jerald, 173

alienation, 88

American Tobacco Company, 43

Anderson, T., and Warkov, S., 71

architecture, 88

Argyris, Chris, 52

aspiration, level of, 88

assessment criteria (see insurance companies)

authority,
    clear lines of, 56
    authority of office, 56
    use of, 59
    structure, 3

authority pattern, 4, 35, 92, 168
    executive, 13, 17, 22
    executive-external, 15, 17
    collegial, 17, 22
    internal coupling, 23

automation, 88

autonomy of organizational units, 23, 24

autopsy rate, see hospital, specification of visibility procedures (professional component)

awareness, see visibility of consequences

Barnard, Chester, 5

Barnes, T., 52

Bass, B.M., 71-72

Baumgartel, H., 59

Becker, Selwyn, and Gordon, Gerald, 77, 78, 113

Bell, G.D., 69

Bennis, Warren G., 52

Berry, Ralph, 40

Blau, Peter, 5
    and Scott, W.R., 59, 62, 65

Blue Cross, 106

Brech, E.F.L., 52, 54, 56

Brown, W., 52

budget, budgeting, 35, 88, 107-108

bureaucracy, 27, 37, 88
    central bureaucracy, 23, 25, 28
    complete, 12, 17, 18, 21, 22, 25, 37; defined 13
    decentralized, defined, 23
    enucleated, 15, 16, 17, 19, 31, 37; defined, 16
    externally coupled, 22
    internally coupled, 21, 22
    optimal, structures, 17, 18
    overcomplete, 20
    parallel, 25, 26

truncated, 13, 14, 17, 32, 37
    defined, 15
    Weberian ideal, 13, 168, 169
bureaucrat, 8, 9
Burns, T., and Stalker, G.M., 52, 67,
    168
Bustillo, Juan Antonio, Professor.,
    viii, 147, 163, 192

C_V, see visibility of consequences
C_V procedures, see procedures to in-
    crease visibility of consequences
Caplow, Theodore, 44, 45
capital, 88, 168
Capitalism, 86
career stage, 88
Center for Health Administration
    Studies (University of Chicago),
    vii
centralization, see decentralization
change, organizational, 37
    and visibility of consequences,
        80
Chicago, see hospitals
climate, 87
    leadership climate, 89
Coch, L., and French, J.R., 62, 82
cohesiveness, 88
collegial authority system (see au-
    thority pattern, collegial), 19, 27,
    68, 88, 144
        collegial coordinating mecha-
            nism, 22
communication, 4, 88, 168
    effectiveness of, 82
    and coordination, 82
    time, 26, 27
communism, 86
competition, 86

complexity, organizational, 3, 4, 18,
    19, 24, 159, 168
complexity of task environment, 24,
    69-76
    (see task-environment)
    (see hospitals, complexity)
compliance relationship
    normative, 33
    utilitarian, 33
computerization, 88
conflict in organizations, 37
    tolerance for, 37, 79
    and visibility of consequences,
        79, 80
contingency theory, vii, 66-68, 75
control, 56, 88, 168
    owners, 91, 92
    managerial or hierarchical, 64,
        66, 95
    collegial, 95
    see hospitals, control
control graph, 53, 55
Cook, Doris, 82
coordination, 7, 8, 13, 14, 16, 18,
    25, 58, 82, 84, 88, 168
    defined, 7-8
    benefits of, 17, 19, 20, 23, 24,
        28, 91
coordinator, 8, 9
coupling (coupled organization), 66,
    67, 92, 94, 95, 168
    internal coupling, 21, 22, 23
    external coupling, 22, 23
craft unions, 15
Crozier, Michael, 52
culture, 86, 88, 147-149, 155-156,
    167

Darwin, Social Darwinism, 43

Davis, Kingsley, 6, 7, 9
decentralization (centralization, decentralized organization) (see bureaucracy), 23, 24, 28, 51, 68, 84, 88, 168
    degree of organizational, 24, 72
    functional, 25, 28
    parallel, 26, 28
decision-making
    collegial, 17
    (see insurance companies)
delegate, delegation, 8
    delegation and enucleated bureaucracy, 24
demand, 126
    unpredictable, 13
    sporadic, 20, 21
    environmental, 20
Denton, J.C. et al., 125, 136, 160
departments, departmentalization, 89
    (see hospitals, insurance companies)
depression, economic, 86
differentiation, 5, 68, 72, 92, 165
disability, 88
discretion, 7, 8
Division of labor, 16, 88
Dubin, R. et al., 40

E.T., see Entrepreneurial Theory
economic conditions, 86
economies of scale, 19, 23, 25, 117
    and the central bureaucracy, 28
    (see Hospitals)
education, worker, 88
effectiveness, 4, 8, 41, 154

and efficiency, 44, 45
efficiency, organizational (the efficient organization) (see hospitals, insurance companies), 3, 4, 5, 7, 38, 66, 77, 85-89, 91, 159
    and discontinued present value, 48-49
    and goals, 38, 39-50, 80, 89, 168
    a model of, vii, 92-95
    as a ratio of outputs to inputs, 40
    specification of procedures and, 53, 82, 92-94
    visibility of consequences and, 78, 80, 92-94
Entrepreneurial Theory of Formal Organizations (E.T.), 4, 5, 38, 46, 51, 53, 65, 66-69, 87, 89, 111, 113, 167, 168
    Description of, 3-38, 70-76, 85-87, 91-93
enucleation (see bureaucracy), 18, 19, 21, 26, 28, 66, 68, 72
environment (see task-environment), vii, 18, 24, 25, 26, 65, 69-76, 84, 87
    environmental change, 26, 67, 80
    environmental demands, 81, 87
    environmental variables, 85-89
    owner and, 86, 87
    stable, 20, 21, 67, 87
environment-organization interaction, 70, 85-89
    complexity of, 19, 21, 25, 28, 65, 68, 159
    diversity of, 19, 20, 21, 87
equipment, quality of, 88

Etzioni, Amitai, 33, 41
experience, worker, 88
exploitation of organizational resources, 30, 31

factor prices, 86
fad and fashion, 87
failure, business, 83
fatigue, 88
Fayol, Henri, 52, 56
Feldstein, Martin, 90
Finney, D.J., 117
fire regulations, 86, 106
Ford Foundation vii
formal organization (see bureaucracy, entrepreneurial theory) vii, 3, 6, 14, 22, 88, 91, 161, 167
    definitions of, 5, 7
formulary, see hospital, specification of production procedures (professional component)
Frank, A. Gunder, 52
French, J.R.P. et al., 62
fringe benefits, 88

Galbraith, Jay, 72-76, 167, 168
General Motors, 28
General Resource, see resource
Georgopoulos, B.S., and Mann, F.C., 57, 58, 59, 71, 82, 160-161, 173
Gerard, R., 64
goal congruence, 33, 79, 80, 81
goal achievement, 41, 42, 91, 168
    (see goals, attainment)
goal(s)
    organizational (see hospitals), vii, 4, 5, 28, 42-50, 144
    attainment, 7, 22, 29, 77, 81, 92, 168

and efficiency, 38-50
owner's, 7, 8, 23, 87
subgoals, 25, 125
and systems-resource approach, 45-46
universal, 43
and visibility of consequences, 79, 144
whose, 43
Gordon, Gerald, and Becker, Selwyn, 29, 52
Gordon, Gerald, and Marquis, Sue, 78
government regulation, 86-87

HAS, see Hospital Administrative Services
Hage, Jerald, 40, 52, 54, 56, 71, 107
Hall, Oswald, 31
Hall, Richard, H. 4
Harwood factory, 62, 82
Hawthorne effect, 88
Heydebrand, W., 71
Hickson, D.J., 41-53, 55
hierarchy, 14, 18, 88
    hierarchic levels, 3, 16, 17, 19, 20
    and information, 25, 38
    hierarchical leadership style, 88, 95
Hill, W.W. and French, W.L., 54
Hirsch, Paul, 166
Hospital Administrative Services (HAS), 101, 105, 142
hospitals, vii, 4, 35, 47, 99-102, 105-145, 159-163, 166, 168-169, 171-173

hospital
  administrative component (non-medical component), 105-124, 141-143, 159-161, 166, 173
  Administrative authority pattern, 21, 101-102
  administrator, 109, 110, 114-115, 119, 128, 129, 131, 137, 142-144, 166
  administrator awareness (see visibility of consequences)
  average length of stay (ALOS), 99, 100, 101, 109, 126
hospital
  board of trustees, board chairmen, 83, 84, 109, 129, 132, 163
  and visibility of consequences, 84, 114, 115, 119, 128, 131
hospital
  communication in, 82
  see specification of visibility procedures
hospitals
  as complex coupled organizations, 21, 101-102, 141, 143
  complexity (C_X) differences in, 116-117, 118-124, 132-133, 136-140, 159, 160
hospital
  control, 54, 57
  (see specification of procedures)
  collective control (medical staff), 161-163
  coordination, 58
  costs, per diem costs, 58, 100, 101, 109, 114, 160
  cost index ($), 105, 106, 108, 111, 112, 113, 115, 116, 117, 118-124
hospital
  departments, 102, 105, 109
  department heads, 111, 113, 114, 143, 160, 173
hospital
  economies of scale, 117, 118, 159, 160
  efficiency (administrative component), 58, 105-108, 111-124, 141-143, 159, 166
  efficiency (professional component) (see quality of care), 125-127, 130-134, 136-140, 143-145, 160-164, 166
  expert evaluation index (administrative component) (EE) (see efficiency), 106, 108, 111-116, 118-124, 141
  expert evaluation index (professional component) (EE) (see quality of care), 125-127, 131-134, 136-140, 145, 160
hospital
  goal attainment, 144 (see efficiency, quality of care)
  goal congruence, 33
hospital, Joint Commission on Accreditation of Hospital (JCAH), 109, 143,
  accreditation, 106
  efficiency index (administrative component) (see efficiency), 106-108, 111-115
  quality index (professional

component) (see quality of
care), 126-127, 131-134,
136-140
hospitals
    man hours, 101
    man hour index (MH) (see effi-
    ciency), 105, 108, 111, 112,
    113, 115, 116, 118-24
    measuring instruments, 171-
    173
hospital
    medical records, 106, 111,
    129, 144
    medical staff, component, 21,
    31, 54
    see hospital, professional
    component, 125-140,
    143-145, 161-164
hospital
    non-medical component, see
    administrativee component
hospital
    occupancy rate (∅), 100, 101,
    107, 108, 109, 111, 112,
    113, 115, 116, 118, 124
    owner, ownership, 84, 114,
    161
    (see board of trustees)
hospitals
    physicians in, 125-140, 143-
    145, 161-164
    board certification of, 126,
    127
    (see hospital, professional
    component)
hospital, 21, 31, 54
    professional component, 101-
    102, 116, 125-140, 143-
    145, 161-164

professional qualifications in-
    dex, 126-127 (see quality of
    care)
hospital
    quality of care, 40, 58, 82,
    125-127, 130-134, 136-141,
    145, 160-164, 166
hospital
    severity adjusted death rate
    (SADR) Index of quality of
    care, (see quality of care),
    126-127, 131-134, 136-140,
    160-164
    size (S), 99, 100, 101, 117,
    134-140, 159, 160, 161,
    162, 163, 164
    medium size, 99, 118-124
    (see economies of scale)
hospital, specification of production
    procedures (Pt) (administrative
    component), 102, 105, 107-109,
    111, 116-124, 141, 143-145, 159,
    160
    perceived (Pp), 107, 110, 112,
    116-124, 173
    budget as a measure of, 107-
    108, 110, 112, 143
    position control as a measure
    of, 108, 110, 112, 143
    salary control as a measure of,
    108, 110, 112
    written job descriptions as a
    measure of, 108-110, 112
    Department head's, 111, 113,
    143, 173
    hierarchically imposed rules,
    160-161
hospital, specification of production
    procedures (P+) (professional

component), 129, 144-145, 161-164
    formulary as a measure of, 129-131
    admitting privileges as a measure of, 129-131
    perceived MD influence as a measure of (Pp), 129-131
    Joint Conference Committee (P+) as a measure of, 132-133, 163
hospital, specification of visibility procedures (PCv) (same as specification of procedures to increase Cv), 155
    (administrative component), 114-116, 118-124, 141-143, 159-161
    (professional component), 125, 127-128, 134-135, 137-140, 143-145
        autopsy rate as a measure of 127-128, 134-135, 137-140, 144
        reports index as a measure of, 128, 134-135, 137-140, 143-144
hospital
    task environment, 70, 71, 125
    (see complexity)
hospital, types of, 99-100
    governmental, 161
    proprietary, 161
    teaching, 48
hospital
    usurpation, 84
hospital, visibility of consequences (Cv), 29, 78, 83, 84, 102
    —(administrative component),
    109-110, 114, 115, 118-124, 141-143, 159
    —(professional component), 125, 128, 131, 134, 140, 144-145
    —and board of trustees, 114-115, 128
humidity, 88
human problem solving, 4
human relations, 49, 59-62, 63, 95
human resources, 7, 14, 32
    (see resources, volitional)
hypotheses, 11, 85, 93, 95, 103, 105
    tests of, 111-125, 130, 140, 145, 147-150, 156-159, 165

I.S., see Initiating Structure
ideology, 86
illness, 88, 126
incentives, 88
industry, 87
informal organization
    and visibility of consequences, 79, 80, 88
    values, norms, cohesiveness, 88
information
    accessibility, 29
    and change, 38
    and efficiency, 83
    and hierarchical level, 25-26
    information systems, 81, 88
    and procedures to increase visibility of consequences, 81, 82
    processing, 72-73, 160, 167
Initiating Structure (I.S.), 53, 57
innovation, innovative activity, 78, 154, 166
input, mix, variables, 3, 4, 88

Instituto de Estudios Superiores de
    Administracion, viii
insurance companies, vii, 4, 102,
    103, 147-158, 163, 165-166, 175-
    192
insurance companies
    assessment criteria, 149, 150,
        156, 157, 165, 183
        instrumental, 149, 150, 156
        economic, 149, 150, 156,
            157, 165
insurance companies
    costs and benefits, 151-153,
        155
insurance companies
    culture and the use of time,
        147-148, 149, 155-156
insurance companies
    decision making process, 147,
        150, 184-184
        rational, 147, 149, 150,
            156, 157
        impulsive, 147, 148, 155
        postponing-neglectful, 147-
            149, 155
        speed of, 155
insurance companies
    departments, 152-153
insurance companies
    efficiency, 147-148, 156-157,
        165
        expert evaluation measure
            of, 150, 157, 191-192
        profit/asset measure of,
            150-151, 157
insurance companies
    managerial technology, 177-
        183
    measuring instruments, 175-192

insurance companies
    ownership, 103
insurance companies
    size, 157-158
insurance companies
    time, use of, 147-149, 155-
        156, 165, 184-185
insurance companies
    visibility of consequences, 147-
        150, 156-158, 165, 186-190
        actual, 151-152, 156-158,
            165
        potential (Cvp), 148-149,
            153-155, 156-158, 165
integration, 68, 72, 88, 165, 167

JCAH, see hospitals, Joint Commis-
    sion on Accreditation of Hospitals
Jacques, Elliott, 54
Janowitz, Morris, 52, 65
job: content, satisfaction, introduc-
    tion to, layout training for, aliena-
    tion from, performance, 88
job descriptions (see hospitals, speci-
    fication of production proce-
    dures), 36
Joint Commission on Accreditation
    of Hospitals, see hospitals

Katz, Daniel, and Kahn, Robert L.,
    41, 44, 45, 62, 65, 66
Koontz, H., and O'Donnell, C., 63

labor market, 86
Lawrence, Paul, and Lorsch, Jay, 66,
    67-68, 69-70, 72, 73, 75-76, 92,
    165, 167, 168
leadership style, 88, 119, 165
Leavitt, Harold, 59

legal restrictions, 86-87
legal sanctions, 6
Lenin, V.I., 63
Lieberson, S., and O'Connor, J.R., 165-166
lighting, 88
Likert, Rensis, 52, 61, 62, 63
Likert Scales, 53, 153
Litwak, E., 52
living conditions, 86
Lowin, A., 62, 63, 66

maintenance, organizational, 44, 45, 88
manager, management, 8, 9, 14, 23, 83, 84, 88, 91, 169
    defined, 8-9
managerial component, 54, 66, 88
    (see administrative component, also hospitals)
measuring instruments
    Hospital Study, 171-173
    Insurance Study, 175-192
Medicare, 106
succession, managerial, 3
manufacturer, 22
March, J.G., and Simon, H.A., 77
Marcson, Simon, 12
market, size of, 86
market research organization, 22
marketing, 88
Maslow, A., 61
McGregor, D., 52
Meltzer, L., 64
Merton, Robert, 58-59
military organizations, 20, 35, 36
monopoly, 86
morale, 36, 41, 44, 45, 49, 88, 168
Morse, N., and Reimer, E., 62, 63

MSO (medical staff organization), 161-164
    (see hospitals, professional component)
motivation, 88, 168
music, 88

needs, individual, 88
    of managers, 88
    achievement, 88
nepotism, 144
Noltingk, B.E., 58

Ohio State University, 57
oligopoly, 86
oligopsonistic relationship, 23
organization (see: formal organization, efficiency, coupled, bureaucracy)
    complex-structures, 21, 64, 88, 92
    decentralized, 23
    dominant form of usurpation in, 33
    maximally coordinated, 18
    organization-environment interaction (see environment), 86-87
    voluntary membership, 33
organizational roles, 8-9
    (see manager, professional, bureaucrat, worker)
output variables, 3, 4, 126
owner (of an organization), ownership, 16, 22, 24, 68, 70, 86, 89, 91, 169
    definition of, 5-7, 10
    the rational owner, 7, 14, 24, 89, 92

goals, 85, 168
and environment, 86, 87
owner's agent, 6, 91
and specification of procedures, 19, 89
and visibility of conse-
quences, 77, 83
hospital owner, 84, 114 (see
hospital, board of trustees)
(see under insurance com-
panies)

P+ specified procedures, 11, 17
P− generalized procedures, 11, 17
P± proportion of procedures which
are specified, 85
(see procedures)
PCv procedures to increase visibility
of consequences, 85-87
(see procedures)
P+R+ (see complete bureaucracy, executive authority pattern), 17
P−R+ (see enucleated bureaucracy,
collegial authority pattern), 17
P+R− (see truncated bureaucracy,
executive-external authority pattern), 17
P−R− (no organization possible), 17
Parsons, Talcott, 44, 45
participation in decision making, vii,
54, 64-66, 68, 88, 111
Patents, 86
patients, 126
(see hospitals)
Pelz, D.C., 64
Pelz, D.C. and Andrews, F., 62, 64,
78, 82
performance, 41, 42, 61, 65, 160
performance ratings, 88

Perrow, Charles, 74-76, 167-169
personnel, availability of, 86
policies, 88
Pfiffner, John, 56
physical strength, 88
physicians (doctors), 31, 35, 58, 125-
140
(see hospitals, professional
component, medical staff
organization)
planning, 88
plant, 88, 106
percent of plant capacity in
use, 88
(see hospitals, occupancy)
Presthus, R.V., 52
prestige, organizational, 86, 88
procedure-resource interaction, 29,
38, 77, 78, 81, 83
procedures, specification of, (P+)
(see hospitals, insurance companies), 9-11, 16, 19, 22,
31, 32, 37, 51-68, 75, 77,
81, 85, 88, 91, 159
specification of production
procedures, 92-94, 159, 165
to increase visibility of consequences, 80-82, 91-94,
159
measurement of, 53-55
ratio of specialized to generalized, 11, 88
speed of, 18, 19, 21, 28
procedural complexity, 28
producers, 8, 9, 19
product, demand for, 86
mix, 88
production technology
unit, mass and process, 66, 165

activities and process, 92-93

production procedure, see procedure, specification of production procedures

production as output, 3

productivity, 40, 61, 63, 64, 89, 119

professionals, 8, 9, 19, 65, 88, 111
  —in enucleated bureaucracy, 16, 17
    specified procedures and, 59, 64
  (see hospitals)

profit, for profit, profitability, not-for-profit, 41-43, 49, 99, 100, 150, 156, 158, 165-167, 169

property rights
    within organizations, 5-7, 9
    Kingsley Davis definition, 6, 7
    public and private, 6
    owner's, and usurpation, 30, 33, 78

public relations, 88

quality, 40, 66

quality of patient care, 36, 40, 58, 82
    (see hospitals)

R— generalized resources, 11, 17

R+ specialized resources, 11, 17

R± proportion of resources which are specified, 85
    (see resources)

R and D (Research and Development) unit, 35
    (see research)

rapid response
    need for, 21
    and decentralization, 24

and environmental complexity, 25

raw material, 86, 88

records, 83
    (see hospital, medical records)

reports, 82
    (see information, specification of procedures to increase visibility and hospitals)

research, 3

research organization, 59, 64

research scientists, 58, 61, 62, 64
    (see R & D, scientists)

resources (R±), 85
    specific and general, defined, 9-10
    volitional and non-volitional, 11, 15, 18, 20, 22
    conversion of general to specific, 23
    cost of storage, 20
    and efficiency, 39
    resource related variables, 88
    slack, 167
    storage of, 9, 14, 20, 89

rest periods, 88

return, 40

ritualization of procedures, 30, 31, 32

Robinson, Webster, 56

Roemer, Milton I., et. al., 126, 160

Roemer, Milton I., and Friedman, Jay, 161-163, 164

Rosner, Martin, 54, 78

Russian Revolution, 63

SADR Severity adjusted death rate, (see hospitals, quality of care)

safety, regulations, 86, 88, 106

scarcity, assumption of, 49
scheduling, 88
Schein, E.H., 64, 68
scientific art, state of, 86
scientist, 3, 78, 82
    (see research)
Scott Paper Company, 25
Scott, W.G., 59
Sears Roebuck, 22
Seashore, S., and Yuchtman, E., 45,
    165
self-actualization, 61
share of the market, 43, 44
Shortell, Stephen, 167-168
Simon, Herbert A., 52
size, organizational, 3, 4, 64, 82-84,
    87, 88, 103
    (see hospitals, insurance com-
        panies, economies of scale)
span of control, 3, 54, 55, 88, 165
Specification of Procedures, 51-68
    (see procedures, also hospitals)
Specific Resource
    (see resource)
Specificity of Role Prescription, 51-
    53
    (see procedures, specification
        of)
Stigler, George, 43
strikes, 86
subgoals, 25, 125
    (see goals)
Success, 41
    (successful companies), 82, 83
Survey Research Center, University
    of Michigan, 61
Sutermeister, R.A., 40, 89
systems
    formal organizations as, 5

systems resource approach, 45-
    46

Tannenbaum, A.S., 55
Tannenbaum, A.S., and Schmidt,
    W.H., 63-64, 66
task, vii
    definition of, 69
    task complexity, 71, 113
    self contained tasks, 73
    manager's task, 84, 85
task-environment, 69-76, 77, 91
    (see environment)
    and industry, 70
    complexity of, 70-71, 91, 93,
        94, 95
    multiple, 92
Taylor, Frederick W., 52, 56, 62
taxes, taxation, 86
technology, 69, 74, 75, 84, 86, 87,
    88, 165, 168
    technological efficiency, 88
    (see production technology)
temperature, 88
theft of resources, 30, 32
Thompson, John, 149, 167, 168
Thompson, Victor A., 52, 71, 74-76
time, historical point in, 86, 87
    Season, day of week, holidays,
        88
    use of, 147-149, 155-156
Time magazine, 18
time span of discretion, 54
transformation process and visibility
    of consequences, 81-82
transportation costs, 86
truncation, 18, 20, 21
    (see bureaucracy, truncated)

U.S. Naval Mine Defense Laboratory,
36
USPHS (U.S. Public Health Service),
vii
Udy, S.H., Jr., 71-72
unintended consequences, 58
unions, 86, 88
universities, 33, 34, 35, 40, 48
urban and rural, 86
Urwick, L.F., 52, 56
usurpation (see hospitals), 7, 24-25,
30, 36
    definition of, 30
    coupled organizations and, 35,
    36
    departmental, 34, 36
    efficiency and, 78
    goal congruence and, motiva-
    tion for, 33, 78
    organizational structure and,
    31-33
    property rights and 30, 47
    visibility of consequences and,
    34, 78, 80

Venezuela
    (see Insurance Companies)
ventilation, 88
Veterans Administration Hospitals,
71, 163
visibility of consequences (Cv)
    (see hospitals, insurance com-
    panies)
    definition of, 29, 77, 92

change and, 38, 80
conflict resolution and, 37, 79
distance and, 29
efficiency and, 80, 93-95, 169
goals and, 79, 80
innovation and, 78
measurement of, 83, 84
operators perception of 33, 34
owner and, 30, 84, 85, 87, 89,
92
perceived and actual, 31
procedures to increase visibility
    and, 80-82, 85, 87, 92-94
usurpation and, 33, 34, 36
visibility procedures
    (see procedures to increase visi-
        bility of consequences, also
        hospitals)
Vroom, V.H., and Mann, F.C., 65

Wage rates, 86
    salary and wage levels, 88
Walker, H., and Lev, J., 108
weather, 86
Weber, Max, 12, 13, 52, 56, 168
Whisler, Thomas et. al., 54-55
White, R., and Lippitt, R., 59
Whyte, W. Foote, 52, 61
Woodruff, A.M., and Alexander T.G.,
    82, 83
Woodward, Joan, 66, 69, 165
workers, 8, 9, 16, 68, 160
work group, the, 88
working conditions and hours, 88